C000076108

PERGAMON GENERAL PSYC

Editors: Arnold P. Goldstein, *Syracuse University*
Leonard Krasner, *SUNY, Stony Brook*

Child Without Tomorrow
(PGPS-36)

PERGAMON GENERAL PSYCHOLOGY SERIES

Child Without Tomorrow

by
Anthony M. Graziano
State University of New York at Buffalo

PERGAMON PRESS

New York · Toronto · Oxford · Sydney

PERGAMON PRESS INC.
Maxwell House, Fairview Park, Elmsford, N.Y. 10523

PERGAMON OF CANADA LTD.
207 Queen's Quay West, Toronto 117, Ontario

PERGAMON PRESS LTD.
Headington Hill Hall, Oxford

PERGAMON PRESS (AUST.) PTY. LTD.
Rushcutters Bay, Sydney, N.S.W.

Copyright © 1974, Pergamon Press Inc.

Library of Congress Cataloging in Publication Data

Graziano, Anthony M   1932-
    Child without tomorrow.

    (Pergamon general psychology series, PGPS-36)
    1.   Child psychotherapy.   2.   Behavior therapy.
3.   Group psychotherapy.   4.   Parent and child.
5.   Community mental health services.   I.   Title.
[DNLM: 1.   Behavior therapy—In infancy and childhood.
2.   Child behavior disorders—Therapy.   WM420 G785c
1973]
RJ505.B4G72   1973   618.9'28'91   73-3394
ISBN 0-08-017085-4
ISBN 0-08-017722-0 (pbk.)

All Rights Reserved. No part of this publication may be reproduced, stored in a retrieval system or transmitted in any form, or by any means, electronic, mechanical, photocopying, recording or otherwise, without prior permission of Pergamon Press Inc.

Printed in the United States of America

This book is dedicated to the memories of Abraham Blum, my teacher and dearest friend, and Melba LaMontagne, my friend and colleague who was a most gentle and skillful child therapist.

We who knew them were enriched.

Contents

About the Author

Anthony M. Graziano (Ph.D., Purdue University) is Professor of Psychology at the State University of New York at Buffalo. After a post-doctoral fellowship at the Devereaux Foundation he taught at the University of Bridgeport. Throughout his career Dr. Graziano has maintained a primary interest in the mental health and general welfare of children and has been active in setting up a number of children's programs and working with parents' and other citizens' groups concerned with children. He is the editor of a book entitled *Behavior Therapy with Children*, and the author of articles on behavior therapy, psychotherapy, psychological testing, history of psychology, mental health politics, and children's rights.

Preface

This book describes our explorations from May 1963 to May 1969 in group behavior therapy with severely emotionally disturbed children. It is a working paper, a sharing of experiences which we hope will be of value to professionals and students and also to parents of emotionally disturbed children, who must struggle continually with their children's often impossible demands and long-term development. Hopefully we will provide at least some practical suggestions and the reassurance that even severely disturbed children can be taught a good deal of "normal" behavior.

The rationales and procedures of our work will be described in detail so that practicing professionals will be able to repeat much of it. We hope our errors will be instructive and only vicariously shared, and the more successful approaches and concepts actively tested or adopted.

We will also share our experiences in coping with the professional-political realities of local communities and discuss the effects of these realities on the initiation and development of social action programs. Excepting private practice, mental health services must rely for support on the local public, giving that community effective supportive or veto power. Thus, the development and survival of a mental health service depend to a major extent on political factors which, we shall contend, frequently ignore concerns such as scientific and humanitarian goals. Yet a helping endeavor such as a mental health program cannot be developed through isolated science, but is thoroughly embedded within and dependent upon complex social contexts. Indeed, the ultimate reality of a program, it will be shown, depends almost completely on social-political factors and not on scientific or humanitarian concerns.

Our major goals in this working paper are to illustrate that severely disturbed children can be taught new, complex, socially adaptive behavior, that non-professionals can be trained as effective child-behavior therapists, that parents are potentially significant as therapists for their own children, that the survival of a mental health program depends upon political realities, and that behavioral concepts and methods are sufficient to bring about significant improvement in severely disturbed children.

Our work, which has required a major part of six years and has involved 161 children, 66 staff, many other professionals, parents and lay persons, was

xiii

initially aimed at developing an effective day-care behavior therapy program for a small group of autistic children. I wish it were now possible to present a highly sophisticated research report, to claim that this entire endeavor has been rational, objective, and scientific, and that we had started with precise assumptions and specific hypotheses which developed systematically into controlled, quantitative experimentation yeilding highly valid and reliable conclusions. A technical writing style could and perhaps should have been adopted, but it would have omitted too much of the reality. As much as we would like to claim objective science in all of our work, we cannot, because in addition to rational science the program was shaped by humanitarian concerns and also by the consequences of its existence in a highly complex and frequently hostile community. Scientific and humanitarian idealism was almost continually confronted by the immediate realities of conflict, bitterness and frustration. There were repeated failures and gloomy depressions, small successes and overdrawn elations, grandiose six-figure budgets for the future and the constraints of penny-pinching realities of the present. Our program was further molded by many personal, professional, agency and community rivalries and, somewhat truculently perhaps, it developed much in isolation with little or no support from or contact with already established mental health agencies. This marked independence contributed much to both this program's strengths and its weaknesses.

Several starts have been made to organize the material and an essentially chronological organization has been adopted. The program to be described began in 1963, but the real beginning was some nine years earlier. We will start our chronology with that event.

Before presenting the details of our program, I wish to acknowledge the contributions of all the laymen and professionals who served on the board and the staff over the years. Particular acknowledgments are due the following persons: Maxine Bond, our first group worker, and Mae Bonnar Johnston, our second, who created a program stability in the early months from which we were able to develop a continuity with other highly capable and devoted people. They included Mattie Samuel, whose gentle, patient and sensitive work, particularly with the younger children, is seldom matched. Ruth Wendell, whom I put in the role of a no-nonsense, high-demand teacher, contributed her affection for the children, her faith that they could learn, and the uncompromising determination that they *would* learn. She labored skillfully and molded a cooperative class out of the collection of originally bizarre and unmanageable children. Jeffrey Kean was directly in charge of the daily conduct of the program during part of the third and fourth year, making both theoretical and practical contributions. Melba LaMontagne, one of the two people to whom this book is dedicated, was perhaps the most critically important staff member. Melba contributed a consistently gentle, unruffled warmth, and her genuine pleasantness combined with her excellent therapeutic skills smoothed the many rough areas and sharp encounters that inevitably arise when working with disturbed children.

Marian Szekeres, Alexander Norwood, and Richard Ryan were notable in working with us during our summer programs. Diana Metz worked with us for two summers and, along with Olive O'Dell and Eugene Boyko, also contributed to the sixth year of the program. Our thanks are also extended to many other staff members, primarily college students who worked for brief periods of time.

Thanks are also due our colleagues, the late Dr. Abraham Blum and Drs. Ralph Blackwood, Paul Harwood, and Murray Levine, all of whom made significant contributions to our program. Dr. Mildred Stanton, Mr. Robert Evans, Daniel Prosser, Gabriel Simpches, and others in decision-making positions for various state departments gave significant support.

A special note of thanks must be written for our friend and colleague Dr. Fred Esposito for his unfailing support from the beginning of the program. Fred contributed at many levels, including theortical analyses and critical evaluations, suggestions and demonstrations for practical applications drawn from his extensive experience with young children, and even many days of some rather skillful carpentry and painting to renovate quarters for the summer program.

Acknowledgments are due also to a number of persons who helped in the preparation of this manuscript, notably, Dr. Wendy Katkin who read and extensively criticized it, Mrs. Erma Rawlings who efficiently typed most of the final copy, Mrs. Irene Hurley who supervised earlier drafts through the typing pool, and Mrs. Tracey Ricci who did much of that typing.

The earlier influence of a number of my university teachers and clinical supervisors must also be acknowledged, notably, Drs. Lawrence M. Baker, M. Ray Denny, Ralph F. Hefferline, Frederick H. Kanfer, Fred S. Keller, Edgar A. Smith, and the late Franklin J. Shaw.

I wish to thank Sheila, my wife, for her patience and support and our children, Amy, Lisa and Michael, whose bouncing enthusiasm for just about everything made this writing task far more pleasant than it might have been.

This section cannot be completed without acknowledging the cooperation of all of the parents whose children provided the major reasons for the project.

A.M.G.
Time Hill Farm
Chautauqua County, New York

CHAPTER 1

Introduction: Clinical Innovation and the Mental Health Power Structure[1]

CHILD WITHOUT TOMORROW

The birth of the first son signaled proud announcements, family celebration, gifts, and congratulations. Difficulties at birth were forgotten as the family settled in to the pleasant but demanding task of helping their new child grow. The infant, a very "good" baby, slept well, made few demands, and lay quietly even when not asleep, often for hours at a time. Eventually his parents wondered, was he "too good," too quiet, too unresponsive, too easy to manage? Holding and hugging him, his mother began to sense an aloneness and to note a consistent lack of response. When she picked him up, she found that he stiffened and arched away, strenuously resisting being held. Try as she might, she could not get him to hug and cuddle, and she knew by his sixth month that he was pulling away from her every attempt at affection.

Frankie soon began to have feeding problems; he often vomited, refused to drink water, actively resisted the change from strained to chopped baby food, began to cry more, seemed in pain, and lost weight. Hospitalized for what appeared to be "intestinal disorders and severe throat infections," Frankie was fed intravenously, had blood transfusions and gastro-intestinal diagnostic tests, and was medicated to relax his stomach and thus reduce vomiting. The parents had noted his unresponsiveness and slow development, but, after their next two children were born and their progress compared, their first-born's slowness and

[1]Much of the content of this chapter first appeared as an article in Graziano, A. M. Clinical inovation and the mental health power structure: A social case history, *American Psychologist*, 1969, 24 (1), 10-13, and is reprinted here with permission.

strangeness were no longer in question. Over the next four years the child moved through, within, but never as a part of his family, as his younger siblings caught up with and rapidly surpassed him.

His childhood seemed without the joy of physical involvement; he did not play with toys or with other children. Aloof, alone, and silent, he sat for hours, apparently staring at a fan or even a corner. He somethimes knotted rope. Most frequently, making a humming sound, he sat near a window, staring, trancelike. Whereas other children his age had already learned to talk, he was still silent. His parents also noted repetitive bizarre motions of head and hands and always, it seemed, that strange humming. Another essential part of his life was his insistence on routine. He always required the same chair or a certain pillow, and even minor changes threw him into a rage.

By the time he was five he was still an aloof, non-verbal little boy who played neither with toys nor people, who could not tolerate even minor changes in routine, who was still not toilet-trained, and who, in general, had never fully experienced childhood. (As we shall see, he was essentially the same four years later.) He had been hospitalized once and examined at several clinics and special schools by neurologists, psychologists, psychiatrists, educators, and speech therapists; he had been thought to be deaf, to have cerebral palsy, and to be aphasic. His parents had tried all they knew, but he remained unresponsive and aloof. He was finally diagnosed as autistic.

The initial impetus for the program to be described came from parents and the program became identified as one for autistic children. Actually perhaps only 10 of the 161 children could be reliably diagnosed as autistic. A brief discussion of autism, not intended to be complete, is presented here because of the importance placed on autism in the early formulations of the program. Rimland (1964) presents the most complete discussion of autism, and the reader is referred to that work.

Rimland notes that complications of pregnancy and birth in autistic children occur at about the same rate as in the births of normal children. The sex ratio, however, is significantly different, with autism affecting primarily first born males (three or four boys to one girl). Autism shows itself at an early age. For the first few months after birth, the autistic child appears quite normal; in fact, many seem exceptionally well-formed, healthy, and alert. Parents usually first suspect that some problem exists when they note the infant's consistent lack of reaching in anticipation of being picked up and his lack of adjusting his body position to adapt to the person holding him. Now alerted, the parents become increasingly aware of emerging strange and disturbing behavior, including "... prolonged rocking and head-banging ... apathy and disinterest ... fear of strangers, obsessive interest in certain toys or mechanical appliances, repetitive and ritualistic play, insistence on being left alone and that the physical environment remain unchanged, and a very unusual language behavior." (Rimland, 1964, p. 7) Toilet training is difficult to establish and feeding problems occur in nearly all cases.

Two of the most common characteristics of children subsequently diagnosed as autistic are insistence on preservation of sameness and severe isolation or aloneness. The child arranges objects in some fixed, stereotyped manner, and any change, even a minor one, cannot be tolerated. One autistic child in our project had a daily ritual of lining up seven dolls in a certain manner; if the position of any doll was even slightly altered, the child reacted with a violent, screaming tantrum that could continue for two or three hours. A different type of "preservation of sameness" was exhibited by another boy who became extremely agitated when we took a slightly different route to summer camp. His agitation began precisely at the point where we diverged from the usual route. Even two years later he refused to ride in that particular car, an easily distinguished, small, green Saab station wagon, although he had no apparent objection to other cars.

The second characteristic, extreme aloneness, is seen in the child's spending hours sitting alone, staring sometimes simply into space, ignoring everyone, and remaining isolated.

Autistic children are difficult to live with, usually show little or no affection, act in ways totally outside the experience of most parents. However, the children are not neurologically impaired, often have special abilities and in what appear to be flashes of brilliance they perform precocious acts not typical of mental retardation. These may include early, even precocious talking (which, however, might be lost later), early good motor ability such as walking; they can have excellent, even phenomenal memories, good spatial ability as tested by adroitness with form boards and jig saw puzzles, and sometimes complex spatial arrangements of toys and other objects.

The parents of the autistic boy introduced earlier embarked on a long search for help and soon learned that facilities were not only scarce but, when they did exist, were extremely expensive. Special schools, residential treatment centers, and child guidance clinics were not equipped to deal with children who were severely disturbed and who posed many treatment problems. Private psychotherapists were prohibitively expensive and thus not available to these parents. They were told repeatedly that there was little hope, and the parents began to picture their son, alone and aloof, detached and silently standing still while the world matured past him. They saw endless, unchanging days fading into each other. While other parents and other children planned for and anticipated optimistic and varied futures, their son, it seemed, would have no tomorrows.

For this boy and others like him, there were no special treatment facilities in 1957. The children remained at home, increasing their demanding dependency on already burdened families and maintaining their essentially negative life situations and deepening abnormal development. Because of this lack of treatment facilities and an equal lack of interest by professionals, the initiative to develop facilities had to come from those most immediately involved—the parents. Although they provided the initial impetus, control of the organization they formed was soon taken over by a small group of laymen (who were not parents of disturbed children). The parents were then grouped into an auxiliary with a representative on the agency's board of directors. Thus, the agency that emerged, the Society for Emotionally Disturbed and Mentally Ill Children, was neither a professional nor a parents' organization.

But the parents were determined to get help for their children and for themselves and eventually convinced a local clinic to create a therapy program for "severely disturbed," ostensibly autistic children but also including schizophrenic and brain-injured children. It was soon realized that the original notion of finding a therapist for a small number of children was a naive concept, far too direct and simple a move for the jungle of political and bureaucratic constraints and professional domains. Further, the simple certainties of traditional psychotherapy were soon eroded by the realities of the task and were found to be of little real use with such profoundly deviant children. As a result, the program evolved away from its initial form and, beginning in 1963, developed a markedly different identity.

In the process of development it became clear that the reality of the program was shaped on at least three major, complex levels: (1) a conceptual-theoretical level, (2) a practical, applied level, (3) a social, political, professional level. In this book we will describe the program's growth by focusing on these three levels as we proceed chronologically. It must be stressed that the political level was no less important than the conceptual and applied dimensions, and that all that occurred with the children was played against the background of complex, constantly intruding political and professional factors.

INNOVATION IN MENTAL HEALTH

The 1960's called for innovation, for creative and bold new approaches to our vexing social problems. New programs seeking humanitarian goals suggested that humanitarian aims and scientific methodology had finally merged into a broad mobilization of those previously unfocused strengths of our culture. Innovation was in the air, but it should be noted that the *conception* of innovative ideas in mental health depends upon creative humanitarian and scientific forces, while their *implementation* depends not on science or humanitarianism but on the broad spectrum of professional and social politics!

The main points of this chapter are: (a) that these two aspects, conceiving innovation through science and humanitarianism on the one hand, and implementing innovation through politics on the other, are directly incompatible and mutually inhibiting factors, and (b) that the pursuit of political power has almost totally replaced humanitarian and scientific ideals in the mental health field. Innovations, by definition, introduce change; political power structures resist change. While the rhetoric of "innovation" filled the Sixties, innovative *action* was resisted; the decade seemed to simultaneously encourage and dampen innovation in mental health. Rationality and humanitarian concern alone are not sufficient to change existing patterns of professional services; we must also contend with the essentially political nature of the mental health profession. Many professional-political factors affected the conduct of this children's program and it should become apparent that a significant portion of our time and effort was devoted to political and social survival.

The laymen and parents introduced earlier formed a group in the late nineteen fifties called the Society for Emotionally Disturbed and Mentally Ill Children (SEDMIC) which had two primary goals: (1) to help to raise funds and work for state legislation, and (2) to find a local mental health clinic which would provide professional services for emotionally disturbed children and their parents. At first encouraged by their own progress, the laymen and parents soon found that the major task of providing professional services to a client population (in this case, severely disturbed children) became lost in a jungle of bureaucratic irrelevancies, individual and agency rivalries, and professional mystique. Another full two years would elapse before a group program for the children was finally begun.

The major obstacles were administrative and political rather than clinical and scientific! There were problems from the beginning concerning the identity of the sponsoring lay group, the definition of roles and division of responsibilities between the lay and professional groups, and problems of financing that included the demands of the local United Agency, an influential fund-raising group. The cooperating clinic was a respected agency with 25 years of service, and its clinical approach was traditional and well-accepted. However, despite its compatibility with the community, it still encountered inertia, confusion, and sometimes active resistance. The program operated for three years providing the only services to severely disturbed children in the area. Gradually, however, the lay group began to question both the clinic's high costs and its conduct of the program. Conflicts emerged over the roles of the lay and professional groups.

The lay people felt they were being displaced or eased out by the clinic's professionals, but were nevertheless still "expected to pay the bills." The professionals, on the other hand, came to see the lay people as well-intentioned but impulsive persons who were trying to control the program, which was clearly a professional function. Threatened and angered, both sides retreated to positions more acrimonious than communicative, and they accused each other of being untrustworthy.

"Don't trust the professionals" and "Beware the laymen" were expressed in countless and diverse ways. To this growing distress, new complaints were added by some of the parents. After four years of parent-groups and three years of children's day-care programs, the children had remained essentially unchanged. The parents angrily let it be known that they had devoted too much time and energy to find few improvements four years later. Assuming that the parents' judgment of no significant change was correct, it is nevertheless not an unusual situation. In fact, lack of therapeutic success with autistic children appears to be the usual case (Rimland, 1964).

The recrimination, criticisms, and general hostilities increased until the original lay group, SEDMIC, withdrew its support from the clinic and set out to create its own independent program. Hiring a psychiatrist and a psychologist as consultants and an R.N. as a child group worker, SEDMIC arranged for the use of a room to house its program. Thus prepared, this small group aggressively demanded financial support from both the United Agency and the State Department of Mental Health. The clinic continued a version of the program formerly sponsored by SEDMIC, and now also demanded continuing support from the United Agency and the State. Thus, the two agencies, the clinic and SEDMIC, were directly competing for the same local, state, and federal funds, with both claiming priority. Several meetings were held with the two groups and federal, state, and local officials, in which the essential issue of who was going to receive the money was discussed.

The clinic explained its psychoanalytically-oriented group therapy program, with major assumptions as follows:

1. Psychoanalytic principles and treatment methods are the only known effective approaches to severely disturbed children.
2. Group psychotherapy is a useful but "weaker" version of individual therapy.
3. Parents of emotionally disturbed children have internal psychodynamic problems of their own which bear a causal relationship to their child's pathology.
4. Therefore, in order to effectively treat the child, the psychodynamic problems of the parents must also be ameliorated.

5. The essential problem in psychotherapy is to bring about significant changes in the internal, psychodynamic conditions that constitute the "core" of mental illness; the focus of treatment then is internally directed.
6. Therapy is essentially a medical endeavor, and the clinic program was properly directed medically.

The clinic, which had operated for some twenty-five years, based its arguments on experience, professionalism, and stability as a successful community agency; it offered to continue the accepted "tried and true psychoanalytic methodology" (sic) and "proper" medical direction.

On the other hand, SEDMIC contended that because psychoanalytic approaches had not resulted in significant improvement for severely disturbed children, the community should support reasonable alternative approaches and not be entrapped by the pseudo-efficiency of a single program to avoid "duplication of services." One alternative was proposed: modification of behavior through the application of psychological learning theory. The major assumptions, which will be more fully discussed in the next chapter, were at variance with those of the clinic.

1. Traditional psychodynamic approaches to disturbed children have not been effective. Meaningful alternatives are needed.
2. Observed current behavior, the acquisition of adaptive behavior, and decrement of maladaptive behavior are the proper focus and content of therapy.
3. Adaptive social learning will occur more effectively in a social group than in an individual therapy situation.
4. The parents of emotionally disturbed children do not generally require psychotherapy, but do need training in reality-oriented, everyday dealing with their children.
5. The essential problem in therapy is to bring about significant changes in overt behavior, and the focus of intervention then is externally, environmentally directed.
6. Because this approach is psychological, it therefore should be psychologically and not medically directed.
7. No significant attempts had been made to provide mental health services to children of lower socioeconomic class and, in fact, traditional psychodynamic approaches would be irrelevant in any such attempt.

Criticizing the establishment, SEDMIC proposed changes which called for new approaches based on a psychological rather than a medical model and furthermore which insisted on including poverty children in the program. Early in 1963, offering psychological learning concepts as alternatives to psycho-analytic treatment of children and arguing that traditional clinics had failed to help low-income children were not well received. From the beginning, then, this group was cast as "radical" and "troublemaker."

Clearly the divisive lines had been drawn on at least three levels: (1) the theoretical level, i.e., the psychoanalytic versus the behavioral assumptions and the methods predicted from them; (2) the professional level, i.e., program direction by a psychologist versus the more traditional program direction by a psychiatrist; and (3) the political level, i.e., the "traditional" faction was in a better position than the "outsiders" to obtain support from the important mental health decision-makers on bases other than the eventual merits of the proposed programs.

In 1963 the weight of support was clearly on the side of the traditional faction—the psychoanalytic, psychiatric, political in-group—and it was no sur-prise when the State Department of Mental Health and the United Agency decided to support only the traditional clinic.

A compromise was possible, however, and the clinic offered to administer SEDMIC'S program, allowing it to develop its psychological-behavioral emphasis. SEDMIC rejected this offer, believing that in order to develop a genuine alternative the program had to develop independently and not under the admini-stration of a traditional psychiatric clinic.

Hoping to avoid competition within the clinical structure, in 1963, SEDMIC proposed to the local university the creation of a small-scale research and training project to develop child therapy approaches from learning theory and to select and train non-degree, undergraduate, and master's-level students as child group workers and behavior therapists. The proposal was rejected because: (a) the project was too radical and would only create continuing controversy, (b) the local mental health professionals had already clearly indicated their opposi-tion to it, and (c) the university, always cognizant of Town-Gown problems, could not risk becoming involved.

The message was clear: the project was opposed by the local mental health professionals; it had already caused controversy, would create more, and the university was no place for controversy!

Denied the university environment, SEDMIC moved to compete within the closed-rank mental health agency structure, soon again encountering the United Agency. That agency's annual fund-raising campaign is carried out with intense publicity, and donating through one's place of employment has become some-what less than voluntary. Operated primarily by business and industrial men, the United Agency had some million and a half dollars to distribute to agencies of its choice, thus giving a small group of traditionally conservative businessmen considerable power over the city's social action programs.

Having been advised that SEDMIC'S proposed program could not long survive, the United Agency's apparent tact was to delay for a few months until SEDMIC'S quiet demise. That delaying tactic was implemented as follows:

1. The United Agency listened to SEDMIC'S preliminary ideas but would not act until it had a written proposal.
2. A month later the United Agency rejected the written proposal because it was "only a paper program!"
3. SEDMIC'S program was started and expanded, but after six months of operation was again denied support because, the United Agency explained, its existence had been too brief a time on which to base a decision. The group was advised to apply again after a longer period of operation.
4. After a year of operation, SEDMIC'S next request was denied on the grounds that the program had to be "professionally evaluated" before the United Agency could act. And who would carry out the evaluation? The local mental health professionals, of course. SEDMIC objected to being evaluated by its competitors but agreed to an evaluation by the State Department of Mental Health, although it too had previously refused to support the program. This was to be the "final" hurdle. If the evaluation were positive, the United Agency would grant funds for the program.
5. Completing its professional evaluation, the State Department returned a highly positive report, and strongly recommended that SEDMIC be supported. Apparently caught off guard, the United Agency was strangely unresponsive; several months elapsed before the next request for funds was again deferred, on the grounds that the question of "duplication of services" had never been resolved.
6. After additional state endorsement and high praise for the program as a non-duplicated service, the United Agency rejected SEDMIC'S next request with: if the state thought so highly of the program, why didn't it support it? "Come back when you get state support."
7. Six months later and nearly three years after starting the program, SEDMIC had a state grant. The United Agency then allocated $3,000 which it said would be forwarded as soon as SEDMIC provided the United Agency with (a) an official tax-exemption statement, (b) the names and addresses of all the children who had received SEDMIC'S services, and (c) the names of the fathers and their employers.

For three years SEDMIC had met all of the United Agency's conditions—it had provided a detailed proposal, launched the program, had successfully operated for three years, had expanded, had received high professional evaluations, had resolved the duplication of services issue, and had provided the tax-exemption voucher. But SEDMIC could not, it explained, provide confidential information such as names, addresses, and fathers' places of employment. The United Agency therefore refused support because SEDMIC was, after all, "uncooperative" in refusing to supply the requested information.

SEDMIC'S final attempts to gain local mental health support was with an agency we shall call "Urban Action," whose function, at least partly, was to help ameliorate poverty conditions through federally supported programs. Arguing that the city had no mental health services of any scope for poverty-level children, SEDMIC proposed to apply and evaluate techniques of behavior modification, environmental manipulation, and selection and training of "indigenous" sub-professionals, mothers and siblings, to help emotionally disturbed, poverty-level children.

The written proposal was met with enthusiasm but, in keeping with the concept of total community focus, the Urban Agency explained, more than one agency had to be involved; it suggested inviting the local mental health association to join the project. The mental health association, of course, was comprised of the same professionals who had opposed SEDMIC'S program from the beginning. Skeptical, SEDMIC distributed copies of its proposal to the mental health association, again referring something new back to the old power structure. Five months later a prediction was borne out: the mental health association returned the proposal as "unworkable" and, in its place, submitted its own highly traditional, psychiatric version, which was ultimately rejected in Washington. Those poverty-level children who received no mental health services in 1963 still receive no services, and there are no indications that the situation will be any different in the next few years.

The "outside" group, its new ideas clashing with the professional establishment, repeatedly encountered barriers composed of the same people and never did receive support from the local mental health agencies, the United Agency, the university, or the Urban Action agency. For the first two years it subsisted on small tuition fees and cake sales organized by a few determined ladies. Eventually, it did receive significant federal and state support. Thus, it carried out its programs in spite of the opposition and lack of support of the local mental health professionals.

Moving into its fifth year, SEDMIC experienced an ironic development. Having successfully overcome all major external obstacles, the agency began to disintegrate internally. Achieved of some status, success, and continuing support, it no longer had the cohesive force generated by battling an external foe. Its own internal bickering, previously overshadowed by the "larger battle," now became dominant, and the agency again splintered along laymen-professional lines. The precipitating factor this time was the professionals' insistence on including poverty-level children, who were nearly all Black and Puerto Rican. A few lay persons, supported in their anger by the professional director of an actively competing agency, objected to the "unfairness" of allowing Black children into the program "free," i.e., supported through a grant, while their own children had to pay a small fee. Poverty funds could not be used to support the more affluent White children, as the lay people demanded, and the professional staff was then faced with two main alternatives: (1) abandon the poverty program and work only with middle-class, White children, or (2) resign from SEDMIC and continue the program under other auspices. The staff decided on the latter alternative, continuing its program until 1969.

Thus, turning innovative *concepts* into concrete programs required a good deal more than humanitarian beliefs and scientific objectivity. The eventual reality of the program depended upon its ability to maintain its integrity throughout all of the political buffeting.

When our program finally ended in May 1969, there were again no available local services specifically for severely disturbed children. However, we had influenced several established agencies to move toward a behavioral model and to accept some severely disturbed children they would not have accepted earlier. In some instances this was accomplished when those agencies hired some of the two dozen full-time staff we had trained. Thus, a public school system, a state agency for mentally retarded children, a state residential treatment agency, and a private school for exceptional children were directly influenced by our programs.

THE LOCAL AGENCIES AS A FIELD
OF PARALLEL BUREAUCRACIES

In spite of the support of the state and of many "outside" professionals, the local agencies maintained a closed-rank rejection of the program. A workable set of relationships among the various mental health agencies had developed over the years. In fact, "inter-agency cooperation," ostensibly in the service of clients, also seemed to provide important reciprocal support for the agencies.

Despite overlap, the agencies were differentiated according to major functions: some were referral sources (schools and churches) some provided services (the hospital, the clinic, the center for retarded children); some were financial supporters (United Agency, Community Chest); some acted as community planners (the Mental Health Association); and some had dual functions (such as the State Department of Mental Health and the anti-poverty agency, both involved in community planning and in funneling federal money to agencies of their choice).

Each agency had its own administrative structure with its own bureaucracy, decision makers, and line personnel. Thus, there existed several autonomous, parallel, bureaucratic structures, some larger than others, but all trying to deal with some aspect of human health. Their work was clinical and practical, dealing with issues of immediate reality. On the assertion of too much pressing immediate work, these agencies had no use for research of any kind, and therefore no adequate evaluation of the few available services was ever made. The agencies tended to give support to each other through their mutual referrals, maintaining an uncritical acceptance of the various territorial claims and never openly questioning the value of their own or other agencies' work.

Gradually, another level of inter-agency cooperation became apparent. For example, the director of the leading mental health agency (which received funds) was also a ranking member of the major mental health planning group (which made recommendations about what agencies would receive funds). Some persons were not only important members of agencies that allocated money, but were also members of agencies that received the money; some sat on boards of several agencies; some positions were held concurrently, while some people "rotated" through the various agencies. In a period of four years, the same relatively few people were repeatedly encountered in various roles associated with one or another of the agencies, making the major decisions regarding local mental health services. In other words, while the parallel bureaucracies making up the "mental health community" were ostensibly autonomous, each with its own demarcated area of functioning, inter-agency sharing of upper-level decision makers occurred, and the situation approached that of the "interlocking directorates" of big business.

There was yet another way in which the parallel bureaucracies cooperated; based on some immediate issue or problem, temporary agency "coalitions" were formed. The composition varied according to the nature of the issue, and the coalition relaxed when the issue was resolved. One such coalition was the original cooperation of SEDMIC and the clinic, while the United Agency stood opposed. Later, when conditions had changed, a new set of coalitions formed, this time finding the United Agency and the clinic together.

Thus, the active mental health field in this city was made up of parallel bureaucracies, i.e., various social agencies which, by virtue of their "expertise," had been granted legitimate social power by the community in the area of mental health. Despite the essential autonomy of the bureaucratic structures, they cooperated closely in several major ways, which tended toward mutual support and perpetuation of the existing bureaucratic structures. This cooperation occurred through (a) normal and clearly legitimate professional channels such as reciprocal referrals of clients, (b) tacit, uncritical acceptance of agency "territories" and functions, (c) inter-agency "sharing" of upper-level decision-making personnel, and (d) temporary, variable-composition coalitions that briefly intensified agency power in order to deal with specific issues.

THE MENTAL HEALTH POWER STRUCTURE

We have described the practice of the mental health professions as a legitimized special-interest segment of a community. That segment (or field) was composed of parallel bureaucratic agencies which, by virtue of their control over professional and financial resources, cooperated in their own mutual support and tended to maintain decision-making power within that field. There thus existed a definable and relatively stable social structure through which agencies shared leadership, made cooperative decisions, and wielded legitimized social power that tended to support, strengthen, and perpetuate the viability of the structure itself. Schermerhorn (1964) notes: "The power process frequently crystallizes into more or less stable configurations designated as centers or structures of power." (p. 18) Clearly, what has been described is a *power structure*, a ". . . Temporarily stable organization of power resources permitting an effectual directive control over selective aspects of the social process." (p. 24)

Polsby (1963), who takes issue with the prevalent "stratification" theory of authority power structures, nevertheless notes the following:

"By describing and specifying leadership roles in concrete situations, (we) are in a position to determine the extent to which a power structure exists. High degrees of overlap in decision-making personnel among issue-areas, or high degrees of institutionalization in the bases of power in specified issue areas, or high degrees of regularity in the procedures of decision-making—any one of these situations, if found to exist, could conceivably justify an empirical concludion that some kind of power structure exists." (p. 119)

We have tried to show that such conditions did obtain, and we therefore conclude that a viable *mental health power structure* existed that made all major decisions in the "mental health field" of this community. Never static, the mental health power structure continues to react to new pressures and to maneuver, in a changing world, in order to maintain and further strengthen itself. In so doing, it becomes a defender of its own status quo. It is our contention that local mental health power structures across the country have become so thoroughly concerned with maintaining themselves that the *major portion* of their commitment has been diverted from the original ideals of science and humanitarianism and it has become invested instead in the everyday politics of survival.

Selznick (1943), writing about bureaucracies, notes:

> "Running an organization as a specialized and essential activity generates problems which have no necessary (and often opposed) relationships to the professed or 'original' goals of the organization . . . (these activities) come to consume an increasing proportion of the time and thoughts of the participants, they are . . . substituted for the professed goals. . . . In that context the professed goals will tend to go down in defeat, usually through the process of being extensively ignored." (p. 49)

Thus, we believe that contemporary mental health practice is carried out within power structures that are primarily concerned with justifying and maintaining themselves, while they pay scant attention to the scope of mental health services and even less to the objective evaluation of quality or effectiveness. They maintain their own self-interest, which conflicts with humanitarian ideals, science, and social progress. Such conflict is clearly evident in the power structures' relationships (a) to their clientele and (b) to any intruding innovator.

Relationship to Clients

Because of the proliferation of agencies with their territorial claims on one community, there must be some means of parceling out the available client pool. Some agencies deal with children, others with adults; some deal with poor children, some with retarded children; some with Catholics, some with Jews; some with immigrants and others with the unemployed. None deal with just people, but all deal with "certain kinds" of people who are categorized and parceled out. To whatever category he might be assigned, it is implicit that the client is in some way a failure; that he has folded up and dropped out; that he is marginal; that he is not as bright as "we," or as well-adjusted as "we," or as well employed as "we," or as nicely colored as "we." There is always an implicit and very real distance separating the clinician from the client; and at the upper end of this breech is the righteous and very certain knowledge of the professional that he is behaving nobly in a humanitarian cause. While the clinician focuses on each "client-failure," society is busy producing several more. We too often fail to recognize that our individual, internally-focused ministrations have little if anything to do with the amelioration of those social conditions that have shaped the individual's disorder in the first place. To say that the mental health professionals have failed to recognize the crucial importance of external *social conditions* in shaping disturbed behavior is another way of saying that *professionals refuse to recognize that we labor to rebuild those lives which we, in our other social roles, have helped to shatter.* Nowhere is this more obvious than in the area of civil rights, where a clinician might occasionally help some poverty-level minority group member and later go home to his restrictive suburb, attend his restrictive club, play golf on a restrictive course, and share a restrictive drink in a restrictive bar with businessmen who hire Negroes last in good times and fire them first in bad times. By fully accepting the "official" power-structure view of the "sick" individual in an otherwise fine society, we clinicians never admit the validity of such non-scientific analyses as Kozol's (1967) shattering *Death at an Early Age*; we therefore need not admit that the restrictiveness of our own lives has anything to do with the frustrations of someone else in another place.

The power-structure clinics tend to limit their services to White, middle-class children with mild to moderate disturbances, that is, to those children with the best chances of improving even when left alone; those children whose parents would be most cooperative in keeping appointments, being on time, accepting the structure, and, of course, paying the fees; those children who do not present the vexing and, to the middle-class clinician, *alien* problems of lower-class, minority groups. Certainly a clinic is much "safer," much "quieter," more neatly run when it limits itself to the most cooperative clientele and, we might suggest, when it *selectively creates a pool of cooperative clients*.

The waiting list is one of the selective devices used to weed out the impatient clients and retain those who are most docile. By insisting on the incredibly lengthy and largely irrelevant traditional psychodynamic study, clinics refuse to deal immediately with a client's problems. Instead, they artificially create a waiting list, which then serves as an objective validation of the continuing "need" for clinic services over the next year or so. The length of the waiting list, is in fact, often seen as a positive indication of the value of the clinic. Thus, in some perverse manner, the slower and less efficient the clinic and the longer its waiting list, the greater is that clinic's claim to importance and to increased money and power! It would not be surprising to find that a clinic efficiently handling all new referrals within an hour would be considered of dubious quality because it had no customers waiting at the door.

Thus, the structure, responding primarily to its own needs for self-perpetuation, has created a mythical client beset by dramatic internal conflicts, hidden even from himself, but apparently little affected by the realities of external social conditions. The professional, with his role clearly delimited by the power structure, continues his myopic, psychodynamic dissection of individuals and never perceives the larger social, moral, or—if you will—*human* realities of that client's existence. The power structure, further insuring its own perpetuation, carefully selects clients who best meet the structure's needs and rejects the great majority who do not. The "most hopeful" but still doubtful psychiatric services are offered mainly to bright, verbal, adult, neurotic, upper-class Whites. In the context of contemporary social reality, the mental health professions now exist as expensive and busy political power structures that have little relevance for anything except their own self-preservation. In this process, we suspect, the client might too often be exploited rather than helped.

Response to Intruding Innovations

The mental health power structure, committed primarily to its own preservation, is alertly opposed to any events that might change it. Thus, when innovation intrudes, the structure responds with various strategies to deal with the threat. It might incorporate the new event and alter it to fit the pre-existing structure so that, in effect, nothing is really changed. It might deal with it by active rejection, calling upon all of its resources to "starve out" the innovator by insuring a lack of support.

The most subtle defense, however, is to ostensibly accept and encourage the innovator; to publicly proclaim support of innovative goals and, while doing that, to build in various controlling safeguards such as special committees, thereby insuring that the work is always accomplished through power structure channels and that no real change occurs. This tactic achieves the nullification of the innovator, while giving the power structure the public semblance of progressiveness. The power structure can become so involved in this pose that the lower-line personnel come to believe that they are working for the stated ideals of humanitarianism, science, and progress although, in reality, they labor to maintain the political power of the status quo.

This has occurred in civil rights and anti-poverty programs, where federal money has been poured into the old local power structures that have loudly proclaimed innovation, improvement, and progressiveness, while all the time protecting themselves by actually nullifying those efforts. After several years of public speeches and much money, it becomes clear to the citizens of the deprived area that nothing has changed. Frustrated and angry, many submerge themselves into non-protesting apathy and others, (perhaps the more hopeful ones) erupt into violence, smashing their world, trying perhaps to destroy in order to rebuild.

Hence, while the power structure continues to proclaim innovation, it expends great energy to insure, through its defensive maneuvers, the maintenance of its status quo. Innovation is thus allowed and even encouraged, provided that it remains on the level of conceptual abstractions and does not, in reality, change anything! The hallmark of this interesting but deadly phenomenon of spending vast sums of money and effort to bring about no change, all in the name of innovation, might be summed up in what I once suggested as a motto for one of those agencies: *Innovation Without Change*. This motto reflects a central tendency of mental health services in the 1960's: maintaining our primary allegiance to the power structures rather than to science and humanitarianism, and continuing our busy employment, creating innovations without changing reality.

Every community (including the mental health field) has its built-in safeguards which guarantee rejection, neutralization, or at least deceleration of any new approaches that do not fit the prevailing power structure. Significant progress in mental health will not be achieved through systematic research or the guidance of humanitarian ideals, since they are neutralized by being filtered through the existing structure. For those scientific and humanitarian conceptual innovations to remain intact and reach the level of clinical application, they must avoid that destructive "filtering" process.

Likewise, progress will not be initiated by or through the power structure, but will depend upon successfully changing or ignoring that structure. It does not seem possible at this point to join the structure and still maintain the integrity of both areas, i.e., the essentially political power structure and the humanitarian and scientific ideals. The two areas are incompatible; science and humanitarianism cannot be achieved through the present self-perpetuating focus of the power structure.

A case in point is the present interest in the development of comprehensive mental health centers. When a community commits itself to the vastly expensive reality of a mental health center and then *refers control of that center back to the existing power structure*, it has created innovation without change. The major result might be to enrich and reinforce the old power structure, thus making it vastly more capable of further entrenching itself and successfully resisting change for many more years.

Our personal experience in contributing to the planning of comprehensive mental health services led us to conclude that the comprehensive centers would provide only "more of the same." Instead of trying to determine the needs of the people in the urban area, and then create the appropriate approaches, the planners asked questions such as: "How can we extend psychiatric services to treat more alcoholics?" "How many beds do we need for acute cases?" "How can we increase our services to schizophrenic children?" "How can we pool our resources for more efficient diagnostic workup of cases?" etc. The questions themselves assumed the validity of the existing power structure and were aimed at *extending old services* rather than determining needs and creating new services. Only the scope of existing approaches was questioned—never the relevance or effectiveness.

Thus, surrounded by the modish aura of innovation, the existing structure not only remains intact but becomes enriched and continues its existence irrespective of the real and changing needs of its clients. By allocating a great deal of money to the existing power structures, whether through mental health centers, antipoverty programs, special education, or other action, we are playing the game of the Sixties –"Innovation Without Change"–and, win or lose, we run the risk of insuring our own stagnation.

In summary, we have maintained that contemporary mental health professions in the United States have developed viable, community-based professional and lay power structures that are composed of mutually-benefiting bureaucracies. Scientific and humanitarian ideals are incompatable with and have been supplanted by the professionals' primary loyalty to the political power structure itself. By virtue of their focus on self-preservation, these power structures (1) maintain a dogmatically restrictive view of human behavior and the roles of the professionals within that structure and (2) prevent the development of true innovations. The basic, self-defeating weakness in the variety of current attempts at innovative social action is their unintended strengthening of the existing power structure, which is incompatible with innovation. Future advances in the practice of mental health will most readily occur outside of the current mental health power structures.

Contemporary mental health professions in the United States base their major decisions neither on science nor humanitarianism and certainly not on honest self-appraisal, but on the everyday politics of bureaucratic survival in local communities. As Murray and Adeline Levine (1970) have pointed out, at the same time as the professions operate to maintain themselves, society changes, and the two grow further apart. Eventually, the mental health professions become grossly alienated from the human realities of the very clients they purport to help, and the professions soon become irrelevant. Admitting no need for critical evaluation, the professional continues to provide services that are, in fact, of limited scope, of questionable value, and of extremely high price. As long as all new developments are uncritically referred back into the control of the old power structure, we will continue to insure innovation without change.

THE LAYMEN AND PROFESSIONAL EXPERTISE

One barrier to inquiry in mental health is the politicizing and bureaucratizing of the profession into rigid, self-perpetuating power structures that too often operate at the client's expense. Another is the complex relationship between laymen and professionals; i.e., any mental health service includes some agreement or contract between them and here, too, stumbling blocks and barriers abound. The program to be described was based on one set of assumptions held by the laymen and another set of assumptions held by the supervising psychologist. These assumptions, seemingly similar at first, eventually diverged and brought to an end the cooperation between laymen and professionals. Pointing out some of those problems might be of use to other laymen and professionals in similar situations.

From the beginning, the laymen's major intent was to provide effective services to a small group of their own children. The focus was on the practical application of knowledge in order to improve the lives of these children. As the laymen perceived it, the professionals had the necessary knowledge and skill to provide the services they desired.

The psychologist agreed on the major goal of service, and an apparent accord was reached. However, he had additional assumptions and expectations that were not shared by the laymen and that were obscured by the glow of agreement between them on the issue of the importance of service. The psychologist assumed that this was an area of limited knowledge and that practical applications, which constituted the program's major goal, would have to be *developed* as the program continued. Here was a primary and unrecognized difference that emerged some four years later as a major destructive factor. The laymen perceived professionals as highly skilled practitioners whose task it was to apply the proven, effective, therapeutic methods they had learned in their long, costly, professional education. Otherwise, of what value was that education? This, of course, is the popular view, actively fostered by both the professions and popular communications media. It is the image of the psychotherapist, particularly the psychiatrist, as an empathic, powerful, and highly skilled professional who, by virtue of his long, specialized training and experience, can take the distressed person in hand and, with competence and assurance, firmly lead him out of his morass and into a brighter, calmer, and more effective life. These skills cannot be provided by laymen but only by professionals. The laymen, then, had an uncluttered view of the relationship between themselves and the professionals: they would define the area to be covered, i.e., therapy services for autistic children, and would hire the necessary professionals, buying their exclusive expertise as competent practitioners. During their first experience with professionals, all parties agreed to that division of labor. After several years of cooperation, the laymen criticized the professionals' conduct of the program, claiming that the professionals were not providing enough service, that they were charging too much, and that the children were not improving. The laymen severed their relationship with that group of professionals and sought other professionals who would provide more services at more reasonable cost.

The laymen did not seriously question the professionals' knowledge or skill; they did not discard their belief that professionals were capable of providing effective services; they continued to believe that there is a body of knowledge and effective practical skills that constitute professional "expertise." Their criticisms were of the personalities of the professionals, which, according to the laymen, made it difficult to work with or "trust" them. Their arguments were on personal levels, directed at the particular professionals with whom they had worked. Their subsequent action was consistent with this view; they discarded those professionals and sought others who, if not more skilled or better educated and trained, would at least be more dedicated, humane, and personable. Again, in their second search for professionals, they maintained their faith that professional expertise was a necessary and real commodity, possessed by all professionals. Their criteria for selection were not based on professional ability or knowledge, which they assumed to be more or less constant among professionals, but rather on the more personal terms mentioned here.

The laymen then embarked on their second search for professional affiliation. But word of their previous difficulties had circulated, and they found repeated refusals by professionals to join their endeavor. It was at this point that I became involved. New to the community and just two years out of graduate school, still expressing idealism and optimism that people are inherently rational and all problems can be solved, I was intrigued by the high-risk challenge offered by these disinherited lay people. My lack of concern for high fees and my willingness to work independently (that is, outside of the existing framework of local agencies) apparently convinced the lay people that they had found a professional who agreed with them in all major respects and with whom they could work. One of the major expectations with which I entered into this work was that effective and practical services to help psychotic children would comprise the major goal of our endeavor, and that all other aspects of professional work would have meaning only as they were relevant and useful in attaining the practical, applied, and humanitarian goals. In this, the laymen and I were in complete agreement, and we would strive together to provide the best services we possibly could. Given this rather abundant initial harmony, where did we differ? What were those initially unrecognized issues that later emerged and dissolved the layman-professional relationship?

APPLICATIONS AND INQUIRY

The basic difference was our respective expectations concerning the practical competence of mental health professionals. Although the laymen assumed that all professionals had the requisite skill to provide effective services for psychotic children and needed only support and dedication to create and maintain those services, I had no such faith in the applied skills of professionals. It was my belief that previous psychotherapeutic attempts with psychotic children were largely failures, that professionals did not have any well-defined, valid body of knowledge or practical applications, and that support for more of the traditional approaches would only serve to entrench our previous ignorance. Therefore, when faced with the task of providing services for a particular group of psychotic children, we would approach the task not by immediately applying the practical techniques we had learned in graduate school (techniques of psychodiagnostics and psychotherapy) but rather by discarding or at least suspending them, and devoting our efforts to the development of appropriate new approaches.

Thus, the crucial problem as seen by the laymen was the *application of known techniques* in order to provide services; for me, it was the *inquiry into the development of effective techniques* in order to provide services. Here, then, was the crux of the unrecognized differences in expectations between the laymen and myself—application on the one hand, and inquiry on the other. The laymen expected that I would apply a maximum of *known* psychotherapeutic techniques to help their children directly. I expected to apply a minimum of known applied techniques and to develop the rest. Beyond providing a humane, kindly, and organized atmosphere, there lay the necessity for systematic inquiry into the details of structuring the environment to bring about maximum learning of adaptive behavior. Our inquiry would begin with observations of the behavior of the children, and we would ask *what* behavior occurs under *what* conditions? Presumably, as our observations sharpened and methods developed, we would gradually abstract concepts to account for observed consistencies and slowly develop and evaluate applied methods. As finer observations and greater control led to more specific hypotheses, we would gradually move to more highly controlled, experimental tests. The constant and increasingly sharpening evaluation would be continually fed back into the program to bring it closer to the major goal of more effective clinical services for psychotic children. The goal of effective service was to be reached by actively integrating research inquiry into the clinical program so that improvement in clinical methods would come about through a continual process of rational, systematic, and controlled (although not necessarily experimental) research. This expectation was, of course, a grossly naive one which assumed that certainly professionals, and perhaps laymen, would agree that the most effective way of gaining knowledge is to carry out systematic inquiry into the problem area. It failed to recognize the degree to which both laymen and other professionals were committed to the position that professionals already possess requisite knowledge, and that further inquiry is not essential.

In a relatively short time we had established an operating program which, as far as could be observed, was as competently run as any. The children seemed to be benefiting, and even casual observers noted the greater order, cooperation, and increasingly "normal" behavior of these children, who had originally behaved in a bizarre manner. Within two years, the expanded program was operating smoothly, and included not only specific programs for children but also direct work with parents, staff recruitment and training, and even provided some services for other agencies. As the laymen saw it, the major goal—direct services for their children—had been realized and, except for some expansion of the number of children and the eventual acquisition of better facilities to house the program, they were generally satisfied with the level and quality achieved. They were puzzled therefore when we continued to modify what appeared to be an already adequate program. They did not understand why we discarded or changed apparently useful aspects of the program, and some of the laymen became concerned that we were going far beyond, and losing, the original intent of the program.

The psychologist, operating consistently with his initial assumptions, saw the smoothly-running program as the *minimum* to be expected from professional work—i.e., what appear to be smoothly running programs are the rule in our highly professionalized field, actually reflecting little achievement beyond some organizing success. It was our belief that almost anyone could bring together children as clients, adults as staff, organize a few activities, call it a "program," and impress the public. Many agencies had done just that. We believed that a professional, whether a psychotherapist or playground director, would at the *least* be expected to organize activities and maintain them in good order. The most crucial contribution of the professional, however, one that arises from what ought to be one of his major responsibilities, is to demonstrate that his activities are effective. To accomplish that, he would have to maintain a systematic and critical inquiry and be able and willing to modify even his most cherished procedures in the light of his own continual evaluation.

Thus, after about two years, the laymen believed they had achieved their program goals and further program changes and research were not necessary. Rather, they felt it was time for "consolidation" of their achievements. I felt, that on the other hand, we had achieved only the minimum of program goals and were finally ready to get on with the real work of continued inquiry, evaluation, and change. Our positions were diametrically opposed—a conservative versus a liberal or perhaps radical view. None of us had the foresight to recognize the developing impasse until it was too late to heal the differences. After another two years, our association ended.

It is interesting to note that the laymen, in their increasingly conservative stance, which was opposed to continued evaluation and change, quickly moved back to a position of close agreement with the traditional agencies and professionals in the community (with whom they had so strongly differed four years earlier). This was another instance of regrouping in the repeated shifting of temporary agency coalitions discussed earlier.

HELPING AND REALITY

We have attempted to show not only the obvious fact that turning the expressed desire of "helping" disturbed children into the applied realities of effective programs is a complex process, but also that it proceeds along at least three related levels: (1) a conceptual level, including the abstractions derived from the continuing inquiry and the theoretical aspects of understanding and predicting behavior; (2) a practical, applied level, involving the everyday realities of a program and its concrete methodologies; and (3) a social-political level of professional domains, public bureaucracies, and personal relationships between and within groups of people such as laymen and professionals.

Our helping attempts consisted of continued inquiry in order to develop effective services, and all of this was embedded within the powerful reality of a complex social context. All of us recognized this social context, or at least parts of it, but we grossly underestimated its impact, believing that "politics" and professional maneuvering were unfortunately sometimes necessary but basically secondary to the main goal of service (as the laymen saw it) or inquiry leading to service (as I saw it). We failed to recognize to what extent the social context touched each of these goals, and that it did so in so many ways that their very nature and form were affected. Thus, the research and the practical applications were significantly shaped by the surrounding social context.

Our failure[1] to clearly recognize this in the beginning stemmed partly from my initial and unquestioned assumption upon beginning this work that scientific and professional endeavor has objective validity of its own and is easily insulated from, and properly carried out independently of personal and social factors. However, it appears now that in reality, in our helping professions, the scientific substance and practical forms are largely determined by non-scientific factors that make up the surrounding social reality. In other words, as much as we may deplore and deny it, in our profession at least, our science is to a large extent determined by our politics. This, I believe, is a crucial point that should be made clear to all professionals and laymen involved in social programs. Mental health programs do not exist in humanitarian and scientific independence, isolated from the more mundane factors of social and political maneuvering; conversely, every mental health program takes on crucial unplanned-for characteristics that are inexorably molded by the extra-scientific context in which that program exists. A program for psychotic children, if housed in a state hospital, will be very different in concept and application from a program for similar children housed in a public school. A program operating effectively in one situation might nevertheless be completely inapplicable in some other place and within the realities of some other social context. Helping, then, is tightly entwined with the non-scientific social context of the people being helped, the people helping, and all of the surrounding persons and general culture.

Mental health programs may begin in concept as humanitarian and scientific endeavors. However, when these ideals are turned to the realities of working with people, the professional has thereby redefined his task. No longer will his major focus be the science of psychology or the philosophy of humanitarianism; it becomes the art and application of politics. The development of a profession, such as the mental health profession, is seen here as essentially the *politicizing* of the original sciences and philosophies. In this view mental health professionals struggle with what is most basically a *political* endeavor. Just as we failed to recognize this in our own work, so we believe that our profession generally fails to recognize and admit the essentially political nature of its task. The result, as I have pointed out elsewhere (Graziano, 1969a, 1969b, 1972), is that while we foster a professional rhetoric that is humanitarian and scientific in content, we ignore the realities of our actions, which are essentially political. Our mental health professions will never function effectively to attain humanitarian and scientific goals unless we recognize the essentially political context within which those goals are pursued, and, therefore, the political nature of our task.

[1] For another analysis of the political-social factors in our program, see Dr. Seymour Sarason's (1972) discussion, pages 24-46.

CHAPTER 2

Assumptions, Facilities and Staff[1]

INITIAL ASSUMPTIONS

Our program, initiated in 1963 (Graziano, 1963) as an alternative to traditional approaches, proceeded toward two major goals—service and inquiry—and was based on several major assumptions. First, it assumed that the effectiveness of insight-oriented psychotherapy with autistic and other severely disturbed children is questionable, as is the validity and reliability of psychodynamic interpretations. An effective program would not operate on the inferential level of psychodynamic interpretations but would instead focus on what could be observed and readily manipulated, i.e., overt behavior and the observable environment. Thus, for these children, *observed current behavior is the most useful content of therapy*.

Human behavior, whether adaptive or maladaptive, is largely learned, and the learning occurs through lawful processes. Thus, maladaptive behavior, as Dollard and Miller (1950) noted, ". . . should be unlearned by some combination of the same principles by which (it was) taught." (p. 7) By focusing on the learning processes, an increase in adaptive behavior and a decrease in maladaptive behavior could be brought about. A second assumption is: *the focus of therapy should be on learning processes that facilitate the acquisition of adaptive behavior and the decrement of maladaptive behavior*.

[1] Portions of this chapter have appeared in Graziano, A. M. The consultant, the client and hidden assumptions. In J. Zusman and D. L. Davidson (Eds.), *Practical aspects of mental health consultation*. Springfield, Ill.: Chas. C. Thomas, 1972, 52-70. Reprinted with permission.

According to these first two assumptions, the essential problem for the children is learning adaptive behavior. The third assumption then follows: *if the essential problem for the children is learning, the essential task for the therapist is teaching*. Therapy becomes a highly specialized *teaching* situation in which the staff develops specific, applied techniques· for teaching adaptive behavior to severely disturbed children.

Much of what needs to be taught involves adaptive social behavior, and social learning should occur more readily in a social group situation than in an individual therapy setting. The group situation should provide more varied and direct stimulation and reinforcement, should provide more opportunities for modeling, should increase imitative learning and vicarious reinforcement, and should generally facilitate positive transfer of the learned behavior by more closely approximating the "normal" world. Thus, the fourth assumption is: *adaptive social learning will occur most effectively in a social group situation rather than in an individual therapy setting*.

Because a learning model has been adopted, it is not necessary to train staff in psychodynamic abstractions. Focus can be maintained on the observed functioning of the children. The staff therefore must be trained in the considerably more concrete approaches involving the observation and direct manipulation of behavior, active modeling by staff, and control of environmental variables. Training staff to work with objective events is more parsimonious and less time-consuming than training them in subjective, abstract inferences. Further, since practical rather than academic ability is required, potential therapists might be found outside the traditional academic framework. Summarizing these ideas, the fifth assumption is: *behavioral approaches are straightforward and parsimonious techniques that can be taught readily to selected non-professionals, including the parents of the disturbed children*.

It is often assumed that, to treat children effectively, the parents must also be treated, particularly the mothers. Approaches to parents have ranged from depth analysis through group guidance, the latter assuming that parents do not need intrapsychic change but "...a better understanding of the dynamics of child-parent relations and of the basic facts of child growth and needs." (Ginott, 1961, p. 164) Agreeing with this, our sixth assumption is: *parents of emotionally disturbed children do not generally require psychotherapeutic treatment but do need supervised training in reality-oriented, concrete, everyday dealing with the children and active involvement in the child's therapy program*.

Our seventh assumption is: *in order to modify complex human behavior we must analyze it into its more specific response constituents and then reinforce those constituents in carefully-planned sequences of successive approximations.*

This programming approach would require a highly structured setting and an intense focus on behavioral details.

In addition to the direct teaching, which would occur through structured programming, direct and indirect teaching would also occur through consistent modeling by staff of organized, adaptive behavior. *The modeling function of staff is assumed to be an extremely important function*; because of its importance, *staff selection must be aimed largely at the selection of those who can most consistently model organized, adaptive behavior.*

Severely disturbed children are often seen as hopelessly complex, with a forbidding variety and subtlety of behavior. But that same complexity may also be an excellent indication that the child has been capable of learning complex behavior, though of a maladaptive sort. If the child can successfully learn complex *mal*adaptive behavior, it seems reasonable to assume that he can also learn complex *adaptive* behavior. Thus, the last and perhaps most important assumption with which this program began is: *all children, regardless of their degree of "emotional disturbance," are capable of learning complex socially adaptive behavior*; it is the professionals' task to provide those conditions under which even the most severely disturbed child will learn adaptive social behavior.

THE TEACHING EMPHASIS

We had assumed that the basic problem for the children was to learn adaptive social behavior. The essential task for the staff, therefore, was to *teach* adaptive social behavior to the children. Because clearly defined methods for accomplishing this had not yet been developed, our basic general task was the development of effective, practical techniques for teaching adaptive social behavior to severely disturbed children. Accordingly, we chose as our area of endeavor to become a specialized *teaching* agency. That is, if the problem is *learning*, then the task is *teaching*.

Entering the demanding world of practicalities and immediate decisions, the concepts must be translated into effective, practical, applied techniques. It was to the development of this technology that we addressed our efforts. The question was no longer, "What might we do?" or "What seems theoretically indicated?", but rather "What will we do now?" or "How do we go about developing effective practical techniques to teach adaptive behavior to severely disturbed children?"

To answer that question we must first determine what behavior we are going to teach, and that in turn requires an assessment of present behavior baselines.

BEHAVIORAL ASSESSMENT

Teaching adaptive behavior would entail both response acquisition and decrement. On the one hand, the children would have to learn age-appropriate, adaptive behavior, which they had thus far failed to acquire. Such deficiencies in age-appropriate behavior would be classed as Behavioral Deficits, which would presumably be overcome as we helped the children acquire the behavior in question.

On the other hand, we would have to bring about a decrease in overt maladaptive behavior, which, by virtue of its occurrence, interfered with the development of alternative adaptive responses. Such repeatedly-occurring maladaptive and interfering behavior would be classed as Behavioral Surplus.

The assessment of surplus and deficit behavior was attempted in three ways, through: (A) highly detailed interviews with the parents, (B) direct contact with the child in our evaluation session, and (C) ongoing observations of the child's behavior during the group sessions.

(A) *Detailed interviews with the child's parents* were carried out and the child's behavior at home was carefully described. Instructing the parents to think of the past two days, we focused on the details of how the child behaved at home. An open-ended interview form was used in which a specific sequence of behavior categories was discussed in detail:

1. Morning Behavior
   a.   arising in A.M.
   b.   washing, dressing, etc.
   c.   interactions with family
   d.   play activities
   e.   breakfast, food, and social factors
2. Eating Behavior—Food and Social Factors
   describe details of lunch and dinner, interactions, amount and quality of food, use of utensils, etc.
3. Activities at Home—All Interactions, Use of Toys, Upsets, etc.
   a.   morning
   b.   afternoon
   c.   after dinner
4. Bedtime and Sleeping
   a.   time
   b.   preparing for bed (resistance, self-help, cooperation, etc.)
   c.   behavior in bed (gets up, sleeps readily, etc.)

    d.   quality and amount of sleep (i.e., seems restful, restless, gets up, etc.)

    e.   nightmares, night fears, etc.

5. Use of Objects

    a.   describe all appropriate and inappropriate use of toys, tools, utensils, games, school material, TV, etc.

    b.   destructiveness or use of objects as "weapons"

    c.   favorite or most-used objects

    d.   feared objects

6. Behavior Toward Animals

    reactions to pets, strange animals, etc.

7. Behavior Toward Persons

    a.   parents and siblings

    b.   other children

    c.   other adults

8. Speech Activity

    a.   amount of speech

    b.   quality (clearness and appropriateness)

    c.   specific words and phrases

    d.   peculiarities

9. Toilet Behavior

    a.   degrees of control

    b.   upset behavior, tantrums, conflicts, etc. associated with bathroom behavior

    c.   recent changes in behavior

    d.   related self-care/cleanliness behavior

10. Tantrum and Aggressive Behavior

    a.   frequency, severity, and duration

    b.   detailed account of the two most recent upsets

    c.   specifically what conditions surrounded the beginning and end of upset?

11. Fears

    a.   current fears

    b.   changes in fears

12. Attention Span

    a.   attentive behavior, duration, directed at what objects or situations

    b.   what objects, situations, or activities are reinforcers?

13. Motor Coordination

The interviews were detailed and structured, moving in orderly sequence from the child's awakening in the morning through his sleep at night. As the session proceeded through the detailed description of the day's activities, the interviewer recorded the information under the appropriate headings listed above. The parents were required to focus on concrete details, giving specific rather than general information, to provide an accurate, detailed, and sequential account of the child's behavior. Many parents, particularly those having previous experience with clinics, tended at first to discuss their interpretations of their child's motives, and active work by the interviewer was necessary to keep them focused on the realities of the child's behavior. After a few such interviews, the parents learned that objective descriptions of behavior were required, and they provided them quite adequately. On later work with the parents, discussed in Chapter 9, they observed the children at home during the day and recorded their observations in notebooks. Those data were then used for further program planning for the children as well as instructive material for the parents.

The parents' reports that were most objective and best validated by staff observations were those obtained in the highly structured interview where specific details were required. When the parents made more casual reports, such as during brief chats as they brought the children in, the reports were apt to be highly influenced by immediately preceding events or their current emotional states or moods. At such times, the parents were apt to voice value judgments and broad statements of overall "adjustment" rather than the more verifiable detailed descriptions of behavior.

As the structured interview progressed, a detailed description of the child's daily behavior was constructed, specifying conditions under which behavior occurred and identifying surplus and deficit behaviors and effective reinforcers. The same structured interview was used periodically to assess the progress of behavioral change in the child.

(B) Another means of obtaining behavioral evaluations was by a *direct initial observation of the child in evaluation sessions*. The usual attempts were made to establish rapport and interact with the child in a play-room situation. Whenever feasible, attempts were made to administer intelligence tests and to obtain drawings and samples of writing or other academic work to help assess developmental levels. Projective tests were not employed. One of the important aspects here was the attempt to determine the class of stimuli to which the child responded most. Thus, reactions to a variety of auditory, visual, tactile, and olfactory stimuli were observed. This sensory testing was not carried out under controlled conditions, and we have no data to report. We believe, however, that experimental investigation of the inter- and intra-individual responsiveness of different sensory modalities is potentially important for practical application to disturbed children.

(C) The most useful method of behavioral evaluation was the *ongoing observation of the child in group sessions*. Regularities of behavioral deficits and surpluses were easily apparent after a week or two of daily detailed observation by several staff. Further, under such close observation, any changes in deficits or surpluses were immediately apparent. The children's deficit and surplus behavior was so grossly apparent that more sophisticated measurement was not necessary.

The major deficits and surpluses of the six children who comprise our focal group are briefly summarized and grouped under several categories.

BEHAVIORAL DEFICITS

The following were the most apparent and common of the behavioral deficits:

1. Social Interaction
    a. little or no positive response to people, no playing with or apparent response to other children
    b. solitary play lacked social relevancy or apparent imitation of adults' social roles or situations
    c. verbal and non-verbal communication was lacking or grossly limited
    d. recognition of concern or respect for the rights, safety, or property of others was totally lacking
2. Physical Involvement with the Environment
    a. marked aloofness from people also evident in aloofness from most common objects
    b. little appropriate use of objects such as toys, books, crayons, eating utensils, etc.
    c. marked lack of physical effort in the general manipulation of objects; for some, even the physical resistance of a light switch was too great to overcome, although, of course, they did possess sufficient physical strength
    d. low level of activity; some had a markedly low general activity level, devoting much of their time to immobile, silent sitting or standing; for others, there were periodic times of immobility, inappropriate to the prevailing situation
3. Verbal Behavior
    a. verbal communication among children and between children and staff was completely lacking in most children and was rare, brief, and bizarre in others
    b. verbal behavior even of a non-communicative type rarely occurred
4. School or Academic Behavior
    a. extremely short attention span
    b. little or no use of writing or drawing implements or any arts and crafts materials; no creative activity of drawing, scribbling, pasting, etc.

      c.   no observed academic skills

      d.   no following of even simple directions, no ability to remain seated together, as in class, for even a few seconds

5.   "Independence" or Self-Care Behavior

      a.   little dressing or undressing by themselves even with hats and coats, although two children reportedly were able to but would not

      b.   three of the six were not yet at all toilet trained; two others were enuretic at night

      c.   all showed marked lack of "safety" behavior and avoidance of hazards

      d.   no helping around the house, even when asked

      e.   general lack of independent, age-appropriate behavior in any situation

6.   General Lack of Flexibility in Behavior

      a.   marked inability to shift from one activity to another

      b.   lack of apparent interest or acceptance of any new objects, events, or persons

      c.   marked restriction in food preferences and refusal to try new foods.

BEHAVIORAL SURPLUSES

1.   Repetitive and Stereotyped Behavior

      a.   markedly stereotyped, repetitive, bizarre grimacing, posturing, and gesturing

      b.   severe, repetitive head-banging, particularly in younger children.

      c.   rocking, in many positions, under many conditions

      d.   repetitive, almost ritualized use of a limited array of objects

2.   Inappropriate Vocal Behavior

      a.   repetitive, "broken record" verbalizing of two children

      b.   loud, shrill screaming, often prolonged for two or more hours

3.   Aggressive and Destructive Behavior

      a.   severe, prolonged, aggressive and destructive tantrums

      b.   physically assaultive to others and selves; some were seriously self-injurious, drawing blood by repeated biting and digging at flesh wtih fingernails or sharp objects

      c.   highly destructive of objects

      d.   high occurrence of sudden throwing of objects

      e.   resistance to change or interference shown in violent fighting against parents and others

4. Eating Behavior
   a. mouthing, chewing, or swallowing inedible material such as dirt, clay, buttons, and insects
   b. violent rejection of certain foods
   c. aggressive grabbing of food from others at mealtimes
5. Hyperactivity
   a. for some, a general, constant hyperactivity even when grossly quiet, such as when sitting or lying down
   b. when active, exaggerated movements and vocalizations
6. Fears
   a. cringing, screaming, and running away from people, dogs, cats, birds, shadows, trees, and in one case, from stones and granulated sugar

BEHAVIORAL BASELINES, DIMENSIONS, AND GOALS

The above summary categorizes only the most apparent surplus and deficit behaviors. In its detailed form this information of each child's behavior at home and in the group constituted detailed behavioral baselines that could be compared with later behavior as observed in the groups and reported in later parent interviews.

The detailed assessments of deficit and surplus behaviors also identified the most appropriate *behavioral dimensions* along which each child should progress, thus roughly outlining individual programs for the child. The assessment that a child lacks social interaction, for example, obviously implies a desirable goal of acquiring social interaction. Each of the behavioral deficits defines its own goal, and the more carefully we assess the behavioral deficit, the better defined is the behavioral goal. The deficit and its goal can then be expressed as a *dimension* along which behavior varies from a low to high occurrence. The low end of each dimension corresponds to the child's current behavior, and the high end defines the behavioral goal. The baseline behavior for a given child and the collective baseline behavior for the group of children can be located on the various dimensions. Obviously, as these children have been described, the behavioral baselines would fall at the low end of each dimension of deficit.

Similarly, surplus behavior can be expressed as dimensions ranging from low to high, with the children's baseline behavior at the high end and the behavioral goals at the low end of each dimension.

Each child's program emerged from this planning and consisted of a sequence of those behavioral dimensions integrated into a total program. Behavioral priorities, sequencing and timing, and procedures to introduce and carry out each dimension were determined for each child. This program construction will be illustrated in Chapter 4.

ACQUISITION OF ADAPTIVE BEHAVIOR
THROUGH POSITIVE REINFORCEMENT OF
SUCCESSIVE APPROXIMATIONS

Having identified dimensions of deficit and surplus behavior and defined behavioral baselines and the desired goals for each dimension, the task remained to help the child progress from his initial baseline levels to the identified goals. With deficit behavior, where the task was primarily that of acquiring new adaptive behavior, successive approximations were employed: the careful, step-by-step, sequential reinforcement and acquisition of new behavior that increasingly approximated and eventually achieved the specified behavioral goal. This approach stemmed directly from the basic assumption that complex human behavior is most readily modified by analyzing it into its specific response constituents and reinforcing them in carefully planned sequences of successive approximations toward the specified terminal behavior. Applied to children, these planned sequences or programs proved to be difficult and complex tasks requiring a great deal of highly detailed planning. Often, at first, a two-hour staff meeting was required to determine the details of even a fifteen-minute sequence to be tried. In our applied, clinical setting, programming was not as controlled and quantified as it might at first appear, and there was a good deal of qualitative guess-work and many blind alleys. Despite their detailed pre-planning, sequences had to take into account unpredicted contingencies rising from a great variety of everyday occurrences. In one sequence to be described later, for example, a four-year-old autistic girl was taught to consistently approach another person for the first time in her life. However, before the results could be validated, the family suddenly left the state for a vacation.

More will be discussed concerning the difficulties in the application of these concepts. For the present, however, it must be emphasized, that the acquisition of new, adaptive behavior was to be brought about through the use of *positive reinforcement* applied in highly detailed, planned sequences of successive approximations leading to the previously-determined behavioral goal. This sequencing, or programming (the same as that applied in the field of programmed instruction), underlies the therapeutic approach we at one point named "programmed psychotherapy." It provided the most basic conceptual and applied tools, and every behavioral deficit of each child was approached in terms of "programming" the acquisition of adaptive behavior—thus, "teaching away" that deficit.

DECREMENT OF SURPLUS BEHAVIOR THROUGH NON-REINFORCEMENT AND THE ACQUISITION OF INCOMPATIBLE RESPONSES

It was originally expected that surplus maladaptive behavior would decrease essentially as a function of the increase in adaptive behavior. Thus, maladaptive behavior would presumably weaken (a) as reinforcement was presented for adaptive approximations but withheld when maladaptive behavior occurred; (b) as the rate of adaptive responses increased and a greater proportion of the child's total output of behavior would presumably become adaptive—and thus his maladaptive behavior would decrease proportionately; (c) as the adaptive responses increased and there would be greater opportunity for the occurrence of adaptive behavior that would be directly incompatible with maladaptive behavior, thus weakening that maladaptive behavior. For example, speaking quietly is incompatible with loud screaming—a person cannot emit both simultaneously; one must be suppressed or weakened in favor of the other. If the child acquires the speaking quietly response, that response will be incompatible with and will tend to weaken the previous loud screaming response.

Thus, assuming that maladaptive surplus responses would decrease as adaptive behavior increased, the primary focus of our initial efforts would be on the acquisition of adaptive behavior. While actively and directly programming the acquisition of adaptive behavior, we would, presumably simultaneously, effect the decrease of maladaptive surplus behavior. The major tasks in this regard were to bend our efforts to the adaptive responses by reinforcing adaptive approximations and withholding reinforcement of maladaptive responses in order to achieve their expected decrement.

As will be described, our expectation that maladaptive behavior would decrease almost automatically as we focused on the acquisition of adaptive behavior was not completely borne out. More active efforts had to be employed to bring about the significant decrement of occurrences of maladaptive responses.

STIMULUS CONTROL

Our assumptions about the learned nature of maladaptive behavior of psychotic children led to an overall approach that focused on identifying maladaptive behavior and modifying that behavior through carefully planned learning sequences, utilizing high positive reinforcement of successive approximations toward defined behavioral goals. The emphasis on careful arrangement of the reinforcing contingencies is explicit in the above summary. An equally important focus is the development of *stimulus control*. That is, while it is important to arrange the reinforcement of behavior in order to strengthen or weaken specified behavior, it is equally important to arrange the discriminative stimuli so that the emerging adaptive behavior will occur appropriately in the presence of usual social stimuli. For example, by using food reinforcement we can teach Karl (an autistic boy) to say, "My name is Karl." However, we must also teach him to respond appropriately with that phrase or some close variation of the question, "What is your name?" If he emits the response, "My name is Karl" in haphazard fashion, having no consistent relationship with the appropriate stimuli, then that verbal behavior obviously has not come under appropriate stimulus control.

The therapy program, as a result, would entail structuring the therapy setting in order to manipulate or manage the reinforcing contingencies and bring about adaptive behavior under appropriate stimulus control. These related ideas will be more fully and appropriately discussed in Chapter 6. At present, let it suffice to say that stimulus control is a central concept in the conceptualization and implementation of the therapy program.

As has been indicated, our focus was on the major deficit and surplus behavior exhibited by the whole group of children, and our efforts were directed to the acquisition by the group of adaptive behavior through behavioral programming. We shall now discuss our attempts to translate the above assumptions into practical teaching techniques.

FINANCES AND EQUIPMENT

Our early support, it will be recalled, consisted of parents' small tuition payments, meager amounts of money raised through cake sales and raffles and, most important, a staff willing to underwrite the program by accepting exceedingly low salaries. Except for the last two years when we obtained large state grants, the program operated on a skeleton budget. The annual expenditures for the total September-through-June operation during the first three years did not equal the salary of one psychiatrist at many child-guidance clinics!

The chronically undernourished treasury made it difficult to carry out and expand the program as planned. Several research projects had to be abandoned because of the lack of even simple observation and recording equipment. Other equipment, such as developmental toys, could not be purchased, and the staff depended on its own inventiveness in creating and scavenging toys. The equipment most fruitfully used in the first year consisted of cast-off books and toys, old magazines, and jig-saw puzzles. A very important item (trading stamp catalogs) was obtained free from local stores. Equipment included two small aluminum exercise ladders, six plastic balls, cardboard building blocks, a sand-box, and assorted small toys such as cars and dolls. Our furniture consisted of old tables, benches, and desks, discarded by local schools. Because there was no outdoor play area, the children were taken to city playgrounds and parks, excursions that proved to be of unexpected value for social learning as well as for recreation.

Ths modest equipment did not hinder the daily program, because sophisticated or expensive equipment is not essential for work with children. However, it did hinder research and evaluation, which delayed the program's rate of improvement. For example, tape-recorded data from the beginning would have been very helpful.

PHYSICAL FACILITIES

Heavy, noisy traffic flows along Main Street, past deteriorating three- and four-story business and apartment buildings. The elevated railroad station is a block away and, just beyond is an oil-coated inlet for industrial barges. Our program was located in a two-story brick armory facing Main Street and immediately surrounded by three bars, a liquor store, a clothing factory, a hot-dog stand, a diner, two gasoline stations, trash-filled backyards, a debris-laden empty lot, and an ancient meat-packing plant—all set against the railroad and barge inlet.

We used two rooms and a hallway on the second floor, with the open hallway at the top of the stairs also serving as our office. The two rooms were large (20 X 35 feet), cheerful and well-lighted by a row of windows overlooking the main street. They were connected by an adjoining door, and cradled between the constant, loud street noises and the unruffled din of the first-floor gymnasium, which sometimes hosted 200 exuberant youngsters.

PERSONNEL

There has been growing awareness that much of what is psychotherapeutic does not necessarily occur only in psychotherapy or by the ministration of a highly-trained therapist. The literature on non-professional therapists and on training parents to treat their own children has grown in recent years and has been discussed by several writers (Ayllon and Azrin, 1968; Guerney, 1969; Tharp and Wetzel, 1969). Early in 1963, however, there was little in the literature about non-traditional therapists (exceptions are Branch, 1963; Holzberg, 1963; Rioch, et al., 1963) and little experimentation with the active involvement of parents in special educational or therapeutic programs for their own children (Berkowitz and Graziano, 1972; Levine and Graziano, 1972).

The selection and training of non-traditional staff, including parent-training, was a major aspect of the program we proposed to the university in 1963. However, the university's refusal and the general lack of support prevented a training program per se; all training was then carried out on a small scale as part of the clinical services, and lacked adequate controls and evaluation. Despite those weaknesses, our experiences lead us to conclude that potential mental health personnel exist in sufficient numbers and are easily located in the general population; they can be readily trained, and there need be *no* lack of effective personnel in children's programs.

Our staff consisted of nurses, housewives with college degrees or only high school diplomas, and male and female students and teachers. Except for the director, none of the staff held degrees beyond the master's level or had previously trained to work with emotionally disturbed children.

Each new staff member accepted the position of "trainee" for a trial period of up to four weeks. They became assistants in an already-functioning group, observing, becoming involved when directed by supervisory staff, and learning our approaches in daily sessions under the immediate and constant supervision of one or two experienced staff. The trainee was also observed for several hours weekly by the program director, with whom he also met several times weekly to discuss his progress. After each daily session the staff met to complete the recording of observations and comments, to discuss the day's occurrences, to plan for the next day, and to discuss the trainee's progress.

More formal staff meetings, held twice weekly, aided both in training new staff and in maintaining close communication among all staff. In this way the new trainee and, in fact, all staff became immersed in the program, were in immediate and continued contact with the children, came to know their behavior, and were surrounded by the techniques and language of the developing behavior therapy. Within only a few weeks, the new trainee had learned basic concepts of reinforcement, shaping, and extinction and had begun to practice some of the techniques of behavioral observation and modification. After six months to a year of this deep immersion, the trainee was ready to head his own group of children, and the program was expanded accordingly. Thus, training consisted of very closely-supervised, daily immersion in the total program and direct and active teaching by the experienced staff.

The first trainee was an R.N. who had never before worked with emotionally disturbed children. She was, however, a mature, reliable, and stable person who had successfully raised her own family and who obviously enjoyed working with children. After close supervision by the director for six months, she became our first group worker and then actively assisted in the training of the next three trainees, as described earlier.

Trainee selection was subjective but careful, based primarily on interviews. New trainees were recruited by: (1) classified newspaper advertisements, (2) notices for students at local colleges, and (3) a standing request to colleagues for candidates.

On one occasion we received 77 replies to the following newspaper advertisement: "Mature, dependable woman, with one or more years of college, nurse's training, or nursery school teaching, wanted to train for work with young exceptional children. Preference given to applicant with grown children." The preference was based on the perhaps doubtful assumption that people who have successfully raised their own children would be more mature, patient, and knowledgeable than those who have not. Despite the preference for mature persons, the applicants ranged from young, unmarried girls to mothers with teenagers, grandmothers, and one great-grandmother.

Based on telephone interviews, 38 applicants withdrew for a variety of reasons (low wages, fear of "that section" of town, time and transportation problems). The remaining 39 attended a meeting where they were given details about the children and their behavior, our methods, and expectations of staff performance. High demands, long hours, and low pay were stressed, with the compensations of possibly seeing severely disturbed children slowly improve. After that meeting there remained 30 applicants for *one* position, all meeting at least the minimum requirements set forth in the newspaper notice. Each was interviewed separately by the director and chief group worker, resulting in *exact*, independent agreement on the top-ranked eight applicants. These top applicants had three personal interviews. We invited the first-ranked person, a youthful grandmother who had long ago completed two years of college but had not worked before, to join our staff for a one-month trial period. The second- and third-ranked persons were hired later, when more positions became available.

Subjective criteria were used in the personal interviews to search for persons who were able to understand and learn concepts as well as applied techniques, who could easily verbalize their own ideas, and who were capable of preparing daily notes and other reports. The potential therapists had to be personally flexible—easily able to accept and to learn ideas conflicting with their own. They had to be able to tolerate uncertainty and to accept unexpected events. They had to be mature, dependable people who were capable of good judgment, steady performance, and highly responsible behavior. There also had to be a quiet calmness, a softness about these people, a gentleness of approach always coupled with a firm, unruffled maintenance of limits. They had to enjoy working with children, to find satisfaction in noting even small steps in minor progress, and to engage in instances of gentle humor as well as the more demanding aspects of the work.

The most important implicit questions underlying those interviews were, "Will these persons be good models for the children?" "Do they already have in their behavioral repertoire the behaviors necessary for constructive, consistent modeling of organized, adaptive behavior?" We assumed that through training we could teach the technical details of working with children to almost any adult—but not every adult is able to consistently model the adaptive behaviors constituting our behavioral goals. Thus, the careful selection of people who would serve as good models, *even without training*, was crucial in work with children. If we could then teach these people technical skills, we would have powerful, capable, child therapists—and we believe that we succeeded.

One might object that the persons sought could not be found, not only because the criteria are subjective and the selection process highly personal and idiosyncratic but also because the criteria appear to be impossibly demanding. We contend, however, that within the limits of our ability to make such subjective judgments, an abundance of such persons can be readily found in the

Table 1. Program Staff and Occupational Areas from which They Were Drawn

Previous Occupation	Regular Program	Summer Program Only	Total
Housewives (no college degree)	7	0	7
Nurses	2	0	2
Teachers	1	22	23
College or Graduate Students	8	20	28
High School Students	0	6	6
Totals			
No. of Staff Hired	18	48	66*
No. of Positions Available	18	64	82*
No. of Applicants	176	208	384

*Sixteen persons were rehired on subsequent summers; thus, only 66 persons were needed to fill 82 staff positions.

general population. There are probably more than enough persons with the requisite personal characteristics to provide services for *all* children of whatever disorder.

During the first four and a half years of the program's operation, 82 positions became available. As seen in Table 1, 18 of the positions were in the regular program, which ran from September to June, and 64 were made available during the four summer camp seasons. Each summer, 16 persons were invited to return to work, and thus the total of 82 positions was filled by only 66 persons. Table 1 also indicates the occupational areas from which these staff members were selected.

As seen in Table 2, the 384 applicants learned of the program through a variety of avenues, from newspaper classified advertisements and bulletin-board notices at universities to personal invitations by the program director. Of the 66 persons hired, 64 were selected through interviews, as described earlier. The remaining two were not carefully interviewed and screened, but had been hired early in the program on the recommendation of a colleague in the mental health professions. It is interesting to note that one of these two resigned within two weeks and the other was later discharged for poor work.

Table 2. Avenues of First Contact with Applicants

"Avenue"	Regular Program		Summer Only		Total
	Applied	Hired	Applied	Hired	
Personal Invitation	4	4	–	–	
Newspaper Ad.	142	4	–	–	
University Notices	19	4	126	22	
Recommended by Poverty Agency	3	1	33	6	
Recommended by Educational Colleagues	6	3	45	20	
Recommended by Mental Health Colleagues	2	2	4	0	
Totals Applied	176		208		384
Totals Hired		18		48	66

Six of the 66 persons hired were high school students from poverty homes hired on a special summer project. They were not intended to be considered therapists, teachers, or group workers. Their responsibilities in the program were clearly limited. This program will be discussed in Chapter 8, which deals with the summer camp.

The remaining 60 staff, composed of housewives, nurses, teachers, and college students, had greater responsibilities and constitute a group we suggest as potential, non-traditional, mental health personnel.

EXPECTATIONS OF STAFF PERFORMANCE

The selective hiring process provided bases for our expectations of the quality of staff performance. We attempted to create working conditions that would communicate these expectations and would support the behavior of staff meeting them. In this section and the next, these expectations will be discussed and the most important support systems described.

We assumed, and attempted to communicate clearly to staff, that those who survived the selective hiring process did in fact possess the qualities we sought, i.e., strong humanitarian values, enjoyment of children, firmness, flexibility, etc. Each new staff member was accepted as a select, highly responsible, and potentially skilled person who had made a personal commitment to learn new skills and carry out tasks at the highest possible level. Each staff member was accorded high individual value and was not perceived merely as someone filling a position. The qualities of the person and the qualities of performance were emphasized; the position, titles, job description, etc., were considered to be of lesser importance.

These assumptions about the staff led to clear expectations concerning the quality of performance. Common group procedures and specific programming for each child provided the basic program structure shared by all staff. Those structures had been developed in staff meetings and were based on a great deal of shared thought and planning. It was important to maintain the basic program structures as they had been planned and to avoid unilaterally introducing changes that had not been carefully thought out and agreed to by all staff. The program structures defined clear goals for the group and for individual children, outlining the general procedures of shaping and determining priorities for these goals, i.e., their order or sequencing.

Thus, a major expectation was that staff would *maintain the program structure with its clear focus on specified goals and would not alter the programming in any way that diverted the program from its goal direction.*

A second expectation, related to the first, was that while staff maintained a clear focus on goal direction, each person would flexibly *contribute his own individual style of functioning to achieve those goals*. For example, if attentive behavior were a goal for a child, then shaping attentive behavior would constitute a program dimension. A child might work with as many as four different staff members in a day, and each would employ his own style. One might characteristically demand a narrow, intense focus on the task at hand in a somewhat stern, no-nonsense manner. A second staff member might operate in a low-keyed, soft approach, easily tolerating a great deal of behavioral variation and reinforcing a much wider spectrum of approximations. A third staff member might characteristically adopt a laboratory-like, emotionally neutral methodology, precisely pinpointing highly specific behaviors in a controlled setting from which all extraneous stimuli and behaviors had been removed. Another staff member, working with the same child, might shape attentive behavior through a boisterous, happy, highly vocal, and physical rough and tumble approach. All would maintain the planned goal direction utilizing positive reinforcement in the programmed sequences; individual styles would be varied, highly valued, and supported. Only when it was judged to be specifically important at some stage of a child's programming would staff be instructed to utilize any specific style for that child.

An assumption about children's learning underlying the high value placed on individual staff styles is that complex behavior, such as attention, consists of a large number of individual acts. By providing a variety of learning settings and of reinforcement, we would presumably strengthen a wide variety or spectrum of individual acts, all sharing the common element of attentive behavior. We assumed that this would provide a greater richness or response depth for the behavioral dimension being taught. The same assumptions were involved in our decision to utilize primarily a group rather than an individual setting.

Thus, staff members were expected to maintain the basic programming and goal direction and, at the same time, use their own personal styles in creative ways to achieve those goals.

Another group of expectations concerned our emphasis on task orientation. Staff was expected to agree fully that *our overriding task was the development and welfare of the children*. The program existed for that reason and all else, including staff personal needs, was secondary, important only to the degree that it affected the main task. It was important, then, to remain sharply aware of all factors that might conflict with that task. Therefore, staff members were expected to *maintain a highly critical self-evaluative alertness*, becoming extremely sensitive to the details of their own functioning with the children and each other.

As part of this, staff members were also expected to be *fully in control of their own emotional behavior*, not allowing any of it to conflict with the welfare of the children. For example, any negatively-toned reactions, such as withdrawal of positive reinforcement, must be clearly response contingent and goal directed, dispensed by staff *purposefully*. Any non-contingent, unplanned responses actually or potentially disruptive of the children's program were assumed due to staff's incomplete understanding of the programmed dimension. In these instances, verbally reviewing the program with staff easily solved the problem. Negatively toned, unexplained, disruptive responses were assumed due to other staff factors such as mood, fatigue, conflicts among staff, dissatisfaction with working conditions, transfer of home or private problems to the work situation, etc. When such problems did inevitably occur, staff members were expected to recognize their behavior and willfully modify or suppress it while working with the children. *Staff members, then, were expected to monitor and appraise their own behavior in relation to the planned programs and, simply, to turn off any interfering emotional behavior*.

These expectations emphasized staff functioning as primarily a task-oriented, conscious or intellectual process. That is, personal problems of staff are private affairs, ideally irrelevant but potentially disruptive of the work task. Staff was expected to prevent or control interfering behavior so as to neutralize its effects. The intent here was not simply to suppress behavior but to encourage the staff's alertness to its own conduct and the immediate attempt to solve both personal and staff-interpersonal problems. If personal problems did interfere with the work task, they became everyone's problems and all of the staff involved were called upon to solve them. There was a great deal of support and reinforcement for attempts to solve those potentially disruptive problems. Additionally, explaining work difficulty on the basis of personal problems was not tolerated, i.e., no support or sympathy was given for persistent work difficulty owing to personal problems. Regardless of any stress in personal lives at home, staff was expected to have a minimum of personal problems at work and, when such problems did arise, it was expected that they would be solved immediately. Our task was to help the children; we did not have much time to devote to personal problems of staff members.

Finally, another important expectation was that, because the work was of such complexity and much of the technique had to be created and refined in a trial and error manner, it was inevitable that staff would make many errors. Errors were inevitable and not necessarily disruptive unless repeated. In fact, a seeming error might turn out to have positive value. Thus, when staff made errors, the expectations were that: (1) errors are a natural part of the task and no criticism was applied to the staff member; (2) the staff would recognize and correct errors, so as to avoid the same error in the future; and (3) all other staff would provide help and support, if needed, to solve any problems of persistently made errors.

These expectations were communicated in a variety of ways, including direct verbal instruction. Outside observers, mainly professionals from other agencies, took exception to our intolerance of staff's emotional problems and were critical of our apparently insensitive explanation that when we (staff) came to work we simply turned off personal problems which would not be tolerated during working hours. Many critics maintained that it was unrealistic and naive to expect this willful control over emotions. Clearly, this task orientation conflicted with the more common personal-emotional orientation of typical clinical agencies. Our observations during the six years were that staff could, and did, successfully turn-off or suppress personal problems while at work, with no apparent cost or substitution of symptoms.

PROGRAM SUPPORTS FOR THE HIGH EXPECTATIONS

Concrete support was needed for behaviors appropriate to those expectations, and a complex working support system was developed.

One of the most crucial basic supports was the shared nature of skills and tasks. Aside from personal style, all full-time staff members were capable of at least temporarily carrying out all staff functions—group worker, group supervisor, teacher, researcher, program planner, program evaluator, parent interviewer, home-program consultant, etc. Further, everyone participated at all levels to carry out any needed task, including those ordinarily relegated to low-level staff. Thus, not only working with children but also sweeping floors, taking children to the bathroom, fixing clogged toilets, painting walls, etc. were tasks in which everyone participated, from the newest trainee to the program director.

This sharing at all task levels seemed to have several effects. (1) It cleared away many occupational status distinctions and thus may have prevented potentially disruptive staff status competition. (2) It helped to emphasize skills rather than occupational status. For example, two staff members were extremely skillful in handling major aggressive behavior. Often, when such behavior occurred, they would be called in by a less-skilled staff member who, recognizing the other's ability, would relinquish his control. This flexibility in swapping staff activity occurred easily and smoothly. Staff developed a variety of non-verbal signals to communicate quickly with one or two simple head motions and facial expressions ideas such as, "Jeff, come over and handle Cathy and I'll pick up where you left off with Freddie." Jeff's response, by hand signals, head nods, and facial expressions, might simply be, "Yes," or "Sorry, I can't leave Freddie right now. Hang on and I'll be there within two minutes. OK?". (3) Closely related to the above, it emphasized the task as a cooperative, shared effort. In a short time the staff developed into an occupationally and personally close team of colleagues and friends. While there are many obvious and important advantages of close, friendly, mutually-respectful working relationships, the major weakness was that every person was a critically important team member and, when anyone left, the character of the team changed and could never be recaptured; it became a different team!

A second important support variable was the public nature of group work, which led to an easy, non-defensive recognition of one's own errors in working with the children. If a staff member in a prolonged, intense encounter with a child even momentarily lost the goal direction (e.g., flaring up, shouting, etc.), this lapse was observed by one or more staff members and immediately became public knowledge. If the staff member did not immediately correct the error, one of the others would. Under these conditions, the staff could do little else but admit the error and then focus constructively on how to avoid the same problem in the future. If necessary, the entire staff provided support and attention, not to the error but to the attempts to correct it in the future.

The public nature of the setting, the mutual support by staff, and the expectation that errors were inevitable in our largely trial-and-error process supported a continual constructive self-critical awareness and non-defensive, objective focus on the correction of mistakes.

Another major support was the communications system, which provided a great deal of direct communication among all staff. This included: (1) non-verbal signals during children's group sessions, (2) direct verbal communication informally throughout the day and in regular staff meetings, and (3) a system of written notes.

The system of signals, briefly discussed above, was used during child group meetings when verbal exchange among staff might be disruptive of a child's learning sequence. Another silent method used during sessions was writing notes to one another in a specific notebook easily accessible to staff. Thus, instructions, changes in routine, comments on performance, etc., would be written to all staff or particular staff members, who would read the notes within minutes. This system also yielded a permanent, dated record, useful in supervising of new staff.

Staff meetings were held briefly every morning prior to the group session and again at the end of each day. In addition, one or two long staff meetings were held weekly.

These systems were set up to provide a communications web which facilitated constant, rapid, in-depth staff communication. No question or problem had to wait a week for discussion or solution; each staff member was up-to-date on daily progress reports for each child. Staff had easy access to each other and to all available information about the children.

The last major support to be discussed is the handling of errors made by the staff. It was noted earlier that because of the largely trial and error nature of our work, particularly the early work, we expected to make mistakes. Further, we assumed that those mistakes would not be detrimental to the child unless repeated, in which case there might be some cumulative negative effect.

Staff performance, including that of the director, was discussed regularly at staff meetings, and errors made during the day were handled objectively as were any behaviors-to-be-changed. In this process staff members were not criticized or embarrassed, but rather directly helped to overcome performance deficits.

The performance expectations and the support systems helped create a working situation in which staff functioned as equal-status colleagues in an important, shared, and humanitarian effort; we had access to, and used, a great many individually important, highly talented people clearly committed to the task of helping children.

Thus far, the selection process and criteria, the behavior desired of the therapist, and the major support systems have been described. Based on admittedly qualitative and personal criteria, 60 persons were hired as trainees to work directly with emotionally disturbed children and six high school students were hired as aides with limited duties. Once hired, how well did these people perform?

Two persons resigned and two others were discharged for unacceptable work. Another eight, all hired during the summer programs, had difficulty handling the children and showed so little improvement during the course of the summer program that they would not be rehired or recommended for further work with emotionally disturbed children.

There was a good deal of variation in performance among the remaining 54, from a minimum acceptable performance all the way to exceptionally fine, consistent work. The finest child psychotherapist I have ever observed is Mrs. Mae Bonnar Johnston, an R.N. with no previous training in this field, who remained in the program for just over two years. There were several other non-traditional persons whom I would have no hesitation in favorably comparing with psychiatrists or psychologists in terms of their ability to carry out psychotherapy with children. Such judgments are qualitative, but are based on a great deal of careful observation. Thus, 54 of the non-traditional staff were judged to be competent, reliable persons who could effectively work as therapists in mental health programs for children. All would continue to need professional supervision, but many, especially those who had worked in the program for two years, could function with only a minimum of guidance. Table 3 summarizes this information.

Table 3. Summary of Information on Non-Traditional Staff

Original Occupation	No. Accepted	Would Be Recommended Again	Would Not Be Recommended Again
Housewife	7	7	0
Nurse	2	2	0
Teacher	23	18	5
College or Graduate Student	28	23	5*
High School Student	6	4	2
Totals	66	54	12

*The five college students who would not be recommended again were all education majors planning to become teachers. Thus, 10 of the 12 persons who would not be recommended to work with children were teachers or future teachers!

SUMMARY AND CONCLUSIONS

During the four and a half year program, 66 persons were selected out of 384 applicants to fill 82 positions. There were thus nearly six applicants for each person eventually hired. Six of the 66 hired were high school students on a special program with only limited responsibilities, while 60, consisting of housewives, nurses, teachers, and college students, had greater responsibilities in carrying out the programs. All staff were closely supervised. Twelve were eventually judged as not suited for the work or for further involvement in this area. Of the 12 judged not suitable, 10 were either teachers or future teachers. The remaining 54 would be recommended to continue, some with stronger recommendations than others.

There is not doubt that an abundance of interested persons did exist and that there were many more applicants than positions available. Based on our experiences, we conclude that locating applicants for positions in mental health programs is a relatively simple task posing no problems beyond the careful investment of time in reaching beyond traditional sources. This appears particularly true during the summer when a vast pool of teachers and college and high school students are available for as long as three consecutive months of full-time work. If that pool were to be utilized, there would probably be ample manpower to staff all of the mental health summer programs needed for children. Further, the teachers, housewives, and college students trained during the summer could continue to be utilized throughout the entire year, even if on a part-time basis, thus maintaining many of the expanded programs of the summer.

With this view, the summer could be a productive, active time with special mental health programs employing and training teachers and college students, utilizing the otherwise empty schools and playgrounds with all of their facilities. This view of course, requires that we accept the assumption that teachers, college students, housewives, high school students, and others can readily be trained in techniques of child therapy. In reality, however, instead of an increased level of mental health activity during the summer, we find that it is actually a time of vacations and curtailed programs. Many child guidance clinics close down for a full month or more during the summer, and after-school programs are abandoned when school is no longer in session. The vacations are for the professional middle-class staff; for the children, the summer brings no respite from their behavioral disorders or their intolerable social conditions. There is no doubt that mental health professionals have not taken advantage of the availability of physical resources and potential manpower, particularly during the summer months.

It became apparent that with careful qualitative selection, potentially good child therapists can be identified in the general population and, their lack of professional background notwithstanding, trained in a relatively short time. We believe that this city is not significantly different from others and are convinced that any city can yield a sufficient number of potentially effective child therapists to provide services for all of its exceptional children!

To find and train these people requires a shift away from traditional professionalism and calls for the exercise of infinite care in both selection and training, essentially still a subjective process of judgments. The current dearth of child therapists in all areas arises not from any real lack of persons with required talent but rather from the severly limiting, self-defensive reactions of mental health professionalism. It may be difficult for many of our colleagues to admit that there might be non-professionals who are superior or at least equal to themselves as therapists.

Thus, we maintain that potentially effective child psychotherapists exist in abundance in any city and can readily be identified and trained if we, as professionals, are flexible enough to seek, identify, and accept them. The mental health power structure has imposed artificial limitations on the supply of child therapists, but this situation need not continue, particularly if we are more concerned with the progress of children than with the perpetuation of mental health professionalism.

CHAPTER 3

The Children

THE ORIGINAL GROUP

Our exploratory work covered nearly six years and included 208 children (161 enrolled, 47 evaluated but not enrolled). Although there was only a small degree of experimental control, the immediately-recorded observations of the many varied behavioral events involving this large number of children observed by many different people over a period of nearly six years provide some degree of reliability and confidence in our conclusions. The observations were recorded daily in looseleaf notebooks both during and immediately following each group session. For each child, a daily, dated record exists, which includes behavioral descriptions, quantitative measures, staff judgments and descriptions of special or unusual occurrences, detailed interviews with parents, and twice-weekly, highly detailed, staff meetings.

The six children who will serve as our examples were all previously diagnosed as autistic, were the most severely disturbed, and they remained together longest, in two groups, for at least three and a half years. They have not been selected because of their high degree of improvement. Rather, they were the most difficult and posed the greatest challenges. This section presents a brief history of four of those children and a description of their behavior during the first approximately six months in our program. Each description provides "descriptive behavioral baselines," and serves as bases for comparison with later behavior. Billy, Frankie, Freddie, and Mary were the original four children in the program and they constituted our only group for the first six months.

BILLY

History

Billy refused to dress, feed, or help himself in even minor ways, and frequent illnesses debilitated him to increasing dependence on his mother. Poorly coordinated physically, he would not run, use his hands, or play with toys or other children. At age four, he entered a once-weekly nursery group, but was frequently ill and absent. The following year another nursery school described him as "withdrawn, bizarre, and phobic." A child psychiatrist, who reported minimal progress in fifteen months of weekly psychotherapy, said Billy was "markedly phobic, ritualistic, psychotic, and neurologically impaired." His parents then enrolled him twice-weekly in physiotherapy for three years, without improvement. At five, after two wholly unsuccessful weeks in one private school, he was transferred to another where he remained for the year. The following summer he was in another school, later in a day camp, and, at six, he began two years of academic tutoring.

At eight, Billy was a hyperactive, highly phobic, highly dependent, and nearly helpless child, poorly coordinated, engaged in markedly bizarre actions and stereotyped motions, and possessing many tics. He still maintained a rigid schedule of eating four times a day and had severe tantrums if his meals were not on time. Invarying in content, his meals consisted of one jar each of strained meat, a green and a yellow vegetable, and fruit. At an age when other boys were already playing rough and tumble games and beginning to experience some independence from home, Billy was still passively sitting at a table, bib tucked under his chin, hands idle, opening his mouth for spoon-fed, strained baby foods. At nine, Billy began three years of a psychoanalytically-oriented group therapy program for autistic children, and his parents began group therapy.

When he enrolled in our program at the age of 12, Billy had already experienced many physical and psychiatric examinations, two or three hospitalizations, five nursery and private schools, 15 months of psychiatric treatment, at least one day camp, three years of physiotherapy, two years of academic tutoring, and three years in a group therapy program. In addition, his parents had undergone group therapy for two or three years. At 12, Billy was tall, gangling, hyperactive, still markedly phobic, and bizarre. His verbalizing was intensely insistent, stereotyped, repetitious, circumstantial, and generally inappropriate.

Initial Behavior in the Program

Still poorly coordinated, Billy had difficulty overcoming even minimal physical resistance. For example, when once asked to select a truck from the toy box, Billy dropped it when it snagged on a bit of thread, saying, "I can't, I can't." His hands and fingers seemed to be extremely weak and would collapse if he tried to use a crayon. He did not use toys or utensils and avoided situations requiring the use of his hands or the coordinated use of his body.

At first, quiet, verbalizing little, Billy soon began testing limits. He repeatedly rode a tricycle to the top of the stairs where the danger became so great we had to stop him. He then began to run out of the room and eventually down the stairs and out of the building. One day, in great excitement, he dashed down the stairs and into the clothing factory next door. The sudden appearance of this hyperactive, darting, tall, gangling boy, leaping and bounding about the assembly line, whooping and giggling in frenzied excitement, waving his long arms, and yelling, "Oooh, oooh, they're gonna get me! They're gonna get me! Ooh. Ooh!" was sufficient to disrupt the work process and cause several of the working ladies to add their own shrieks to the confusion. The harried staff pursued him around the factory, finally catching him and leading him out. As the factory was getting back into operation, Billy laughed, giggled, jumped, and bounced in intense excitement over the whole escapade.

Later, he began to leap to the windowsills, dangle his legs out, and shout to the pedestrians two stories below, "Whee, whee, look at me! Hey, look at me." When removed from the windowsill, Billy dashed back to it or hopped up on the radiator, jumping up and down, yelling, "Look at me, look what I'm doing." One day, while he was being ignored for this provocative behavior, Billy filled a pail with sand and emptied it out the window toward a pedestrian two stories below. He then leaped and danced around the room, laughing and giggling, shouting, waving the pail, and becoming increasingly uncontrollable. As each new limit or rule was set, he provocatively tested it. He began to entice the other children also to test these limits, for example, dragging a smaller child out into the hall and shouting, "Look what Freddie did. Look where Freddie is. He's in the hall. Look what Freddie did!"

Within two months, Billy had broken one window, torn down one set of drapes, broken the radiator mountings, and bombarded several hapless pedestrians. As he became increasingly hard to handle, his direct interaction with staff increased; however, it was anything but adaptive. Billy's intense involvement with the bare arms of the staff is an example. At first only touching their arms, he then grabbed them, hanging on, stroking, kissing, and biting them. Billy did not brush his teeth or clean his mouth, and when the staff's arms became coated with his saliva the smell was strong and unpleasant. At the sight of a bare arm he became highly excited, leaping, dancing, waving his own arms, and shouting as he held on to the staff member's arm: "It's pretty. It's a pretty arm. Pretty, pretty, pretty, arm. What a pretty arm. What a pretty arm. It tastes just delicious. Delicious! Like spaghetti and soup!" "I like the arm. It's a pretty arm.

I want to see it move. Does it move? I want to see it move. It's like a cat's tail. I want to take it home. Can I take it home? Can I have your arm? Can I? Let me take your arm. Please? Oh, please? Please, please may I have your arm to take home? Please, please give me your arm to take home? I love your arm. It's a pretty arm. Oh, please, please, please!"

His intense focus on arms faded, and he began to carry on limited conversations with the group worker while he clung to the arm. For example, he would say, "That's a pretty arm. What does the arm do when I say that? Does the arm like it? Does the arm like to be called pretty? Does it? What does the arm do? What does the arm say? Did the arm say it's pretty? What does the arm say?" About four months later, Billy was saying to the same group worker, "Your're pretty all over, not just your arm. All of you. You're pretty all over. You're all pretty. You're pretty all over." His focus continued to shift from an intense and narrow response to an arm, to a more verbal response to the whole person.

His intensity of behavior was also evident in his many fears of illness and injury. When removed from the windowsill, he became very frightened and shouted in a high rapid voice, "You won't throw me out the window, will you? Please, oh please, don't throw me out the window."

Billy was extremely phobic, fearing many round objects, for example— stones, balls, lumps in granulated sugar—because they "might roll" and injure him. He feared hills and inclines down which things can roll, and books because "they bite"; he bounded away in seeming panic from anyone with a cold, and he refused certain food because "it chokes you." If asked to try a cookie, for example, he became highly agitated and shouted, "Please don't shove it down my throat like at that other school! Will you shove it down my throat and choke me?" His diet was limited to soft foods such as stews, soups, and spaghetti, and he would not chew even a soft sandwich.

Billy became extremely excited when other children lost control, and he would bound about shouting, "Help, police, help, oh help, police!" Generally excited, he would not focus on any constructive group activity. Aware of his disruptions, he frequently referred to his behavior, and one day explained that his "bad deeds" were "only a movie" and were not committed by him at all.

Billy was not without humor, and we frequently suspected that while he was literally pulling our arms, he was also, at times, figuratively pulling our legs. When he likened the taste of bare arms to "spaghetti and soup" and went on interminably about how "deeeelicious tasting" it was, there really seemed to be humor behind his very wide grin. There was no doubt, particularly after several months, that Billy sought appreciative audiences. His loud statement, "My, what a gorgeous arm," seldom failed to send Frankie into loud and sustained giggling, and Billy seemed to make sure that Frankie was watching him before making the statement. Frankie was an effective reinforcer for that behavior. Another example was his repeated insistence that there was a "beautiful rosebush" in the hall. "Did you see that pretty rosebush in the hall?" "Rosebush answers the telephone." After informing us of this, Billy would laugh and bound off, perhaps to his perch on the windowsill, and yell out the window at the passing people, "We have a rosebush in the hall! We have a rosebush in the hall! Rosebush talks on the telephone." Billy's reference was his little joke. There was, indeed, a lady named Rose who sat at a desk in the hall, and Billy was quite taken with her. His joke never failed to stimulate him into a laughing, giggling loss of control.

Billy's speech was understandable but rapid, repetitious, and aggressively insistent. Some of his favorite expressions were, "Do you have a kittie? Do you? Do you? Do you have a kittie? What's your kittie's name? Does your kittie have a tail? What's the name of your kittie? Where is your kittie? Will I ever see your kittie?" or "What does the furnace do? What does the furnace do? Does the furnace say anything? Does the furnace like it? What does the furnace do? What does the furnace do? Do you have a furnace?" One phrase that Billy apparently found quite pleasant and rapidly repeated sometimes for 15 minutes without a pause was "look at the big bus." When repeated rapidly, this became, "loogadabigbus, loogadabigbus, loogadabigbus, etc."

There are obvious psychodynamic interpretations that most clinicians would make of behavior such as intense caressing and sucking of bare arms. Billy's report that an open book was "biting" when he put his hand into it, his leaping upon the backs of the group workers, and most of his other behaviors lend themselves to easy and immediate psychodynamic interpretations. Instead we tried to describe the behavior as observed, and later attempted to account for it by identifying the relevant patterns of stimulus control.

FRANKIE

History

Like Billy, Frankie had a history of feeding problems, hospitalizations, many examinations, and different treatment attempts. He wore orthopedic shoes, underwent unsuccessful speech therapy for six months, and also spent several years in the psychodynamic therapy program with Billy while his parents were treated in group therapy. Unlike Billy's hyperactive behavior, Frankie was characterized by behavior deficits. At the age of nine, when we first saw him, he was small, thin, and pale. His motor coordination was poor, and his walk was unusual—bent at the waist, his upper body nearly parallel with the floor, his long legs rigid. Frankie walked by stiffly thrusting out one leg and falling slowly onto that foot, then the other, and so on, never looking right or left. Markedly aloof, he objected to physical contact and never allowed anyone to touch his head; yet, paradoxically, he would allow his mother to kiss him only on his head. When contact was necessary, such as in dressing, he fought strenuously by falling, kicking, and crying, to the intense frustration of his parents.

Initial Behavior in the Program

At times he simply sat alone on the floor, ignoring the others and only occasionally turning his head when his name was called. If other children approached, Frankie ignored or pushed them away. By the sixth session, Frankie allowed another child to stand near him for several minutes. During the seventh session, he spontaneously climbed into a therapist's lap and snuggled against him for ten minutes, making crooning sounds. From that point on, he was observed to have more frequent, although brief and limited, interactions.

Frankie began to watch the other children and by the 29th session (6 weeks) he had become an alert but passive observer, particularly responsive to Billy. While Billy lost control, Frankie sat huddled over, the knuckles of both hands covering his mouth, his eyes alertly following Billy. In this unchanging position for as long as an hour, Frankie giggled loudly at Billy's behavior, occasionally saying, haltingly and explosively, "Billy—OUT!" Frankie's reactions stimulated Billy to even more extreme provocations causing Frankie to giggle for even longer periods, which stimulated Mary into intense aggressive behavior because Frankie was "too noisy."

Frankie's active participation occurred rarely, but with careful and slowly applied structuring he could be engaged briefly in scribbling with crayons, listening to stories, or pointing at and identifying pictures in books. These periods of activity gradually increased, but during the first 100 sessions, or approximately five months, they were few, brief, and sedentary. Frankie's speech was limited in rate, content and quality, consisting of only nine spoken words, five of which identified family members. Frankie's speech was slurred, slow, guttural, and explosive, as if he marshaled a quantity of breath deep in his chest and then pushed it out through stiff, immobile lips. However, Frankie soon began using many sounds to identify pictures and objects. Apparently fascinated by tools, he made a "zzz" sound to pictures of an electric drill, car, or airplane. Although generally silent at home, he had obviously learned to recognize many phrases, single words, names, and uses of objects, but had not learned to produce the appropriate verbal sounds. Speech was an area of severe learning deficit.

Frankie made his needs known by pointing, grunting, or reaching for things which would then be provided by his parents. Mostly, he waited passively for other people to detect or anticipate and then meet his needs. Within eight weeks, he was counting aloud to ten, although we would not have recognized the sounds as numbers if they were not accompanied by the use of his fingers. By the 29th session (6 weeks), Frankie had learned many new words, and was appropriately using phrases such as "Billy go out" and "Daddy paint ceiling." It appeared as if there had been considerable earlier "latent" learning at home, perhaps needing the structure and rewards of the daily group sessions to be more frequently emitted. Parents and clinicians often report that a child "really knows much more than he's showing," and Frankie seemed to suggest just that. Frankie's involvement with the world was minimal, and his use of objects extremely limited. At age nine, he still did not play with toys, but was often observed lining up kitchen utensils on the floor. In the first 100 sessions, he was much the same as at home, usually remaining seated, quiet, and inactive. During his first ten sessions, the only objects he actively handled were cookies and paper cups, a picture puzzle, and once he remained in the sandbox for about five minutes, picking up toys but not using them appropriately. Over the next 30 sessions, Frankie began to roll and retrieve a ball and to touch though not ride a tricycle. By the 40th session, he was spinning the wheel of the upside-down tricycle, but still would not ride it. He began to color with crayons, to roll clay, and to handle puzzle pieces.

On the 75th session, noting his interest in tools, we purchased a set of plastic carpenter's tools for him, and Frankie's activity began to center around those and a large doll house. Frankie would remain kneeling in front of the doll house for long periods, simply idle or using his plastic tools and making various buzzing sounds to imitate power tools. All of his motions were extremely slow and poorly coordinated. Even turning his head in response to his name was a slow process. As noted earlier though, his periods of aloof withdrawal developed into a passive but alert observing of others. Thus, although his physical activity and tempo changed very slightly during the first 100 sessions, his aloofness decreased and Frankie became our quiet observer.

At the age of nine, he was not yet toilet trained, still wore diapers, failed to signal his need to the group worker or to go to the toilet himself, and soiled his clothes daily. Frankie did not run, jump, throw or catch a ball, or swing a bat. Like Billy, he did not manipulate objects and would not overcome even minor physical resistance such as that afforded by a light switch. Thus, while Billy was engaged in his high degree of hyperactivity, Frankie tended to remain in one spot and he either passively observed or appeared not to be even involved enough to observe.

As described earlier, Frankie had a history of eating difficulties and, at the age of nine, he still retained a few of those difficulties. He would eat only one meal daily, usually the evening meal, at which time he ate quite substantially. He preferred very soft foods and even gagged on a piece of cookie. Although he readily drank most liquids he refused to drink plain water.

Like the other children, Frankie exhibited several fears. He was afraid of dogs, strangers, vacuum cleaners, fans, motors, a few television commercials, and trees. He made these fears known by pulling back, flinching, ducking, grunting or screeching when such stimuli were present. Frankie's resistance was characteristically passive. There were many occasions when he refused to move and often remained standing, perhaps with his hat and coat on, holding his lunch box and simply refusing to cooperate. He frequently dropped to the floor in the hall, huddled against the wall, saying nothing an entire morning. Talking to him, coaxing, or pleading had no effect on this behavior.

In summary, when Frankie began in the program he was a thin, pale, nine-year-old boy, poorly coordinated and extremely slow-moving. He was generally not physically involved in the group, but he did begin alertly observing the others and did a good bit of giggling as he watched. His active vocabulary consisted of nine understandable words; the few occasions when he communicated he did so by pointing and grunting. He was not yet toilet trained, did not play with toys, and very rarely actively manipulated objects. Although he ate snacks well, he broke every cookie into very small bits before putting them into his mouth, and even then he gagged. Frankie had no acting-out tantrum behavior, but would frequently become immobile and maintain a marked resistance. There is no doubt that his level of functioning was far below that of most nine year olds.

FREDDIE

History

Freddie's development and behavior, like Frankie's was characterized by severe deficits. Freddie had older sisters and was born in an easy, uncomplicated, normal delivery after a healthy, full-term pregnancy. He sat up at seven months of age and walked at ten. He was weaned without difficulty at one year and toilet trained by about three, although he still has occasional accidents. Freddie's parents did not seek help from the mental health profession until the child was approximately four years old, although his mother had been growing progressively concerned from the time he was approximately six months old. Freddie's mother indicated that his general behavior and lack of responsiveness, his apparent deafness, incessant crying at night, general irritability, and his later lack of language development caused her considerable concern and prompted her to speak to her pediatrician on many occasions.

Unfortunately, the pediatrician did not take the mother's concern seriously and attempted to placate and reassure her that the child "was fine," that she "worried too much," and was "looking for things wrong with the child." Freddie was physically well-developed, with a strong body and excellent motor coordination, and he was markedly free from even the usual childhood illnesses. The pediatrician, apparently focusing only on the immediately visible physical condition of the child, refused to acknowledge any validity in the mother's concern for the child's behavior and social development. It was not until Freddie was four and a half years old, and his behavior was obviously disturbed, that the mother took him to a more appropriate clinic.

Freddie was very "irritable" (he was nearly five before he slept through an entire night without waking up and crying). His crying was raucous, intense, loud, and thoroughly distressing to his parents, who could quiet him only by rocking him in his crib or carriage. Rocking seemed to soothe and quiet him, but he resisted any other close physical contact. His most resistive behavior was during his bath, when he kicked, screamed, and fought so strenuously that two adults were needed to hold him. Unlike Frankie and Billy, Freddie did not have severe eating problems and he never needed hospitalization. Freddie ate sufficient amounts of food, but insisted on a diet heavily favoring large quantities of milk, ice cream, cake, candy, juice, and other sweets. Although indifferent to other food, he did eat them, thus insuring a nutritious variety. At age four and a half, his vocabulary consisted of ten word-like sounds, with none used in direct communication. Freddie was described as being a child who "understands everything said to him" but who communicated non-verbally by "growling inside," pointing, grunting, leading parents by the hand to the desired object or place. If they did not understand him, he would have a brief but intense tantrum. He was often noted to screech suddenly in a loud, shrill manner without any identifiable stimulus for that behavior.

At age four, Freddie was diagnosed as an autistic child and was placed in the psychodynamically-oriented group therapy program with Billy and Frankie, and he remained in that program for one and a half years. When he entered our program at six, he was still non-verbal and generally non-communicative and frequently screeched for no known reason. He ignored or fought adults and feared children. Physically healthy despite a diet heavily saturated with sweets, he was able to ride a tricycle, use a fork and spoon, use an eggbeater to make pudding (which he avidly devoured), pour from a bottle without spilling, and climb even the most vertical and highly polished furniture. In spite of his frequent tantrums and his obviously good physical abilities, Freddie was an inactive youngster, extremely quiet, unresponsive, and described by his mother as having always been "indifferent" to people, things, and activities. His daily behavior at the age of six was described by his mother: "Freddie walks around the house. He looks around, looking for sweets. He won't go out at all in the winter. He goes into closets, drawers, pulls out some things. If I sit down for a minute, he sits with me, usually quiet but sometimes he makes sounds. I try to get him to watch TV but he only glances at it for a minute and won't sit and watch it. He's not noisy. He just wanders. He just spends his day wandering around. He pokes and noses around. It's the same thing all day, every day." This behavior, which continued until bedtime, was punctuated by sporadic tantrums during which he would emit piercing screeches, kick objects such as the refrigerator, and, on occasion, hit someone. Tantrums were brief, occurring when he was even minimally frustrated (if he were mildly reprimanded or when he could not find cookies or sweets, for example). Bedtime was almost always violent. His mother was forced to follow the same unvaried dressing sequence every night—any deviation caused a severe tantrum. His favorite pair of pajamas had to be available every night. Bathing remained a problem, as he screamed and fought, refusing to go near water.

Initial Behavior in the Program

At six and a half, Freddie was a quiet, non-verbal, minimally communicative youngster with little interaction and use of objects. His life consisted of idly wandering about the house, frequent intense but brief tantrums, inexplicable, sudden screeching, and a continual, insistent searching for sweets. On his first day with us, Freddie appeared to be the most acutely disturbed of the three children thus far described, impressing us as tense and agitated. Over the following ten days he remained extremely agitated, screamed, threw and broke toys, and ran into walls.

He was well-coordinated and easily climbed the exercise ladders. Despite his good motor coordination, however, Freddie was not actively involved with the objects or people in the room, but seemed to prefer standing quietly immobile, making few sounds, and facing the window overlooking the street. Freddie did not use many objects appropriately, but certainly had greater facility and more willingness in using his hands than either Billy or Frankie. He frequently licked things, appearing to be tasting and smelling them.

Freddie was stimulated by the sight of food. Sitting with the others during snack times, he quickly devoured his snack and took whatever else was in reach, even out of the hands of another person. He did not enter into any of the group play and rarely responded to the staff. When Freddie did react to other people, it was with a blank, unfocused expression and with no apparent regard for the person. He gave every indication that the other person was only an object to be manipulated briefly and then dropped in the same way he would drop any other toy. There were times when Freddie touched and caressed other children, but his behavior was the same as if he were holding a doll, truck, or piece of clay. The other children's protests and attempts to pull away had no effect on Freddie's behavior and he simply continued his manipulating, finally stopping, apparently of his own accord.

Freddie continued to operate within the group as if the rest of the group were inanimate objects—disrupting the play of the other children by taking things from them, sometimes breaking and throwing toys out of the window, often running into another child as if the child did not exist. Freddie screamed and screeched frequently with no apparent external stimulation, but any change in routine would stimulate a screaming, sometimes destructive, though brief tantrum. When his mother arrived at the end of a session, Freddie frequently threw himself on the floor and screamed. His speech was extremely limited, almost non-existent at first, and he rarely communicated with the others. When he did communicate it was on a non-verbal level, generally by pushing or pulling another person's hand.

It was not until 16 sessions (or approximately 40 hours) had been completed, that Freddie spoke the first clearly communicative word of his life "cookie," which we had been working on daily for two weeks. Later in the same session Freddie repeated the words, "new puzzle." Both words referred to objects which had been previously observed to be highly reinforcing for him. The staff, hearing Freddie's speaking voice, was surprised at its quality—high-pitched but very guttural. Freddie's vocal production increased, with more pre-verbal sounds and, on the 25th session (approximately 63 hours), he clearly said, "tick, tock, clock" and "Donald Duck," two of the stimulus objects the staff had been using. Interestingly, his voice sounded quite like that of Donald Duck in the animated cartoon movies. We were unable to determine if he were imitating the cartoon character or if his characteristic guttural speech was only coincidentally like Dondal Duck's. On the 42nd session he said, "school bus," and by the 100th session (about 300 hours) Freddie had clearly produced a total of 16 different words! Freddie's behavior during the first 100 sessions is described in the following excerpt from observations of a typical day:

"Freddie arrives before the other children, walks slowly down the middle of the room, stops, and ignores the staff's greetings. Suddenly he raises his arms, leaps from the floor, runs to the other end of the room and stands in front of 'his' window. Staff talks to him. Freddie makes a humming sound but not in response to the staff. Freddie continues to smile at no specific thing that can be identified. Occasionally his mouth moves and small sounds, guttural and meaningless, erupt. Other children are coming in but Freddie does not show recognition of their arrival, remaining at his window for 15 minutes, ignoring all approaches. Freddie moves from the window suddenly with a long screech, leaps and runs in his sideways, galloping fashion to the middle of the room, and picks up the arm of a doll that had just been broken by Mary. Throwing back his head, he puts the arm of the doll in his mouth, smells it, throws it up into the air, screeches, leaps, slowly walks around the room, and returns to his window where he silently remains for the next 20 minutes. Later, standing in front of his window, he throws out a ball, a doll, and a wooden truck. When Billy begins to leap from the table to windowsill with Frankie giggling and pointing, Freddie gallops across the room, screeches once and stops, stands still, with an unfocused, faraway look in his eyes and an enigmatic smile, occasionally humming and making guttural sounds for 15 minutes. At snack time, Freddie gallops a few steps, walks to the snack table, makes some guttural sounds, sits down, and then, as he has been trained, gets up again and goes into the bathroom with other children and washes his hands. He returns to the snack table, sits down, and rapidly devours all his food. He grabs a cookie belonging to one of the other children and stuffs it into his mouth. While chewing that cookie, he reaches for one belonging to still another child who prevents him from taking it. Freddie hunches over, leaning out over the table, looks around and rapidly snakes out an arm and grabs at but misses, another child's snack. Freddie then bows his head, clasps his hands in his lap, and emits a long, loud screech which sends Billy bounding off, screaming, 'Help, police!' Leaping onto his windowsill, Billy continues shouting down at the street. For the remainder of the session Freddie disrupts the play of every child by grabbing toys and sometimes throwing them out of the window. Later Freddie goes to the table where the snacks are kept, rummages, taking all of the cookie remnants. He then waves his arms gallops across the room, stands still for approximately five minutes—chewing, making humming sounds, and smiling.

"Freddie then sits in the sandbox. While Frankie holds a truck, Freddie pulls and paws at him. When brought over to the table, Freddie does not resist; he readily sits down and constructs a new puzzle. Closely directed, Freddie then picks up crayons and scribbles on a paper. The use of puzzles and crayons lasts approximately five minutes. Freddie gets off his chair and slowly moves back to his window where he ramains for the rest of the session. When his mother arrives, he throws himself on the floor, kicking and screaming. At no time during the session was there anything resembling speech or eye contact or a clear response to verbal stimuli. In this session he did respond, however, to being physically led to the table where he then used the puzzle and crayons." (15th session)

Freddie was easily upset by even minor change in the daily routine. It took him several days to decrease his peak of agitation after his first day in the program. Each time the program was in any way modified, he again reacted in an agitated fashion. When our walks outside began, Freddie had great screaming tantrums. One day, after he had accepted the group walks he threw himself onto the sidewalk and kicked and screamed in front of a store in response to the staff's suggestion that the group enter. Another day, on our way to camp, we took a slightly different route than usual. Freddie, generally quite calm on this ride, became extremely agitated and has ever since strenuously resisted riding in that particular car.

Another time, during the 75th session, two visitors arrived. Under other conditions such as at home Freddie would probably have ignored them. Here, perhaps because they were not part of the routine, he reacted by running around the room, screaming, and throwing toys out the window. (Heavy screens had been put up inside the windows as a safety measure, but Freddie quickly learned how to open the screen's small door designed for access to the window latch.) Generally, Freddie's response to changes in routines was to screech and scream, sometimes to throw himself on the floor, and to hit himself on the head with his fist or forearm, all the while screeching.

In summary, at six and a half years of age, Freddie was a severely disturbed autistic child functioning on a very infantile level and relating minimally to the environment. During the first 100 sessions he did show some behavioral change, becoming more responsive, more verbal, and less generally agitated.

MARY

History

Mary was born at term and appeared to be a well-formed but small child. During her first year, Mary was a difficult child, constantly and inconsolably crying. Eating showed no particular difficulty and weaning was readily achieved at about two years of age. Walking, however, was late, and she was 27 months old before she began walking unassisted. In her fourth year, Mary still walked as if afraid; if she had even a minor fall, she screamed long, loudly, and inconsolably. Toilet training was not achieved until after her fourth year, and Mary continued to be enuretic through the next ten years. At four years, Mary began using the words "mama" and "dada." By five, her speech was more frequent and more complex, although still an infantile echoing and never conversational. When Mary was three, her mother had become convinced that her development was slow and that some of her behavior, such as incessant crying, was not normal. As in some other cases, she was advised by a pediatrician that some children take longer to develop than others and all one could do was wait. When she pressed this issue with the pediatrician, she was apparently told that there seemed to be nothing wrong with the child, despite the presenting complaints (i.e., a three-year-old not yet toilet trained, not sleeping well, who had been walking for less than a year and was still extremely unsteady; tearful, constantly frightened, and inconsolable when she fell or was frustrated). It was not until the child was five that the parents sought other than pediatric help, and the child was diagnosed as autistic. At six, she began a year of psychiatric treatment which resulted in no noticeable improvements. The psychiatrist's fees amounted to one-third of the father's income, and was too great a financial burden to continue. Psychiatric treatment had been undertaken partly to help Mary adjust to kindergarten and accelerate normal development. However, after starting school and psychiatric treatment, Mary "went all to pieces," returning from school each day in an agitated, tearful condition, "very nervous" with "her legs all wobbly," and "discoordinated." Mary's behavior continued to deteriorate and her agitation increased through that winter until Christmas, when she was taken out of kindergarten.

The following year, when she was seven, Mary was enrolled briefly in a special class, but she was abusive and aggressive, disrupting the class with her screaming and countless aggressive outbursts. When she was seven and a half years old, Mary joined Billy, Frankie, and Freddie in the psychodynamically oriented group therapy program, during which time she did begin to calm down. She remained with them for approximately two years, but at the end of that time Mary was still a disturbed and difficult-to-manage child. When she was approximately nine and a half, Mary was taken out of the psychoanalytically-oriented program and, along with the three boys, formed the original group of four children with whom we began.

Described as "too much for one couple to handle," Mary's care was shared by her parents and close relatives. She was moody, hyperactive, unpredictable, and exceedingly difficult to manage. Frequent intense, prolonged tantrums were brought about by even minor occurrences. For example, at the age of nine and a half, if she looked into a cupboard and saw that there was no baby food, she launched a long screaming tantrum. When she began in our group, her behavior had been basically unchanged for several years, although in the previous group treatment she seemed to have become somewhat less intense.

A typical day for Mary, as described by her parents, began with awakening between 8:00 and 10:00 A.M., immediately turning on the phonograph, and rocking for more than an hour. Absorbed in her motor activity and the music, she did not interact with anyone.

Mary later sat at her own table in the living room and, while watching television, ate a substantial breakfast. Her actions were slow and she appeared to be intent upon the television programs, the breakfast seemingly only incidental.

At about 11:00 A.M. Mary, passive, was dressed by her mother and went outside. Thus far through the morning there was usually little verbal exchange between Mary and her family. From approximately 11:00 until noon Mary remained outside, usually with her tricycle and always alone, never playing with the other children. Because of her past aggressive behavior, the neighbors had forbidden their children to play with Mary. Mary was called in for lunch but did not eat very much. After lunch she was taken to school, returning home at approximately 4:00.

In the car, Mary sat in the back seat, apparently taking no notice of the car, its occupants, or the world outside. Returning home, Mary usually remained outdoors until dinner, which she ate alone in front of the TV set. Mary ate a good meal of baby foods and sometimes mashed potatoes and gravy but not meats or other adult food. Throughout the day, her tantrums were frequent and caused by even minor frustrations. After dinner Mary again listened to records and rocked, again seemingly "lost" in the activity. Thus far in the day, Mary had still had minimal verbal interaction with anyone at home. Bedtime, at approximately 9:00, was always a problem. Mary ordinarily resisted going to bed—screaming, biting, scratching, hitting, kicking, and in many ways delaying the entire process and creating extreme difficulty for her parents. Once she had been readied for bed, she went through a nightly ritual of rearranging things in her room twice over. Only then would she go to bed. Mary frequently awakened after midnight and wandered around the house, often making noise by turning on the record player, for example. Mary took a long time to fall asleep but, once asleep, slept restfully. She was alone, aloof, withdrawn from involvement with people and her environment. It seemed, however, that when she did contact her environment she reacted with intense, aggressive tantrum behavior.

At age nine, her speech was unclear, infantile, and meager in content. She was afraid of strangers and animals. She seemed to have considerable fear of falling down, and would scream inconsolably when she did fall. Mary was described by all observers as a tense child with rigid, sometimes spastic-like movements, often wild posturing, gesturing, bizarre movements of her hands, arms, and legs, and prolonged pounding of her fingers on hard surfaces. Her behavior was generally unpredictable—she would suddenly stop what she was doing and become highly aggressive, attacking whomever happened to be near. She seemed constantly embattled with the world and anyone in it. Sometimes she seemed overwhelmed by the world, and retreated into inactivity or stereotyped rocking involvement with music. At other times she reacted violently, becoming abusive and destructive.

Although careful about walking and timid on stairs, Mary was not alert to other common dangers, often standing on the second floor windowsill, dangerously pressed against the glass, or dashing into the street, wandering away from home. At night, this preadolescent girl, standing nude, framed in her window with lights behind her, upset neighbors, and her father finally had to opaque the window. All of the children so far described were extremely difficult for their families, but Mary was the most intensively persistent, distressing, and difficult.

Initial Behavior in the Program

Mary was a tall, thin, pale nine year old who constantly gestured, postured, and rocked back and forth on her feet. Through the first 100 sessions she was either directly aggressive or coweringly alone. Mary came up the stairs one step at a time, her body bent at the waist, both arms up with her hands covering her ears, head bent forward as if hiding. She clutched a paper bag which contained her snack, and, because her hand was also covering her ear, the bag hid one side of her face. Once in the room, Mary immediately sat on the floor huddled against the wall, hid her head by twisting her body, nearly tucking her head under her arm, and remained there until we finally managed to get her to respond to us.

She did a great deal of crying the first few days, hiding huddled in corners and at every minor sound, repeating, "What's that? What's that?" "It's too noisy? It's too noisy?" Mary's posture (her head hidden, hands against her ear, elbows out) was invariably interpreted by observers as one of frightened defense, keeping anyone who tried to get near her at elbow's distance. She was described by a group worker as "a tall, thin, willowy, extremely tense and agitated girl who exhibited grotesque hand motions, kept her head hidden, and whose most frequent words for the first month were, 'What's that?' Her defensive, alert retreat was her most frequent and basic behavior during her first 100 sessions. Invariably, if Mary were in huddled retreat while a group worker attended to another child, Mary would covertly observe the group worker for perhaps 15 or 20 minutes and then suddenly and rapidly attack, throwing sand, crayons, toys, or whatever was at hand in the face of the staff member. At other times, Mary came out of her defensive retreat to sit quietly for five or ten minutes, coloring with crayons. But even that activity usually ended with Mary suddenly throwing her crayons in the face of the nearest group worker.

The playing of phonograph records never failed to stimulate rigid posturing and rocking. With her body bent forward at the waist, head down, arms along her side parallel with her body and bent upward at the elbows, wrists limp and hands loosely flopping, one leg out in front of the other, she persisted in a tense, rigid, flat-footed rocking back and forth until the record stopped. Thus, Mary's behavior generally fell into four categories: (1) defensive, alert head-hiding retreat, (2) sudden, direct aggression, (3) infrequent and brief periods of coloring with crayons, and (4) rigid, stereotyped rocking when records were playing. In the first three behaviors Mary remained alert to everything, but when rocking she seemed oblivious to all but the recording.

Mary frequently provoked the other children by deliberately running into them as she rode the tricycle, hitting or throwing toys at them, or taking away toys and breaking them. When a child reacted, Mary cried and became upset. One day, while she was being aggressive and destructive, she threw and broke the bottle of fruit juice used for snack. After being told that therefore there could be no snack, Mary attacked Frankie, hitting him on the head because, "There's no juice." On another day, Mary suddenly moved from her defensive retreat, kicked Frankie, and poked a finger into Freddie's eye. She then became extremely agitated and tearful when Freddie screeched. As he continued to screech, Mary threw crayons at him because he was "too noisy."

Even when at her best with other children, Mary invariably ended up by being physically aggressive. Apparently attracted to Cathy (who later joined the group), Mary frequently hugged her, but with increasing agitation, and in just a few minutes would be hurting her. Cathy, who had violent temper tantrums, would be stimulated by Mary who in turn would be stimulated by Cathy and would then become extremely agitated and retreat and cry. Her interaction with the other children seemed to follow a sequence in which she stimulated a child into aggressive action and then tearfully retreated. Another example of this was her aiming the tricycle at Cathy and running into her with considerable force, laughing all the while. Cathy, never one to accept this kind of behavior, immediately hit Mary, in response to which Mary cried, cringed, became extremely agitated, and ran off to huddle against the wall. Cathy, now having been stimulated by Mary, was off on a wild, screaming, destructive rampage, while Mary huddled against the wall crying, and seemingly terrified of what was going on. There were countless incidents where Mary's provocative behavior completely upset the group and her subsequent behavior was that of a noncomprehending victim innocent of any provocation. She seemed to not comprehend fully the relationship between her behavior and the behavior of the others. Later, after she had been with us for about a year, Mary began asking about the consequences of her behavior. For example, she often asked, "Will you spank me if I do that?" A frequent question asked by Mary, which seemed to be asking precisely how far she could go with us, was "If I kick you in the ass, what?"

Snack time was particularly difficult for Mary as it necessitated close contact with all the children seated around the table with the staff. She was alert to everything the other children had in their snacks and always preferred the other children's food. Mary sat in a huddled position, shoulders hunched forward, back rounded, head down, and hands resting lightly on the table or in her lap. She did not appear to be aware of what was going on, but was watching, peering up from her lowered head, and would rapidly shoot out an arm and snatch food. The other child, depending on who it was, would then passively accept this or become upset. Cathy, for example, when treated in this manner, would stand up, scream, and overturn the snack table. Mary's eating habits were poor—she crumbled her snack, threw cookies into the faces of other people, and spit up her chewed and well-salivated wads of cookie. There was one period of approximately 10 days during which Mary daily picked up her juice and poured it on a particular staff member. Each time Mary did this she reacted as if the others had no right to be upset by her and she would become agitated. She often giggled when she did this. In fact, Mary had an almost constant grin. She grinned, laughed, giggled, and cried—almost always inappropriately.

The children frequently took short walks around the city block. While on these walks, Mary covered her ears with her hands, particularly if trucks were going by. Usually fairly well-behaved on walks as long as her hands were being held, on a few occasions Mary threw herself on the sidewalk, screamed and kicked, and in a very shrill, loud voice yelled, "He hit me! He hit me!" while the harried group worker tried to pick her up, anxiously watching the passers-by as they slowed down and gathered, having heard the child's screams. On at least two such occasions, some irate stranger threatened to call the police.

Mary exhibited several fears, including strong reactions to loud noises, strangers, any change in routine, and any suggestion of being hurt. When Donald, a husky, booming-voiced six-year-old boy joined us, Mary deliberately ran into him several times with the tricycle. When he did not react to this except by moving away, she finally hit him on the head with a plastic toy. At that, Donald said "Stop" and Mary immediately jumped off her trike, ran against the wall in seeming terror, screaming, "He hit me! He hit me!" Donald, looking very perplexed and rubbing the top of his head, could only say, "Boy, she's crazy!" There was no doubt that although Mary had reportedly improved during the previous two years of group therapy, she was still far from an easily manageable child.

During the first 100 sessions Mary continued to be highly aggressive and provocative, and she frequently injured the other children by hitting, scratching, or biting them. She was certainly the most alert of the children and one of the fastest movers. Her aggressive outbursts often caught the staff by surprise not only because the movements were rapid but also because her basic behavior was an almost completely opposite passive retreat rather than an active outgoing aggression. Of all the children in the group, Mary had the best ability to agitate and upset the others. Out of the first 100 sessions, Mary was absent 25 times and late 31 times. Estimating the average lateness to be half an hour, she was out approximately 15 to 16 additional hours, or the equivalent of another six sessions. Thus, Mary missed the equivalent of 31 of the first 100 sessions.

THE FOCAL GROUP

After 100 sessions (approximately five months) had been devoted to the original group, several new children were added and new groups formed. As will be discussed in Chapter 5, Freddie, Frankie, and two new children—Cathy and Gerry—were grouped together to form what will serve as our focal group for the remaining discussions.

CHAPTER 4

Structure, Stimulus Control, and Initial Strategies

STRUCTURE AND STIMULUS CONTROL

Our general task was to teach socially adaptive behavior to children who presented grossly severe deficit and surplus behavior. The approach would be based on an educational-psychological social-learning model, using behavioral principles as the basis for developing the major applied techniques. The initial behavior assessments necessary to plan the program sequences had already been made through parent interviews and observations of the children. Having some assumptions about the nature of maladaptive behavior, the direction to be taken in developing therapeutic approaches, and some knowledge of the children's behavior, the next question was approached: under what conditions would the basic teaching task be carried out? Based on the assumptions discussed earlier, it was decided to use a group rather than individual therapy approach, a classroom rather than a play therapy model, and a highly structured rather than a permissive social atmosphere.

Highly structured, our approach would include the staff's active leading and shaping of the children's behavior. Programming would require detailed planning and environmental arrangement by the staff, who would have to be clearly in control of all major aspects of each daily session. We would continuously focus on guiding or teaching the children to achieve previously determined clearly-defined goals.

An important guide in planning our program was the book, *Educating Emotionally Disturbed Children* by Haring and Phillips (1962). Noting that treatment programs traditionally emphasized a permissive and unstructured social atmosphere, those authors assumed that "... children suffer from emo-

71

tional disturbance because they lack order or structure or definiteness in their daily living at home and at school, and that within the confines of the school program, it would be desirable and constructive to rectify past excesses in habits, attitudes, and achievement." (p. 10)

Basing much of their approach on previous work with brain-damaged children, including that of Strauss and Lehtinen (1947) and Cruickshank, Bentzen, Ratzeburg, and Tannhauser (1961), Haring and Phillips created a structured, psychotherapeutic classroom approach to emotionally disturbed children. They wrote:

> "Educational procedures used with brain-injured children appear to offer equal advantages to hyperactive, emotionally disturbed children. Apparently principles such as controlled extraneous stimuli, reduced social activity, and ordered presentation of the materials to be learned are basic to successful classroom experiences of emotionally disturbed children." (p. 65)

In the Haring and Phillips study, one of the criteria for inclusion of a child was his prior school attendance for one or two years. The children with whom we began, however, had not been in school for that time, had shown little or no academic achievement, and generally did not have even the verbal skills of a preschooler. Thus, none of the children in our focal group would have been selected for Haring and Phillips' program. We were to attempt to adopt many of Haring and Phillips' suggestions and apply them to a considerably more severely disturbed group of children. If structure, reduction and control of extraneous stimuli, and planned, orderly presentation or programming of material produced good results with brain damaged children and with the sample of disturbed school children described by Haring and Phillips, it seemed reasonable to expect that similar approaches would have some positive effect on autistic and schizophrenic children who exhibit behavior very similar to but more severe than that which they described.

We attempted to carry Haring and Phillips' concept of structure a step further. "Structure," as a verb, refers to the active arranging of elements to form some unified, interrelating whole; as a noun, it is "something made; any enduring arrangement, grouping, pattern or articulation of parts to form a relatively stable system or whole" (English and English, 1958, p. 529). Like Haring and Phillips, the word "structure" is used here both as verb and noun: as a verb, "structure" will mean actively controlling the sounds, lights, objects, time sequences, etc.; as a noun, it will point to the relatively stable arrangement of those elements.

Structure is implicit in the organization of stimulus elements in the environment and it is functionally related to the behavior of the children; it is this relationship that is of crucial importance. Structuring, then, should be carried out with reference to the relationships between the stimulus items and the particular behavior to be affected by that structure. Structure is important only in relation to the desired behavior, only in terms of the success with which the structure affects the probability of that behavior's occurrence.

The probabalistic relationship between stimulus and response has been termed "stimulus control" (Skinner, 1938; Keller and Schoenfeld, 1950). Haring and Phillips' central concept of structure thus resolves itself into *active strategies to create a stable environment with carefully interrelated elements in order to bring about and maintain stimulus control*; structure is most useful and best understood within the context of stimulus control.

STIMULUS CONTROL AND CONTINGENCY MANAGEMENT

The focal group's behavioral baseline included such severe, generalized surplus and deficit behavior that little appropriate behavior ever occurred. Given stimuli ordinarily found in social situations (i.e., speech, gestures, facial expressions, common objects and activities), these children seemed either not to respond (behavioral deficit) or to respond in some massively inappropriate manner (behavioral surplus). In order to make up deficits and to reduce surplus behavior, our immediate focus was on the acquisition of new, adaptive behavior. However, altering the rate of already existing behavior or bringing about the acquisition of entirely new behavior make up only part of the task. That is, in addition to changing the rate and type of response, we must also focus on changing the probability of the behavior's occurrence *in the presence of normal social stimuli*. Not only must responses occur, they must occur appropriately. Therefore, the task of teaching socially adaptive behavior would not be one solely of response acquisition and decrement; it would also include the equally important task of bringing about stimulus control.

There are several functional relationships that can exist between stimuli and responses (Skinner, 1938; Keller and Schoenfeld, 1950; Terrace, 1966): (a) the discriminative function, (b) the eliciting function, and (c) the primary and secondary reinforcing function. Contingency management refers to the reinforcing function; it is the technology of manipulating the functional relationships between an emitted response and the reinforcing events (stimuli) that follow and are contingent upon that response. Thus, when a child emits some desired behavior such as a verbal response, positive attention to another child, sharing or cooperating, etc., the therapist attempts to strengthen it by quickly presenting reinforcing events. In operant conditioning contingency management refers to the relationship between a response and the reinforcing stimulus that *follows* the response. Stimulus control, on the other hand, refers to the relationship between a response and a stimulus that *precedes* the response. The stimulus might *elicit* the response (respondent conditioning), such as a bright light eliciting pupillary contraction or a sudden, loud noise eliciting a startle reaction. Or the stimulus might *occasion* the response (operant conditioning), such as when the ringing of a telephone occasions picking it up and emitting the vocal response, "hello", or when the verbal stimulus, "Turn off the TV, children, it's time for bed," occasions lachrymose protests and perhaps tantrum behavior. In either case, eliciting or occasioning, stimulus control refers to "... the extent that the presence of a stimulus controls the probability of a response." (Homme, C. DeBaca, Cottingham, and Homme, 1968, p. 428) It is thus a probabalistic relationship; the greater the probability of the response, the greater the stimulus control.

RESPONDENT CONDITIONING AND STIMULUS CONTROL

Stimulus control is most readily evident in classical or respondent conditioning, i.e., as an eliciting function—for example, a sudden, loud noise elicits a startle reaction. In each instance the relationship between the natural or unconditioned eliciting stimulus and the respondent behavior is an automatic, physiologically-determined reflex that is the same for all normal organisms of the same species, age, and sex. The S-R relationship is also one of high probability. By increasing or decreasing the frequency of the eliciting stimulus, we can bring about a corresponding although not unlimited change in the frequency of the respondent. In addition, such S-R relationships obtain throughout the lifetime of a healthy organism.

Eliciting stimuli are (a) unconditioned stimuli—those that derive their eliciting power or stimulus control from the natural, innate characteristics of the organism and (b) conditioned eliciting stimuli—those that derive their control over the respondent through the process of conditioning. With Pavlov's dogs, the unconditioned stimulus—food—elicited the unconditioned response—salivation; a bell presented repeatedly immediately prior to the food soon became a conditioned stimulus which elicited the conditioned response—salivation.

Thus, while the nature of the unconditioned S-R relationship remains essentially the same with repeated elicitations and throughout the organism's lifetime, through conditioning, a wide variety of stimuli can come to acquire high degrees of control over that behavior. In both cases, whether the stimuli are conditioned or unconditioned eliciting stimuli, the probability of occurrence of the respondent in the presence of the eliciting stimulus varies according to lawful relationships. Under certain conditions, the probability of occurrence of the respondent is extremely high. That is, unconditioned stimuli have a high degree of stimulus control over the associated respondent behavior, and previously neutral stimuli can acquire high stimulus control through conditioning.

The relationships between eliciting stimuli (unconditioned or conditioned) and the associated respondent is therefore one of stimulus control. As noted earlier, it is a relationship expressed in terms of the probability of occurrence of the response when the eliciting stimulus is presented.

OPERANT CONDITIONING AND STIMULUS CONTROL

In the respondent paradigm, stimulus control refers to the eliciting function of a stimulus, and it is based in physiologically-determined reflexes. In operant conditioning, stimulus control refers to the discriminative function of stimuli preceding responses. The discriminative stimuli do not directly elicit responses, but they "set the occasion for" the response. The ringing of the telephone occasions an answering response; a loud cry from an infant occasions investigation by the mother; the verbal instructions to Cathy, an autistic girl, to "...finish this page of arithmetic" occasions a screaming refusal. Thus, in the presence of discriminative stimuli, certain related responses have a high probability of occurrence. They are under stimulus control.

In both respondent and operant conditioning, stimulus control is brought about through repeated pairings that strengthen or reinforce the S-R relationship. However, as noted earlier, the stimulus function in operant conditioning is discriminative while that in respondent conditioning is eliciting. Further, the pairing in respondent conditioning involves two stimuli, conditioned and unconditioned, while in the operant paradigm pairing involves the discriminative stimulus, the response, and the reinforcing stimulus. That is, it involves the pairing of S_D-R-S_R rather than CS-US-R. Further, in the respondent paradigm, the CS-US pairing constitutes reinforcement, while in operant conditioning the reinforcement follows the response and can be any event that increases the probability of occurrence of that response in the presence of the discriminative stimulus. In operant conditioning, stimulus control is effected by reinforcing events that follow the response. By manipulating those events in the presence of the stimuli that are to become discriminative stimuli, the probability of occurrence of the behavior in the presence of those stimuli can be controlled.

Controlling reinforcing events so as to strengthen or weaken behavior is referred to as *contingency management* (Homme, *et al*., 1968). Integrating the technology of contingency management with that of stimulus control, i.e., arranging not only reinforcing events but also "synchronizing" the reinforcers with the controlled presentation of stimuli so as to effect desired stimulus control, has been labeled *behavioral engineering* (Homme, *et al*., 1968). The special case of the clinical application of behavioral engineering to the problems of maladaptive behavior is what we have termed *programmed therapy*. Both respondent and operant conditioning are aimed at modifying stimulus control, which can be said to be the central objective of the application of conditioning principles. It will be seen that a major central concept in our therapeutic program is also that of stimulus control.

PSYCHOTIC BEHAVIOR AND STIMULUS CONTROL

When we describe the children's behavior as deficit, surplus, or inappropriate, we are saying that it is not under the control of the same stimuli that occasion or elicit the adaptive "normal" behavior of most children. All of the psychotic children could and did exhibit a variety of approximations of adaptive social behavior. For example, they would all, at least briefly, sit in a chair. But they did not generally sit when asked to, or when dinner was served, or when taken to the bathroom, or when riding in an automobile. Normal children in a playground during recess will scream, shout, run wildly while flapping their arms, exhibit grotesque motions and posturing, wild, eye-protruding and tongue-lolling grimaces, and unprovoked attacks on each other which often result in real, if mild, injury such as bloody noses and scraped knees. So, too, will psychotic children. They, however, will not limit such surplus behavior to the playground but will emit it at unpredictable times in church, supermarkets, school, restaurants, and at home. Parents, teachers, and others cannot specify the discriminative stimuli for such behavior. They are therefore unable to either explain, control, or modify it. Parents of psychotic children commonly complain that their children behave inappropriately, unpredictably, and "for no reason at all."

Normal children, through their history of repeated reinforcement of socially expected or appropriate behavior in the presence of normal social stimuli, soon come under stimulus control. The normal cues thus become discriminative stimuli that come to occasion appropriate responses. Psychotic children do emit much of the same behavior as normal children and, particularly with regard to surplus behavior, often at a higher rate. Psychotic children are not, however, under the control of the same stimuli as normal children. Although they do acquire a repertoire which includes many normal and age-appropriate behaviors such as sitting, walking, eating, etc., they nevertheless fail to emit the behavior appropriately (perhaps at least partly because they have had difficulty in making the basic discriminations necessary for the development of discriminative stimuli).

Thus, in addition to modifying responses we must also bring those responses under stimulus control so they will be appropriate and adaptive. In the subsequent development of our program, we found that it is not especially difficult to teach new behavior to an autistic child. For example, "My name is Ricky Blackman," when uttered by an autistic child with that name, might appear to be a considerable achievement. However, the child must learn not only to emit the phrase, but to do so appropriately—i.e., to respond with that phrase in the presence of certain stimuli such as, "Hello, what's your name?" and not in the presence of other stimuli such as, "What would you like for lunch, hot dogs or scrambled eggs?"

As discussed earlier, the children with whom we began were characterized by severe response deficit and surplus; they failed to make appropriate responses under given stimulus conditions and made grossly inappropriate responses in the presence of those stimuli. When we speak of the appropriateness of normal behavior and the inappropriateness of psychotic behavior, we are referring primarily to the social expectation that stimulus control will operate—that is, in the presence of certain stimuli, the probability of occurrence of certain responses is high. Most people behave quietly at church, happily at parties, and mournfully at funerals, indicating the shared, culturally defined, and learned social nature of discriminative stimuli, and their power in consistently occasioning the same or at least highly similar behavior.

Autistic and psychotic children, however, do not share in this network of stimulus control, and until they do, they will continue to behave inappropriately—failing to respond with behavior that has been generally agreed upon as expected or appropriate under given stimulus conditions. Our therapeutic task was to combine the manipulation of environmental structure with appropriate reinforcement so as to bring about stimulus control and contingency management—increasing the probabilities that the children would respond to normal social stimuli with some variation of normal social behavior.

STIMULUS CONTROL AND THE PROBLEM OF
ATTENTION WITH PSYCHOTIC CHILDREN

The usefulness of stimulus control as an organizing concept can be seen in its application to what has been commonly voiced as a major problem in working with psychotic, retarded, or brain-injured children—gaining and holding their attention. The children are said to be hyperactive and impulsive, and to have extremely short attention spans. They do not easily focus on stimuli as demanded by parents, teachers, and therapists but instead rapidly shift from one seemingly irrelevant object to another or maintain a fixed, rigid focus on a small array of things for very long periods.

The short attention spans and the long, inappropriate perseverations of psychotic children are often used to explain difficulties such as those encountered when standardized psychological testing is attempted, to explain the child's failure to make academic gains, and, more recently, to explain failure in attempts to modify behavior through conditioning.

Attention is selective, focusing at any moment on only a limited portion of the total available stimulus array. The focus of attention at any time is determined by a variety of factors, including (1) stimulus factors such as stimulus size, intensity, contrast, repetition, and movement and (2) internal or organismic factors such as motivation and set or expectancy. The problem of attention of psychotic children is most often discussed in terms of a lack of or confusion of motivation related to the children's general psychopathology. This inferred condition, "lack of attention," is then used to explain various failures of the children.

Instead of inferring the central condition of "attention," we might more profitably conceptualize it as the lack of "attending behavior" which is simply another instance of the lack of stimulus control. The psychotic child who fails to attend to his therapist despite all efforts to make contact illustrates that his attending behavior has not been adequately reinforced in the presence of easily discriminable stimuli and has not yet come under stimulus control.

When a child is paying attention to his teacher, he is under stimulus control of that teacher and/or setting. Attention, according to Skinner (1953), is the traditional label for stimulus control, a "controlling relation . . . between a response and a discriminative stimulus." (p. 123) This controlling relation develops because the individual, such as a child in school, is repeatedly reinforced for complying with the teacher's instructions to "pay attention."

Terrace (1966) noted, "The use of attention as an explanatory principle . . . is begging the question, and seems to be nothing more than a mask for our ignorance concerning the establishment of stimulus control." (p.289)

The problem of gaining the psychotic child's attention can be resolved into that of establishing stimulus control over "attending behavior" and is, in essence, no different from establishing stimulus control over any other behavior. The basic approach to establishing stimulus control is the same: specify the terminal behavior (attending), structure the discriminative stimulus conditions, and *reinforce the desired behavior in the presence of the stimulus*.

STIMULUS CONTROL AND PROGRAM STRUCTURE

In summary, *structuring* would consist of specific strategies and organization of the daily program in order to facilitate stimulus control and contingency management. It would aim at clearly interrelating discriminative and reinforcing stimuli and behavior, and thus would necessitate strategies to maximize stimulus values to improve discrimination by the children. For example, we would attempt to reduce stimulus complexity, to utilize contrast (i.e., to maximize one stimulus complex against a low stimulus background), and to vary other stimulus dimensions such as intensity and motion. As will be seen in the following descriptions, we attempted to present each learning situation simply, concretely, and clearly differentiated from other learning situations. In terms of our daily program, this approach resulted in clear differentiations among the various parts of the program. For example, when academic work was initiated, it was labeled "school time," was always held in the same physical space clearly marked off from the rest of the room, and always occurred at the same point in the daily sequence of activities. By means of this differentiation the discriminative stimuli for academic behavior were presumably more easily discriminable and would more rapidly acquire stimulus control.

The structure of the program was relatively gross at first, but became increasingly refined as the children gradually came under stimulus control and developed to higher levels of adaptive behavior. The following sections will outline the daily structure with which the program began. This structuring was accomplished through a variety of dimensions including (a) time-scheduling and activity-sequencing, (b) determining and controlling content of activities, (c) "zoning" physical space according to activities, (d) setting and maintaining clearly-defined behavioral limits, and, (e) as much as possible, planning and systematically controlling other important discriminative, eliciting, and reinforcing stimuli.

The discussion will now focus on the details of the program's attempts to modify the behavior of these children. Although the program changed in many ways as the children developed to new levels, from our assumptions, trial and error, and many long hours of intensive work, a reasonably consistent approach to the children emerged.

THE DATA COLLECTION

Our basic method for data collection was detailed behavioral observation and immediate long-hand recording of those observations. In addition to data gathered in parent interviews, initial evaluations, and reports from other professionals, there was a daily log for each child on each day of the observations of each staff member. It is possible to reach back, in some cases as far as six years, and read accounts of each child's behavior on any given day. Behavioral changes and trends for each child over time become readily apparent and are easily abstracted from the daily notes. Further, by putting together the individual descriptions for a day or a longer period of time, it is possible to reconstruct the total group's behavior and the trends for that period.

The log also yields other important data including the staff's behavior towards the children, conditions impinging on the group such as the weather, visitors, interruptions, unexpected or unusual occurrences, illnesses, brief contacts with parents, etc.

Before describing the daily schedule, it should be pointed out that the initial structure was also determined partly by the availability of space, personnel, and funds. Thus within the limitations of two rooms available for only three hours daily and with only two part-time staff, the program was launched.

THE DAILY SCHEDULE

Each weekday morning from 8:30 to 9:00, the staff met for a brief planning conference, reviewing the previous day's notes and planning strategies for the coming session. These informal meetings proved to be extremely important in staff communication around both immediately preceding events and planning of the coming day's activities.

9:00 A.M., Arrival Time. The children were scheduled to arrive at 9:00 A.M. As their mothers brought them in, they were cheerfully greeted by the staff who helped them in the routine of removing and hanging up hats and coats. Lavish verbal praise was given, and the children slowly learned to care for their clothing. This brief teaching situation, which was repeated each time the children went in or out of the building, was designed to help overcome some of the more obvious deficits in self-help behavior. After the children helped hang up their coats, they were taken into the first room for an hour's "verbal" session.

9:00-10:00 A.M., "Verbal" Session. The intent of this euphemistically-labeled "verbal" session was to focus on age-appropriate social and verbal behavior. The room was structured to accomplish that, containing a table around which were six chairs and on which were books, puzzles, crayons, clay, paper, and pencils. The two staff members remained at the table, which was situated at one end of the room near the window. The rest of the room was empty and as uniform and little-stimulating as possible. The intent was to mass the social and verbal stimuli at one end of the room, thus presumably increasing the probability of the children responding to a variety of social stimuli near the staff, who could reinforce them immediately. By massing the stimuli, it was hoped to increase their responding, the reinforcement, and, in this way, their learning.

The remainder of the room was empty and remained constantly available just a few steps away as a low-stimulation area into which the children could move. If a child moved into that area it was taken as a signal to the staff that he had reached his limit of stimulation and should be left alone. Later, the child would presumably return to the high stimulation area and join the more social and higher level of activity. Thus, the room was roughly zoned from minimum to maximum stimulation areas. The children entered the room at the low-stimulation end and then, depending upon plans for that day and the assessment of the immediate situation, were brought to the high-stimulus end or were left to seek their own place. Throughout the hour they were free to move within and between the different zones.

10:00-11:00 A.M., Play Session. After an hour's "verbal" session, the children were taken into the adjoining room which contained an assortment of toys similar to those found in most kindergarten rooms. Like the first room, this second one was zoned in terms of activity. At one end were the bathroom, sink and clean-up facilities, the snack table and chairs, and the shelf for books, table games, and arts and crafts supplies. At the other end, near the windows, were the sandbox, toy box, and small, toy kitchen. Between the two ends of the room was a large open area containing a rocking, boat bouncing board, climbing ladders, large cardboard blocks, a doll house, and a tricycle.

During this time the children could devote themselves to free play, utilizing their own choice of a variety of materials and not restricted to the verbal focus of the previous hour. The staff was to work with the children, stimulating and teaching gross physical activity, cooperative play among the children, and the use of toys. Although the focus here was still on cooperative social behavior, the major emphasis was motor and physical rather than verbal as it had been during the first hour.

10:45-11:00 A.M., Snack Time. Designed primarily to help teach a variety of socially appropriate and cooperative interactions, snack time (as will be discussed later) was one of the most powerful therapeutic strategies.

11:00-11:30 A.M., Brief Play Session and Clean-Up.

11:30 A.M., Departure. The staff again taught the children to put on coats, hats, and other clothing as necessitated by the weather.

The time periods in this schedule were not intended to be maintained precisely, only approximately. The general, working rule of thumb to determine at what point the program moved from one activity to another can be stated as follows: "Make every effort to get children to enjoy the activity before moving to another activity." Thus, if the verbal session was not progressing well and it was approximately 10:00 A.M., the staff made every attempt to reduce the demand and frustrations and get the children to enjoy the verbal session if only for one or two minutes before moving to the play session. Likewise, if an activity had been going well but the therapist noted small signs that one or more of the children were beginning to lose interest, he would change the activity while interest was still relatively high. The staff attempted to avoid spoiling a good activity by letting it go too long and letting it become associated with aversive cues. These scheduled times, then, were only guidelines helping to structure the activities. The periods might be longer or shorter than scheduled, always depending upon the staff's judgment as to how well the session was progressing and what was occurring at that time.

While the length of time of the activity periods varied, their sequence was not altered unless it were completely unavoidable. At first, if changes in sequence were attempted, some of the children had violent tantrums that lasted for the remainder of the day. Later, when their verbal ability and general control had improved, the children pointed out or commented upon even the most minor variation in routine. They soon learned that the sessions were predictable. As the program continued and the children developed new levels of functioning, the scheduling had to be altered in many details, but the basic aspects of approximate time scheduling, content structuring, zoning of physical space, sequencing activities, and setting and maintaining behavioral limits remained as important basic aspects of the program.

BEHAVIORAL GOALS

As noted earlier, behavioral goals were defined for each child by evaluating gross behavioral deficits and surpluses. Within the structure described above, programming was attempted to achieve those behavioral goals. The goals were constantly re-evaluated, often discarded or changed as new information became available from the continual observations and as new behavioral levels were reached. The major behavioral goals specified as common to all of the children were: (1) Increased social interaction, including general positive responses to other people, playing and behaving cooperatively, verbal and non-verbal communication, and concern for or respectful behavior toward the rights, safety, or property of others. (2) Increased physical involvement with the environment, including appropriate use of common objects such as books, toys, utensils, etc. and the manipulation of common tools and useful objects such as doorknobs and light switches. (3) Increased appropriate verbal behavior. (4) Increased school or academic subject skills. (5) Increased independence or self-care behavior, including use of clothing, toilet, and personal care behavior, avoiding hazards, household helping. (6) Decreased repetitive and stereotyped behavior such as headbanging, ritualistic mannerisms, grimacing, rocking, etc. (7) Decreased inappropriate vocalizing such as screaming and repetitive verbalizing. (8) Decreased aggressive and destructive behavior. (9) Decreased bizarre eating behavior. (10) Decreased general hyperactivity. (11) Decreased fears.

The focal group (to be discussed in Chapter 5) consisted of Frankie, Freddie, Gerry, and Cathy, and, as will be seen from the behavioral descriptions of these children, one of their common and most obvious deficits was their lack of response to people or to a wide range of other objects. One of the major behavioral goals was to teach appropriate social behavior. But how were we to begin when the children did not even respond to the staff, to each other, or to most of the objects around them? Frankie and Freddie were particularly low in response rate or operant level, spending most of their time in quiet inactivity. Cathy and Gerry operated at a higher rate of behavior but were restricted in the number and kinds of stimuli to which they would respond and in their variety of responses.

Gerry, who will be introduced later, devoted his time to circling the room, screaming, and destroying things. Cathy spent her time spinning in a small circle and crooning TV commercials. None of the four children made any consistent, positive, or approach responses to people. One of the first goals, therefore, was to increase the general response rate of Frankie and Freddie and to interrupt the fixed behavior of the other two while simultaneously increasing their response rate to a wider variety of stimuli.

The children were brought into the structure described earlier, which was designed to maximize the probability of social responses that could then be reinforced immediately by the staff. The children would thus be moved along to the behavioral goals in a step-by-step sequence.

The situation presumably was structured so that minimal social responses would be readily made; that is, the initial responses expected of the children were assumed to be already part of their response repertoire and, under the environmental conditions provided, had a high probability of occurrence. The staff observed and waited for the children to emit a desired response such as picking up a crayon, moving toward the therapists, or speaking even briefly. When a desired response occurred, they were to move in quickly, providing immediate reinforcement. Immediately reinforced, the response would occur more frequently and the children could then be successfully "shaped up" to higher levels of behavior.

However, within the first three weeks it had become apparent that this approach would work only slowly if at all. The children were not shaping up as had been expected. In subsequent discussions of the disappointing results, it was decided that there were two major weaknesses in this approach. First, the children simply did not emit sufficient social responses that could be reinforced. Their initial or baseline response level was so low that wait as we might simple social responses were rarely forthcoming. Frankie continued to remain unresponsive in one spot, Freddie maintained his immobile vigil at his window, occasionally screeching, Cathy continued spinning on her toes, and Gerry still circled the room, screaming. All remained aloof from each other and the staff, and none even began to use the toys, books, crayons, and other objects provided. The strategy of waiting for emitted responses was proving to be a slow approach at best.

The second weakness was even more serious, involving the near impossibility of effectively using reinforcers. That is, even if the children had emitted suitable responses, those responses could not be strengthened because none of the stimuli we identified as reinforcers seemed to have any reinforcing value for the children. They were unresponsive to social reinforcers such as verbal praise, prizes, a pat on the head, hugs, and so on. Food, as a primary reinforcer was tried but found to be impractical most of the time. Cathy, Gerry, and Freddie could not be intruded upon long enough for food to be administered; if food were put in their hands, they simply dropped it. It was not practical to follow them around and quickly put food in their mouths after every desirable response. Frankie was nearly always immobile and would not have to be followed around, but he characteristically ignored everything, including food, which might be put before him or in his hands.

Thus, even if the children occasionally emitted desired responses, those responses could not be strengthened because the stimuli used as reinforcers were either ineffective or too difficult and impractical to administer. The dilemma became clear: ineffectual reinforcers were being used in an attempt to strengthen responses that were not being emitted! Within its first three weeks, the program had reached its first therapeutic blind alley.

At that juncture we decided that before success could be achieved in shaping social behavior in children with such gross behavioral deficits, at least two basic steps had to be achieved. First, there had to be a greater general rate of responding by the children. However, since it appeared prohibitively time-consuming to wait upon the operant emitting of responses by the children, the therapists would have to assume a much more active role in directly stimulating behavior by more careful control of the environment. These responses would then be reinforced and shaped into increasingly social behavior.

Second, as the children seemed to lack what might be called a reinforcement-value hierarchy, another aspect of the therapists' new and more active role would be not only the discovery of existing personal or idiosyncratic reinforcers for the children but the direct development of new normal reinforcers. The therapists would therefore have to identify stimuli that are reinforcers for most children but had no reinforcing value for the children in our program. In some manner, previously neutral stimuli would have to come to assume high reinforcing value.

It becomes clear that in working with children with such gross behavioral deficits it is obviously necessary to shape up social behavior and, less obviously but equally necessary, to *create the reinforcers* that will then be used to teach social behavior. Most children of five or more years have acquired a great depth and variety of reinforcers, and their behavior could be affected by many stimuli including verbal praise, a positive nod of the head, or even a gold star. The children in our program, however, had a dearth of previous experience, their behavioral deficits also extended to reinforcement deficits. Establishing workable reinforcers became a major therapeutic task. This entire area of determining existing reinforcers and creating new reinforcers requires basic research—i.e., "How do stimuli acquire reinforcing value for children?"

In summary, it was originally planned to bring about an integrated and significantly more age-appropriate and socially effective level of behavior for all children by specifying categories of behavior and establishing learning sequences that successively approximate behavioral goals. However, within three weeks it had become apparent that more basic preparation was needed before those sequences could be employed and social behavior developed. The focus of therapy then shifted to attempts to (1) increase the children's general rate of behavior through active stimulation and (2) identify and actively develop effective reinforcers to use later in the social-learning sequences.

ACHIEVING AN INCREASED GENERAL RESPONSE RATE AND IDENTIFYING AND DEVELOPING EFFECTIVE REINFORCERS

Focusing on the above two goals, we became increasingly active over the next few weeks in direct stimulation of the children. To a degree much greater than the children had experienced before we provided verbal, physical, visual, and auditory stimulation. We did a great deal of talking to the children, giving them verbal praise, instructions, or just keeping up a soft patter of comments. We placed things such as toys and crayons in their hands, closing their fingers around the objects to help them hold on to them for even a few moments. The children were frequently touched, gently prodded and pushed, and even tickled. We moved them around, often dragging them after us or prodding them before us, picked them up, carried and even danced with them. We played, sang, talked, enticed, wheedled, coaxed, fed, and at times shouted loudly.

Consistent with our structure, this high level of stimulation was presented in as controlled a manner as possible, attempting to deal with one major stimulus dimension at a time and to avoid what might otherwise become a vastly chaotic and confusing situation. The high stimulation was presented only at the "high-stimulation" zone of the room, for example, and the children could move off into the low-stimulus end at any time.

The dimensions of stimuli varied from one period to another. Thus, verbal stimulation was maximized during the initial verbal session but was de-emphasized during other periods such as recess, which focused on gross motor activity. At other periods, the stimuli maximized were art materials, music, toys, food, and so on. A large variety of stimulus dimensions were employed in this way, but at any one period only one of the dimensions was maximized while the others were de-emphasized. Further, consistent with our structure, there was a predictable sequence of activity and thus of the stimulus modalities.

In this way the children were subjected to a high degree and varied kind of stimulation presented in as controlled and non-confusing a manner as possible. The general tenor of the program was quiet, controlled, and slow; the main attempt during this initial phase being to stimulate the children individually rather than through the application of some gross, general stimuli to the entire group.

The general approach to this intensified stimulation was consistently characterized by a quiet, soft, but highly insistent gentleness. In essence, the strategy was a gentle but unswerving forcing of ourselves on these aloof and unresponsive children. We no longer waited for the children to approach us; instead we intruded upon them insistently, though gently, trying all of the sensory avenues. As we plied them with stimuli, we carefully observed their reactions in order to determine not only what responses they were making but also which stimuli were the most potent in producing the responses.

Frankie and Freddie had started approximately five months earlier than Cathy and Gerry, and the attempts to increase general response rate and discern reinforcers was well under way when the last two children began. However, in order to simplify the exposition, we shall describe the events as if they had occurred concurrently. It should be pointed out that the advantage of having started sooner did not last, and Cathy and Gerry later caught up to and surpassed the first two.

What was the reaction of children so insistently subjected to a variety of stimulation? At first, their response was a continuation of their general and uniform aloofness, totally ignoring the therapists. The children continued to behave as they had at home, apparently having simply transferred their usual behavior to this new situation, making no noticeable modifications because of the new setting. Despite the lack of response, the therapists continued to bombard them during the verbal sessions, with a barrage of verbal stimuli, books, pictures, crayons, paper, puzzles, and other objects, during the play periods with toys of many kinds and during snack time with cookies, cakes, milk, fruit juice, and sweet, artificially flavored drinks. None of these stimuli had any noticeable effects at first—the children merely ignored the objects or used them indiscriminately, showing no change in their behavior.

After a week of insistent stimulation, a small change was noted: the children began to exhibit a slight turning and moving away from the therapist. For example, when the therapist insisted that Freddie hold a toy in his hand, the child remained aloof for several minutes, turned his head slightly away from the therapist, and (as the gently insisting stimulation continued) stepped just far enough away so the immediate physical stimulation ceased. This was observed repeatedly with all of the children over a period of weeks; it soon became clear that they had acquired a new facet of responding—now not only consistently ignoring us but also escaping from us. This escape behavior was carried out with an economy of involvement, simple, direct, and smooth. There were no unnecessary new motions or sounds, and the children seemed to be behaving as little as possible, exerting only the minimum effort needed to achieve the successful escape.

The staff meetings began to take on a somewhat gloomy cast as the developments of the first two months of our efforts were reviewed. Just as the strategy of shaping emitted responses had apparently run into a blind alley, so our second strategy of actively stimulating new behavior seemed to result in driving the children away from us to escape our approaches. Based on the detailed observations discussed in staff meetings, the following inferences and predictions were made: If the observed new behavior was in fact escape behavior, the stimuli from which they escaped must be of a noxious sort. Thus, when the therapists persisted in talking, touching, prodding, showing, and giving and taking away objects, they were presenting noxious stimulation. Since the removal of noxious stimulation can serve as a reinforcer, the cessation of the therapist's insistent approaches should reinforce whatever behavior had just been emitted by the child. It was concluded that we had at last found a consistent reinforcer that appeared effective with all of the children—*the removal of noxious stimulation*. Like any other effective reinforcer, it could presumably be used in carefully programmed sequences to teach higher levels of social behavior.

For these autistic children, the therapist's constant intrusion into their isolation was apparently noxious, while cessation of the noxious stimulation was reinforcing. Learning sequences could be planned that varied from one child to another but shared the basic approach of occasioning an escape response which was then negatively reinforced by withdrawal of the noxious stimulation. The basic approach was as follows: the therapist approaches a child and persists in presenting verbal or other stimulation until the child makes a response desired by the therapist. Immediately upon response, the therapist ceases his intruding and leaves the child alone for some period of time. He repeats the process later. Employing this technique seemed to result in a rather quick behavior shaping of turning or stepping away from the therapist. The following examples are taken from the daily notes recorded during the first week of this attempt:

Freddie has been standing at the window for the past 20 minutes, making no sounds or movements. The therapist walks over, puts his hand on Freddie's shoulder and softly says, "Hi, Freddie. What's out there?" (No response.) "Are you looking out the window?" (No response.) "Look over there, across the street. See, there's a lady looking back at us. Do you see her?" etc. After approximately ten minutes of no response to the continued verbal stimulation, Freddie abruptly moves a few steps away from the therapist, who immediately ceases the stimulation, walks away, and leaves Freddie alone.

Having arrived first this morning, Frankie walks in and ignores the greetings of the staff. He walks slowly to the center of the room, stops, and stands holding his snack bag in his hand. The therapist moves to him, "Good morning, Frankie." (No response.) "Frankie, good morning. Look at me, Frankie." (No response.) "You know, Frankie, I'll bet some day you're going to surprise us and all at once we'll hear you say, Good morning, Mrs. B, Good morning, Dr. G." (Frankie continues to stand still, remaining unresponsive.) "You know, when we meet each other first thing in the morning, we always say hello." (No response.) After more than five minutes, Frankie turns his head slightly towards the therapist, who smiles but immediately stops talking.

Gerry, one of the two more active children, has been working on a small doll, apparently trying to pull its head off. The doll has strong elastic bands inside and is not coming apart easily. The therapist approaches, touches Gerry's shoulder, and speaks to him. Gerry continues pulling at the doll and screeching. After several minutes of getting no response, the therapist puts his hand on the doll, blocking Gerry's hand. Without interrupting his loud screeching, the child attacks the therapist's fingers, pulling them from in front of the doll. This is repeated several times until Gerry rapidly walks a few steps away. The therapist then leaves him alone and Gerry returns to his screeching and pulling at the doll.

After several weeks, all of the children shared two highly predictable behaviors: First, they remained aloof most of the time. Second, after a few minute's stimulation, each child responded directly to the therapist in a variety of new ways, including turning his head toward or away, stepping away, screeching, or grunting. Those responses were obviously socially primitive, and they achieved escape rather than cooperation. However, despite their limitations, they were consistently predictable responses to other people, and the children were obviously no longer completely aloof.

This technique was continued, now aimed at enlarging their meager new repertoire of responses. Gradually, and at rates that varied among the children, other new responses were negatively reinforced by cessation of noxious stimuli. The therapists continued to apply stimulation to the children in this phase, but did not immediately desist when the children moved away or made any of the other newly-learned responses. Instead, the therapists were now seeking different, more socially-oriented responses. They moved after the children, continuing to stimulate, attempting to occasion a new response, and desisting when that new response did occur. For some children, the next response reinforced was a grunt, holding up a hand, or perhaps *moving toward and even touching the therapist*!

More stimulus objects were used, including books, pictures, crayons, clay, and toys, and the children eventually learned to move toward the therapists and to take and handle the various objects offered before being reinforced by withdrawal of the intruding stimulation.

Within six weeks (approximately 25 to 30 sessions), the group was operating at a noticeably higher rate of behavior. The children were increasingly moving around the room, toward as well as away from the therapists. They were handling more toys and other objects, making more vocal sounds, sitting at the table longer, and handling books and crayons although not yet appropriately. In general, the activity rate had increased noticeably, and the children were now making a variety of responses, all at a simple level. The children were far more active generally and more responsive to the external stimuli than they had been just a little more than two months earlier. Each child behaved in more varied ways and seemed not only to have developed responses to a greater variety of stimuli but also to have acquired more responses to the stimuli. To be sure, their new and higher rate of behavior was still simple, but the previously stated goal of actively stimulating a higher general rate of response was clearly achieved.

In the process of increasing the response rate, the therapists simultaneously approached the second goal—identifying stimuli that seemed to have the greatest reinforcing power. During this phase of the program, the staff sought not only to increase the rate of response but also to identify and utilize more stimuli as reinforcers for shaping behavior and thus to further increase the response rate. The major reinforcer thus far used was the cessation of noxious stimulation but, as successful as it appears to have been as an initial tool, this could hardly continue to serve as the only reinforcer, particularly as the children approached more socially adaptive levels of behavior. Having made the initial gains through the employment of noxious stimulation, it was now necessary to develop more positively-valued reinforcers as alternatives. A repertoire of reinforcers would have to be developed as it was expected that some would eventually lose their reinforcing value through satiation, and different reinforcers would be required to strengthen different kinds of behavior.

Reinforcers were found in many forms and in what might seem to be the most unlikely places. They were identified by the staff as we carefully observed the children's reactions to the variety of stimuli. Those objects which were observed to apparently stimulate interest and to be associated with some sustained new behavior were tentatively labeled as reinforcers and were then tested through use in attempts to stimulate and strengthen new behavior. For example, as Frankie and Freddie were plied with picture puzzles, books, crayons and toys, they were observed to eventually appear interested in certain stimuli, reaching for them occasionally, rather than ignoring or escaping from them. After Freddie had learned to move to the table and stand next to it we began to use the variety of objects on the table as stimuli, and found that he soon began handling a simple picture puzzle of an airplane. While at the table with the therapists and, occasionally, some other child, he began manipulating the pieces, remaining involved with them for several minutes. No other stimulus had resulted in this kind of active involvement. Assuming that the airplane puzzle had some reinforcing value, the therapists began using similar stimuli to test whether there would be any generalization of response. Thus, we approached Freddie with other puzzles, and with pictures of airplanes, and he began to show interest in them. Gradually, using the pictures as reinforcers, the therapist would seat himself at the table and reinforce Freddie's approach behavior. Soon the child easily responded when called by moving to the table and standing there while the therapist pointed out the airplanes and maintained a steady, calm, and "soft" verbal patter. Freddie was gradually pulled into a more active participation, pointing out pictures and eventually naming many of the objects. This activity of looking at pictures with the therapist became a regular daily event. As it was increased in time, it was also gradually generalized from pictures of airplanes to nearly all pictures and from the first therapist to the others, as well as to the children. Thus, observing Freddie's apparent interest in pictures of airplanes, the therapist moved him along a behavioral sequence that culminated in simple but relatively sustained cooperative activity with both therapists and children.

It was observed that Frankie began to show interest in pictures of tools in a colorful trading stamp catalog. These pages were then used, much as described above for Freddie, to stimulate and reinforce sequences of sustained activity. This included actively looking at tool pictures with the therapist, turning pages to find the pictures, pointing them out when named by the therapist, imitating their sounds, and verbally approximating their names. ("Zzz" became "zzaw" and then "saw" "rrr" became "rrill" and then "drill.") Soon Frankie was actively participating—searching for, finding, and naming a large variety of things in many different books. Later, by the 25th week, his interest in tools was used to increase his physical activity as well. A set of plastic carpenter's tools was purchased, and Frankie used them to actively engage in play, interacting primarily with the staff but also with the other children. By this time, the effective reinforcers included not only removal of noxious stimulation but also the presentation of objects such as puzzles, food, etc.

As noted, reinforcers were of varied kinds and differed from one child to another. One of the staff's primary task was to *identify potential reinforcers*; this required constant, active trial-and-error stimulation of the children and careful, detailed observations of their responses. Once identified, the reinforcers were used to move the child along a behavioral sequence. A child occasionally would seem to become satiated with some reinforcer, and another would have to be substituted. The reinforcers did not have to be sophisticated or expensive items—one of the most effective was the trading stamp catalog.

Thus, we sought to identify useful reinforcers by observing the children's reactions to the variety of stimuli presented. If some response was observed to occur consistently to a particular stimulus, it was inferred that the stimulus was effective in stimulating that response. Further, if a response increased after presentation of a particular stimulus, it was inferred that the stimulus had reinforcing value. With such observations and inferences, it appeared theoretically possible to construct learning sequences in which desired behavior would be both stimulated and reinforced or just reinforced when emitted. Thus, observing Freddie's and Frankie's increased approach responses to particular pictures led to the inference that those pictures had reinforcing value. If so, then those stimuli presumably could be used to strengthen emitted responses.

It is not clear how particular stimuli came to attain reinforcing value. In Frankie's case we had speculated that tools had perhaps acquired reinforcing value at a time when his father carried out extensive construction at home. As for Freddie, we were hard-pressed to even speculate about the origin of the apparent reinforcing property of airplanes.

Reinforcers apparently did already exist for these children, and needed only to be ferreted out through careful observation and then systematically employed. This identification and employment of reinforcers is illustrated by our work with Diane, an extremely autistic four-year-old girl who joined us two years after the group's beginning. She was a child with severe behavioral deficits: Diane had never spoken and was seldom heard to make vocal sounds except for crying; she was not toilet trained, could not even minimally feed or dress herself or care for any of her own needs in any way; she was incapable of avoiding even simple hazards and would, for example continue striding across the top of a table until she simply fell off the end; she never played with toys or handled any objects and was seldom observed to even open her fists; she was totally aloof and had never been observed to approach another person unless, on occasion, seemingly by accident.

Diane's surplus behavior consisted of constant crying throughout a whole day, interrupted only by sleep, and a markedly-stereotyped, rapidly-emitted wrist-rubbing. In this, she rubbed the insides of her wrists together, followed by inserting an entire fist into her mouth. This behavior resulted in severe chafing of her wrists to the point of bleeding, a grotesque distending of her mouth, and a constant flow of saliva dripping down her lips, chin, and arms, causing them to become severely chapped and irritated.

All direct attempts to interrupt her severe behavioral surplus were to no avail. Likewise, training sequences to overcome behavioral deficits were having no apparent effects on her behavior. For example, an attempt was made to teach Diane to hold a cup and drink from it. There was no apparent learning even of this simple task for an entire year, in spite of the presumed reinforcing value of milk or juice. (Diane eventually did learn to hold the cup long enough for one tiny sip, after which she simply dropped the cup, spilling its contents.) Other training sequences such as toilet training, simple approach responses, or just opening her fist were equally useless. Diane could not be stimulated into activity, did not "escape" our insistent stimulation (therefore rendering useless the reinforcement of removing noxious stimulation), and did not respond in any consistent fashion to any stimuli. Food and liquids were not effective reinforcers; toys, persons, and other objects were ignored. After many months it was noted that, out of the varied and insistent stimulation, the only stimulus that seemed to reach her was the tinkling sound of "Frère Jacques" played by a tiny music box. She sometimes turned her head when the music box played, leading to the inference that the music might not only occasion a positive although minimal response but might also have reinforcing value. Diane's slight and only momentary turning of the head was as meager as a response as the music was as a stimulus. Nevertheless, they were the only relatively consistent stimulus-response and possibly effective reinforcer that had been identified. It was decided to use the music box as a reinforcer to shape up two important responses and to develop a new reinforcer. The responses to be acquired were approach responses to a therapist (or reduction of her continuous aloofness) and a decrease in wrist-rubbing. The new reinforcer to be developed was to be verbal stimuli. We were to attempt to reduce the wrist-rubbing, fist-in-the-mouth sequence and her marked aloofness, both well established responses. In addition, we were to attach reinforcing value to verbal stimuli. The following situation was established:

Each day a therapist sat on a low bench for a half-hour period. The bench and therapist were always in the same position. Diane was allowed to move anywhere within the room. Another therapist observed and recorded (a) the number of wrist-rubbing sequences and (b) the amount of time Diane spent near the therapist. Remaining "near the therapist" (that is, approach behavior) was defined by the act of stepping into a rectangular area delimited by the nine-inch square floor tiles. The area was eight by five tiles (72 by 45 inches). Thus, the standard setting throughout the experiment was the placement of the bench and the therapist, the observer, and Diane—free to move anywhere within the room.

There were four phases:

Phase I (talk only). This was the baseline phase, where the therapist attempted to stimulate approach responses by verbally calling, coaxing, and commanding Diane, and giving the child verbal praise whenever she did approach.

It was predicted that in Phase I Diane would continue to ignore the therapist and to rub her wrists together.

Phase II (music only). In this phase the therapist no longer spoke to Diane. Rather, whenever Diane made an approach response (i.e., stepped into the 72 by 45 inch area), the music box was turned on. However, it would not be turned on if Diane were near the therapist but also engaged in wrist-rubbing. The music was turned off if Diane stepped outside the area or if she commenced wrist-rubbing. The music box was turned on and remained on *only* when she was near the therapist and was not engaged in wrist-rubbing.

It was predicted that if the music box was indeed a reinforcer, both her stereotyped wrist-rubbing and her aloofness would decrease.

Phase III (music and talk). In this part of the experiment, the approach response and cessation of wrist-rubbing were still reinforced by the presentation of the music box. However, the presentation of the music would be preceded each time by a brief verbal statement by the therapist. The verbal statements here were much the same as in Phase I, but unlike Phase I they were immediately followed by the music box. Thus, as Diane made approach responses *without* wrist-rubbing, the therapist made a rewarding verbal statement and then turned on the music box. Both the music and soft verbal patter continued until she stepped away or began wrist-rubbing.

It was predicted that aloofness and wrist-rubbing would continue to decrease since the music reinforcement was still forthcoming.

Phase IV (talk only). This was the test phase in which the conditions of Phase I would be reinstated. Here the therapist again used verbal statements to coax and reinforce both the approach behavior and the cessation of wrist-rubbing. The music box was not used at all.

If the training interpolated between the first and last phase had had no effect, we would expect wrist-rubbing and aloofness to be at the original high level. If, however, the music had been reinforcing and had successfully shaped up both approach and desisting of wrist-rubbing behavior, we would expect the last phase to at least begin with a low level of aloofness and wrist-rubbing.

If verbal stimulation were noxious, we would expect the last phase to show an increase in aloofness and wrist-rubbing as the noxious verbal stimuli punished approach behavior and cessation of rubbing. However, if the music were truly reinforcing, we could expect not only a decrease in wrist-rubbing and aloofness when reinforced with music but also that the therapist's verbal statements would have acquired reinforcing value through association with the music. If so, then in the final talk-only phase, we would expect the aloofness and wrist-rubbing to continue decreasing as approach and control of wrist-rubbing were being reinforced by talk only.

In summary, (a) if music were not reinforcing, we would expect aloofness and wrist-rubbing to show no change from Phase I; (b) if music were reinforcing, we would expect Phases II and III to show a decrease in wrist-rubbing and aloofness compared with Phase I; (c) if the therapist's talking did acquire secondary reinforcing value, we would expect wrist-rubbing and aloofness to remain at a low level in the test phase where the approach behavior and control of wrist-rubbing would not be maintained by the reinforcement of talk only.

The data, presented graphically in Figure 1, clearly show that aloofness and stereotyped wrist-rubbing decreased as predicted. In fact, in the test phase where talk only was again emphasized, aloofness decreased to zero over the last four sessions, while wrist-rubbing decreased to zero during the last two sessions.

For the first time in her life, Diane made definite approach responses to another human being and remained with that person for as long as half-hour periods. Further, for the first time since it became a stereotyped, repetitive response, wrist-rubbing dramatically decreased.

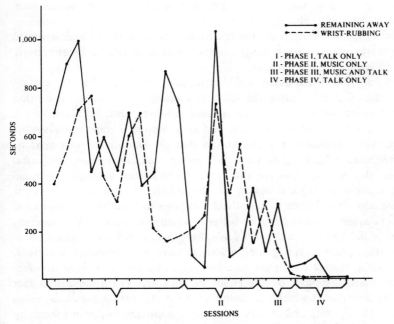

FIG. 1 DECREASE OF ALOOF AND WRIST-RUBBING BEHAVIOR

The major objectives had been achieved: a reduction of aloofness, a reduction of stereotyped wrist-rubbing, and the development of the reinforcing value of talk by the therapist.

It also should be noted that Diane's mother, who had purposely not been told the details of this experiment, voluntarily reported near the end of the experiment that the child was suddenly showing affection at home for the very first time. We are tempted to conclude that Diane learned the approach response through reinforcement by the music box, that approaching people had generalized to her home, and that verbal stimuli were now reinforcers.

There are many obvious weaknesses in this demonstration. First, the two responses—wrist-rubbing and aloofness—might have been better dealt with separately than together. Second, the entire plan had to be shortened when the child's mother unexpectedly announced that they were leaving for their summer vacation sooner than we had expected. The number of sessions in each phase therefore were not equated. The test phase included only six sessions whereas it would have been preferable to have a number equal to the original baseline sessions. Finally, it would have been helpful to have continued the experiment withholding all reinforcement and predicting that the behaviors would soon return to their Phase I level.

Within all of these limitations, the results do tend to support our contention that reinforcers must be actively sought and, once determined, can be effectively programmed into training sequences.

The explanation of the behavioral changes noted in the focal group rests on the assumption that stimulating the children constituted a noxious condition while withdrawing the stimulation constituted reinforcement. Such did appear to be the case as the children were observed to develop new behaviors when the stimulation was withdrawn. The contention that *the stimulation was noxious and its withdrawal reinforcing* is supported through careful, repeated, empirical observation. However, it lacks the more precise and powerful support that can be had in a more controlled test of the hypothesis. It should therefore be possible for some researcher to test the hypothesis that autistic or psychotic children can acquire new and adaptive behavior when reinforced by the cessation of insistent verbal, physical, and other generally human-social stimulations.

If our assumption regarding the noxious value of our stimulation is correct, there are two questions that must be asked regarding the subsequent development of approach responses by the children. They are: (1) If we did in fact shape escape behavior in which the children turned and even moved away from us, how did an opposing and in fact antagonistic *approach* response eventually develop out of this? (2) If our stimulation was in fact noxious, how was the negative value overcome so that the children would not only approach us but would remain with us? Basically, both questions concern themselves with a central problem of how the therapists, beginning as noxious stimuli, eventually came to acquire positive value. By what process was this transformation from negative to positive value achieved? How did we bring about their approach behavior and how did we divest ourselves of negative value?

The development of approach behavior can easily be seen. Escape behavior was not only escape, because much of the time the situation was created in which a child in escaping from one therapist moved *toward* the second therapist. This movement was frequently created by having one therapist present the active stimulation while the other therapists positioned themselves in such ways that the child, had to move toward and even make contact with them in moving away from the first therapist. When such contact was made, the stimulation ceased; it was often noted that the child briefly remained in physical contact with the second therapist who was not only associated with the cessation of intruding stimulation but also maintained a quiet, protective role. The effectiveness of this strategy by a pair of therapists—one assuming the provocative, devil's advocate role, the other maintaining a protective or nurturing role—was seen most clearly about two years later with Randy, a young autistic boy who will be discussed later.

A similar strategy was used in moving children *toward* other children. Again, the escape behavior was utilized by the therapist to create a situation in which the child moving away from the intruding therapist would directly move toward another person, either child or therapist.

In addition, as noted above, once other stimuli and reinforcers were identified, they too were actively used to occasion and reinforce approach responses to the therapist and to other children. The examples of airplane pictures and puzzles for Freddie and tools for Frankie illustrate this point. The same was true with Cathy, for whom dolls were extremely reinforcing. In Gerry's case, the use of plastic pull-apart animals that could be assembled proved to be useful. With Gerry, the reinforcement was not in terms of assembling the pieces but rather in pulling apart an animal that the therapist had assembled. Whatever the reinforcement identified for each child, it became apparent that a wide variety of positive reinforcers were eventually available which were appropriate and useful in many different situations. Children *could* be reinforced for approach responses, and although the cessation of noxious stimulation continued to be an important major reinforcer, its importance soon began to recede as other reinforcers were more consistently used.

The second question—of overcoming the negative value of noxious stimulation—is perhaps more difficult to answer and requires more speculation. As indicated above, as the therapists became increasingly associated with positive reinforcers, their previously acquired negative value presumably diminished. However, another factor seems to have been involved—it appears reasonable to infer that in spite of the apparent effectiveness of the use of noxious stimulation the therapists had never acquired strong negative value.

It is suggested here that the voice and actions of the therapists reached noxious value at high levels of intensity, at which they intruded on the child. It was noted that the children did not escape from the mere physical presence of the therapists—a therapist could remain near a child for long periods if the therapist remained quiet and not intrusive. We are suggesting that the children escaped from the stimulation of an intensive level of the therapist's voice and touch, but not to lower intensities of the same stimulus complex. Noxious value was apparently carried by the most intrusive or salient aspects of the total stimulus complex presented by the therapist. This is consistent with earlier literature which points out that it is often characteristic of the autistic child to respond only to that portion of the environment immediately intruding upon him. Rimland (1964) and others describe autistic children who, when intruded upon, attack that portion of the person's body immediately involved in the intrusion. For example, if by stepping close to an autistic child one disrupts the child's stereotyped behavior, the child might attack the person's intruding foot or hand, as if the limb had no connection with the rest of the person. Autistic children appear not to perceive other human beings as total entities but to perceive only their various parts as they intrude upon them.

In our case, the children apparently responded negatively to the intrusion of the sounds and touch of the therapists, but apparently did not associate the intrusion with the same therapists behaving at lower levels of intensity. The therapists later divested themselves of negative value through their eventual repeated association with positive reinforcers. That could be achieved not only because of the power of the positive reinforcers but also because at low intensities of stimulation the therapists had never been aversive. It was the *intrusion* that was noxious and not the therapists per se.

We are suggesting that early in our program the children did not perceive the therapists as total entities. Rather, they perceived a variety of stimulation—sights, sounds, smells, etc.—some of which were aversive, some positive and some neutral. They did not associate and organize these separate perceptions into common perceptual units; they did not perceive that various groups of these stimuli had common sources—i.e., particular therapists. Thus, a therapist might drive a child away from him by behaving aversively and just a few moments later, by behaving quietly and gently, have no aversive effect.

We observed that eventually the therapists acquired a mixed value, carrying both positive and negative (aversive) properties, with positive value predominant. The children did learn to organize their perceptions of therapists, perceiving each as a complex whole that was sometimes neutral and sometimes positive or aversive. When their perceptions were finally organized and they perceived that the therapists had negative as well as positive properties, how was the potential pre-potency of the negative value avoided? The process appeared to be one of building up the therapists' positive value and simultaneously reducing their negative value. When the children had been responding with escape behavior from the noxious stimulation, they had not perceived that stimulation as part of the therapist. Therefore, the therapists were not seen as noxious and had not acquired negative value. As time went on, the children became increasingly alert and involved in external stimuli; they spent less time in their own aloof absorption, and, in their increased involvement with things, they were interfered with less easily. That is, while previously stimulating Freddie with a picture puzzle would have resulted in his obvious escape responses, now Freddie not only accepted the puzzle but often spontaneously moved to it, picked it up, and used it himself. The puzzle no longer constituted intruding, noxious stimulation. The same was apparently true with the other objects used as reinforcers, all of them becoming increasingly positive in value, with the children therefore less "intruded upon." Thus, the children escaped less because they were being intruded upon less. Their increased involvement in the environment and their acceptance and use of things is another way of saying that the children were more aware of what was occurring; they were perceiving more of their environment and, of course, accepting more of it. It is at this period of heightened awareness that the children began to finally associate the therapists' voices and actions with the therapists, and presumably to perceive the therapists as a totality. By the time these associations were formed, the stimulation of voices and action was less noxious because it had become less of an intrusion; when the children finally associated the voice with a therapist, the voice had already lost much of its negative value.

In attempting to answer these two questions, we have speculated that the negative value did not pose a major problem to be overcome later because the children were positively reinforced for approach responses and, in addition, the therapists had never in fact developed strong negative value. Also, by the time the children began perceiving the therapists in their totality much of the negative value of verbal and physical stimulation had already been decreased.

The most important point in this chapter is that children with massive behavioral deficits must be *stimulated* to increase their rate of variety of responses. From the new, higher rate, the therapist then selectively reinforces those that are most adaptive and that can eventually serve as alternative adaptive responses to replace the current lack of responses and the existing maladaptive behavioral surpluses.

In actively stimulating a higher more varied response rate, several strategies were used—beginning with the presentation of intruding noxious stimuli, which were withdrawn when the desired response occurred. This appears to have been a successful early strategy that gradually gave way to the increased use of positive reinforcers such as food, toys, and verbal praise.

An early concern that through the consistent association of the therapist with noxious stimulation he would acquire negative value and would hence lose his therapeutic effectiveness was not borne out. The use of noxious stimulation did not in any observed way detract from the eventual effectiveness of the therapist. In fact, as will be illustrated by Randy's case, the use of insistent intrusion by a therapist seemed to lead to a rather dramatic apparent increase in the therapist's *positive* value.

At five and a half years of age, Randy was an aloof, non-verbal, non-toilet-trained boy, who was incapable of caring for himself in even minor ways or of avoiding simple hazards. Randy devoted his waking hours to severe head-banging and constant, loud crying. The head-banging was carried out by either banging the front, back, or sides of his head against hard plaster or concrete walls or floors repeatedly or (usually while standing) hitting the sides of his head with his fists. The blows were repeated, severe, and accomplished with both fists whether in succession or simultaneously. His head was bruised and discolored, his eyes often blackened, and his scalp showed bald areas.

Randy was constantly in action—crying, head-banging and rapidly walking. The latter behavior continued, with no apparent destination. If out-of-doors, Randy wandered long distances until encountering an obstacle. When in a room, he wandered until he encountered a wall, where he immediately sank down, huddling against the confines of wall and floor, and continued his rapid head-banging and crying.

Unless actively engaged by a therapist, Randy quickly found his way to a wall, where he withdrew as described above from all association with the others. As long as Randy persisted in huddling on the floor and banging his head, the therapists were unable to engage him in group activities. Therefore, one of the first steps would be to teach him more adaptive alternative behavior, which would make him more accessible to further training. A "standing-up" response was both more adaptive and also antagonistic to "lying-down" behavior. Further, holding his arms down with fists below the level of his shoulders was similarly antagonistic to raising them and hitting his head. It was decided to teach Randy to remain standing or to sit appropriately, as on a chair, and to keep his arms down, fists below shoulder lever. A program much like that used in the earlier focal group, whereby one therapist would act as the "intruder" and another as "protector," was outlined.

Randy had already exhibited minimal approach behavior to one of the therapists but none to me, presumably because I had had little direct contact with him. Accordingly, I served as "intruder." Whenever Randy huddled on the floor or wall, the intruder pulled him up, saying that he would not let Randy lie on the floor. Likewise, whenever Randy hit his head, he would be stopped, his arms held away and below shoulder level. Whenever Randy was standing or appropriately sitting, without hitting his head, the intruder desisted. The second therapist softly held and comforted Randy whenever the child moved to him. However, as soon as Randy either slid to the floor or hit his head, the protector therapist would say, "Oh no. None of that," and would move off. At this point, the intruder quickly moved in again, pulling Randy to his feet or holding his fists away from his head. Thus, head-banging and lying on the floor immediately called forth the loud, insistent, none too gentle intruder, while more appropriate approach behavior resulted in the very gentle, soft, comforting therapist.

This plan was put into effect one morning. The intruder walked into the room, greeted everyone, and immediately moved in on Randy who was huddled on the floor, banging his head. For the next 20 minutes, a completely physical encounter was maintained in the room as I pursued and Randy (crying and banging his head) moved everywhere ineffectually seeking escape. At the end of 20 minutes Randy had had enough, and a most unexpected event occurred. He not only remained standing but, contrary to our expectation, actually moved *to* me, looked directly at me, and made physical contact. In the second scheduled training session, there was no need for me to pull Randy off the floor, since he not only remained standing but also stayed close to me.

From that point on, Randy remained off the floor and was gradually stimulated into more appropriate activity. For example, once he remained up, he could be engaged in rolling a ball, at first by himself and soon in direct play with the therapist. Within a few weeks, playing with the ball had become an obviously reinforcing pasttime, and the ball was then used to reinforce other social behaviors. These included hand-clapping (instead of head-banging), a few words, approach to staff, and finally, active play with another child. Within four months, Randy's behavior was far more social than it had been. Both lying on the floor and excessive crying had completely ceased, while head-banging had been noticeably reduced. Randy was active, involved in play with another child, approached the therapists, and acquired several words including "ball" and "da da." One of the unexpected occurrences, as noted above, was that the intruder did not acquire negative stimulus value. Randy did not seem to dislike or fear this therapist. Rather, after the first encounter, Randy regularly would easily approach the intruder therapist and pull him into an active game of rolling the ball.

In this chapter we have attempted to explain and illustrate our attempts to achieve three important goals early in the program: (1) a variety of environmental structure; (2) an increased rate and variety of response, and (3) the identification and development of reinforcers. In the next chapter the first 100 sessions of the original group (Billy, Frankie, Freddie and Mary) will be described. An attempt is made to trace the behavior of each child as the first two behavioral goals were sought. At the end of 100 sessions, the next two children (Cathy and Gerry) were added.

CHAPTER 5

The First 100 Sessions

THE ORIGINAL GROUP

The group met five mornings each week from 9:00 to 11:30. During the first nine sessions the children appeared tense, fearful, and agitated. Billy, for example, repeatedly asked, "Will you hit me?" pleading "Please don't throw me out the window!" or "Please don't choke me!" He neither waited for nor seemed to perceive any answers. He was able to read a few signs and the names of stores across the street but either perseverated on the same verbal phrase or inappropriately shifted to another, making conversation impossible. Mary was verbal but could not hold a conversation. Neither Frankie nor Freddie responded to verbal cues or verbalized, and during the first nine sessions there was little interaction. A typical session during the first nine would find Frankie sitting silent, inactive and unresponsive; Billy, agitated, shouting, "Look at the big bus" or "What does the kitty do?"; Mary, crying, huddling in corners, occasionally coming out to throw something or hit someone; and Freddie, periodically screeching, standing at his window or silently eating whatever sweets he could reach.

The two therapists moved among the children, attempting to stimulate more behavior and finding their reinforcements meager. The tenth session showed some change toward more group cohesion. The following description is taken from notes written during and immediately after that session.

The Tenth Session

Frankie arrives first at 8:55 A.M., trudging slowly up the stairs, urged by his mother. He walks in slowly and stands, arms at his side with his snack bag hanging from his hand, unresponsive to the staff's greetings. A therapist takes Frankie's limp hand and speaks softly, "Hi, Frankie. How are you today?" Frankie blinks slowly with sleepy-appearing eyes and continues to stand silent and immobile, his eyes not focused on the therapist.

Ten minutes of soft and unsuccessful attempts to stimulate a response in Frankie have passed when Freddie enters. We had seen his mother park the car, get out and stand, trying to get the resisting child out, finally pulling him, still silent and hanging back, across the street and into the building.

His progress up the stairs was presaged by loud shrieks that rebounded from the metal stairs and hard plaster walls. Hauled to the second floor, Freddie was led into our room where his mother bids us "Good luck" and leaves. Freddie enters. He appears tense, walking slowly toward Frankie who is still standing as before. Freddie ignores all greetings, halts briefly at Frankie's side, screeches, leaps forward, flaps his arms, and again stops—facing a blank wall. With a smile on his face, Freddie stands for the next minute while Frankie, finally responsive to Freddie's scream, slowly turns his head and looks toward him. One therapist speaks to Freddie who emits a loud, long, high-pitched screech and runs across the room flapping his arms to where he faces "Freddie's window," remaining there for the next 20 minutes, occasionally screeching but generally silent.

At 9:10 Billy, who is not usually late, rushes up the stairs and into the room in great agitation, slams the door shut, and bounds across to the window where he stops and faces the window. Bizarrely grimacing with tight, quivering head and neck, Billy begins a fast rapping of his two index fingers against the windowsill, making a loud "tsss" sound. He responds to the therapists in his characteristic monotone: "Yes. Hello. Yes. Oh. Hello," but otherwise ignores them. For the next 20 minutes Billy and Freddie remain standing at the windows, ignoring each other.

Frankie had been led to the table where, with intensive individual attention by one therapist, he begins to look at pictures in the books held out for him. After about 15 minutes he clearly identifies a picture of a car, which was, of course, highly reinforcing for the therapist. After another five minutes Frankie turns and, for the next half hour, watches Billy.

The other therapist alternates between Billy and Freddie, trying to seat and engage them with pictures or crayons. Freddie screeches at her approach, while Billy moves away from her. Mary, frequently late, now enters, walking with her back rounded forward, head down, hands covering her ears. Her snack bag, clutched by one hand, is hiding one side of her face, and she is heard repeating, "It's noisy? It's noisy?" Ignored by Frankie and Freddie, only glanced at by Billy who then seemed to be more agitated, Mary makes no response to the staffs' greetings. She moves sideways to the wall and slides down to the floor crying, "Who he? Who he?," as she vaguely points with her fist at Freddie whom she had known for two years, her left arm outstretched and still covering one side of her face. Mary screeches, "He gonna hit me?" and throws her snack bag, hitting Freddie in the back. Freddie and Mary seem to freeze, neither child making a sound. Mary is seated on the floor, her right side against the wall, knees drawn up, head down and covered by her left arm. Mary's right arm is still extended in Freddie's direction after throwing the snack.

Agitated, Billy begins bouncing higher and higher, making vocal sounds and rapping his fingers. Frankie, still immobile, continues to watch Billy. Mary and Freddie briefly remain silent and motionless, and then Freddie screams—a loud, shrill, long scream—causing Mary to convulsively pull her head down to her chest, draw up her knees even further, cover her head with her arms, and scream loudly: "Go home, Go home, Go home." Huddled on the floor, she sobs noisily while Freddie again silently smiles and faces his window. Frankie continues to giggle and look at Billy who is becoming increasingly agitated.

The therapist gets up to calm Billy, who leaps away keeping the table between them, feinting, dodging, giggling, and saying, "Ooh, Ooh, don't get me, don't get me! Ooh! Ooh!" The therapist, aware that he is reinforcing Billy's disruptive behavior, sits down and returns to Frankie, who is slowly turning his head, keeping Billy in sight. Billy continues to laugh, rap the table with his fingers, and he invites the therapist to chase him. After several minutes of no response, he returns to his window. Frankie, always moving more slowly than the rest of the action, is now turning his head back to look at Billy at the window.

Freddie continues to stand silently, while Mrs. B has succeeded in getting Mary to her feet over to the table and seated across from Frankie. Mrs. B then renews her attempts to engage Freddie and Billy. The other therapist sets out paper and crayons, inviting the children to join in coloring. Frankie turns toward the table and picks up a crayon, but he only holds it, and does not use it to color. Mary hunches over the table and watches the therapist coloring on paper. She picks up the crayon, rapidly scribbles for a few seconds, then stops and says, "What that? What that?" Mrs. B succeeds in bringing the other two boys to the table and now all four children are seated together for the first time. A calm ten minutes follow. Frankie still holds his crayon, Mary scribbles, Freddie smiles and makes gurgling sounds much like an infant, and for the first time, Billy awkwardly scribbles three or four lines (holding the crayon with the thumb and the small finger of his left hand) and then abruptly leaves the table. Mrs. B brings him back and the two therapists manage to keep the four children quietly seated while the therapists softly praise their behavior, explaining pictures in books, and so on.

Mary begins to speak in a more agitated fashion and suddenly raises her arm. Mrs. B, anticipating a thrown crayon, smoothly stops the child and gently holds her arm without the other children becoming aware of it. Mary has reached her limit of sustained quiet behavior. Wishing to end the brief session without upset in order to preserve its positive value, the therapists wait for about two more quiet minutes and then announce that it is time to move to the play room.

It is now about 10:05. Mrs. B, carefully controlling Mary by holding and talking quietly to her, takes her into the play room while the others follow. Each child has been asked to carry some of the books, crayons, and papers. All but Mary do so. In the play room Freddie drops his book in the middle of the floor and runs into a corner near the sandbox where he stops, screeches, flaps his arms, and then stands still, smiling silently. Frankie stops abruptly and stands there, causing Billy to bump into him. Billy drops his books, leaps over to the window, raps his fingers, and says, "Loogadabigbus, loogadabigbus" (i.e., "look at the big bus"). After being helped to put his book away, Frankie is led to the sandbox by a therapist who gets both Freddie and Frankie involved in the sand.

Freddie makes cooing and gurgling sounds and wraps his arms around Frankie's head. Frankie, pulled and prodded, makes no response. Mary, having been calmed by Mrs. B, is again huddled on the floor, but is now watching Freddie and Frankie, and is saying, "Who he? Who he?" in a strained, high-pitched voice. Mary finally joins Frankie and Freddie. Helped by a therapist, the three children squat at the sandbox, fingering sand for about 15 minutes. They do not verbalize or interact but, for the first time in the play room, remain together in a play-like situation without upsets. All attempts to engage Billy in playing have failed, and he continues rapping his fingers on the windowsill. When the therapist acknowledges Billy's interest in looking out the window and asks Billy what he is looking at, Billy replies, "loogadabigbus!" When asked "Which big bus?" Billy replies, "Yes, what does the kitty do? What does the kitty do?" As the therapist tries teaching Billy to extend his conversation, Billy becomes increasingly agitated and bounds around the room, finally running out the door. When not chased, he returns and is still quite agitated. He keeps asking, "What does the kitty do? What does the kitty do?" The other children are becoming restless, having nearly reached their limits of controlled behavior, and the therapist announces "snack time."

Frankie is chosen by the therapist to set the snack table, which he does well but slowly, putting out paper cups, napkins, cookies and fruit juice. Frankie sits down when told, Mary has to be led to her chair, and Billy sits down by himself. Freddie remains at the sandbox for several minutes before moving to the table. The two therapists attempt to maintain a quiet, calm order, and snack time goes fairly well for about five minutes, until Freddie takes Mary's food, causing her to cry in seeming terror, "He hit me! He hit me!"

At Mary's crying, Billy raps his fingers on the table, stamps his feet, and runs to the window shouting, "Help, police! Help police!" We calm Mary but cannot entice Billy back to the table. Freddie by now has snatched as many cookies as he can cram into his mouth and hold in his two hands and Frankie (sitting next to Freddie) has begun to giggle. When the scene is again quiet, Frankie and Mary go back to finish their snack, while Freddie is told that he may have no more because he had already eaten his, Billy's, most of Mary's, and some of Frankie's. Freddie knocks over his cup of juice, screams and runs away from the table.

It is now 10:30, and Mary helps clear up the snack table. While Frankie continues to sit, Billy raps his fingers on the windowsill and Freddie stands by the sandbox. A few minutes later Mary turns on the record player and begins her stiff-legged, stereotyped rocking described earlier. Freddie begins screaming, Billy becomes more agitated and bounds around the room, and Frankie remains at his seat, giggling even louder. The therapist turns down the volume of the phonograph, but the children have already been stimulated.

Billy bounds around, in and out of the room. He urges Freddie to throw sand on him. Freddie screeches, grabs a truck and a doll, which he breaks and throws them out the window. Mary, apparently just beginning to respond to the fact that the phonograph has been turned down and seeing Freddie break the toys and throw them out the window, runs over to him and kicks him, saying he "broke the music." At this point Mary is crying loudly, Freddie is screaming, Billy is bounding and rapping his fingers, and Frankie is still seated at the snack table, loudly giggling. After about ten minutes of this peak of excitement, Freddie abruptly stops screaming. Billy calms somewhat, Frankie quiets and Mary stops crying but becomes physically more active—throwing sand at the therapists, laughingly walking on top of the snack table, and doing other things which had earlier been structured as "not allowed." By about 11:00 the group has settled into a fairly quiet period, and Billy's behavior changes quite radically. He seems agitated but is quiet, remaining at the window and occasionally slowly walking around the room.

Freddie remains quiet, unresponsive to the therapist or the other children. Frankie returns to the sandbox, where he sits and looks at Billy. Mary remains active, although the therapists manage to keep her from provoking the other children. From 11:00 until about 11:10, the children are taken for a brief, orderly walk around the building. Upon returning to the room, Mrs. B succeeds in getting Billy, Frankie, and Mary to sit down while she reads a story. Freddie does not join them and Mary breaks up the session half way through the story by hitting the book out of Mrs. B's hand and giggling loudly. The last 10 or 15 minutes of the session find the children physically separated but apparently more aware of each other. Frankie is intently watching Billy, Billy is watching

Mary, on two occasions Freddie walks over and touches one of the therapists, smiles and walks away again. At the end of the session, Mary laughs, giggles and puts on everyone's jacket but her own. She laughs particularly hard when she puts on Billy's jacket—the largest one.

When Freddie's mother arrives, he drops to the floor and screams. Dragging him out, she says, "Now its *your* turn to wish *me* luck." Freddie continues to scream as he is hauled down the stairs, across the street and into the car. The screaming stops abruptly when his mother gives him cookies.

Changes Over the First 100 Sessions

Reviewing the daily notes, we saw changes from the first to the 100th session, five months later. The children generally appeared more relaxed, alert, and responsive to the group setting. Their physical proximity and group interaction increased, particularly in the last 20 sessions. For example, we had noted that all of the children spent a noticeable amount of time in solitary rocking. Assuming that such rocking was reinforcing, we used it as a way of increasing group interaction. Obtaining a wooden rocking boat, we encouraged the children to sit in it and rock. Soon all four children sat in the boat together and rocked, while the group worker sang songs and verbally reinforced their physical proximity and cooperative rocking. This became the first activity that involved all four children in a physically interactive situation. The frequency and duration of their physical proximity also increased as did their general activity level, and all but Billy began to use toys appropriately.

The staff maintained verbal stimulation, and the children began responding to it. There was a noted increase in the appropriateness of Billy's and Mary's speech, while both Freddie and Frankie began using not only single words but also phrases. All children exhibited more positive behavior to each other and the staff. The parents, in carefully detailed interviews, indicated that these behavioral changes were paralleled by similar changes at home. They were surprised at the degree of behavior change that had occurred within only about two months.

As the children became more responsive and active, they also became increasingly aggressive. By the 100th session (about 20 weeks) both Billy and Mary were so hyperactive and Mary so aggressive that they became our major management problems. There was no doubt by the 100th session that significant behavioral changes had occurred—the children were more alert, aware, responsive, active, and aggressive. Following is a brief summary of the behavioral changes observed in Billy and Frankie, who showed the greatest initial changes.

In the first 100 sessions Billy's general response level increased in both socially adaptive and disruptive directions. Billy became more verbal as the staff tried to shape longer periods of verbal interaction. For example, when he said,

"Look at the big bus," we responded with "Where?" or "Point to it," etc. At first Billy retreated, voicing inappropriate phrases such as "Is there a lighthouse?" We insisted, however, and pressed him for an answer to "What big bus?" until finally one day he replied: "There," pointing out the window. We immediately ceased the pressure. Our next step was to get him to focus on the bus, to look at it, and describe it to us. We asked him about the color of the bus, the people in it, its destination, and so on. We pressed many questions, desisting when Billy, backing away, answered appropriately. Soon the following limited conversation occurred. Billy: "Look at the big bus, look at the big bus, loogadabigbus, loogadabigbusloogadabigbus!" Therapist: interrupting him: "What big bus? Where, Billy?" Billy: "There. The green one." Therapist: "The green one? Where is it going?" Billy: "Down Main Street, to the park. It's the Newton Avenue bus."

The elements of Billy's accurate verbal response had previously been laboriously built up. Although his voice was flat and the whole delivery quite mechanical, it was a closer approximation of normal verbal behavior. In succeeding sessions his speech became more animated as well as more normally conversational, and we were able to hold conversations about varied topics. Billy became more attentive as stories were read to the children, and he began using crayons and picture puzzles. Using his hands was still an awkward and reluctant process. His responsiveness to the other children increased considerably, but not always positively.

Billy began to cooperate and help in several small ways—helping to clear up before and after snack, picking up toys, and holding the hands of smaller children during walks. Assigning such simple tasks resulted in brief but controlled and cooperative behavior. Other less positive changes also occurred. His general hyperactivity increased; he leaned out the windows, leaped from one sill to another, stamped upon the radiators; he pulled, stroked, smelled, sucked, bit, and salivated on the therapist's arms; he pulled hair and at times actually swung himself from the group worker's hair. He giggled loudly almost constantly, seeming to have a broad grin regardless of the surroundings, and was perpetually in intense motion, dashing around, in and out of the room. On one occasion he dashed wildly downstairs, and I had to retrieve and carry him back up, cradled in my arms, lanky limbs dangling and waving, while he giggled wildly and shouted, "hey, hey, hey, take me to Rosebush!"

Frankie, the least active and slowest moving child in the group, was non-verbal, not toilet trained, played with no toys, and made few responses to people. The most apparent change was at first puzzling. Frankie was aloof, always appearing to be abstracted and "far away," but about the 15th session he suddenly and very obviously "looked different" becoming "in touch," "with it," and one staff member wrote that there was now "life in his eyes." The same phenomenon occurred later with Freddie, Cathy, and Gerry. All observers agreed that "something" had happened and the children simply "looked better."

After much discussion and additional observations, we concluded that the change was genuine; the children were beginning to focus their vision directly on us and to maintain eye contact. This change suggested a new alertness and "life" to their faces, and made us aware that up to that time they had rarely focused directly on us or maintained eye contact. We observed the same phenomenon in other children who later joined our program. In previous descriptions of autistic children, writers have been intrigued by their facial expressions, which are not so much blank as pensive and suggestive of deep thought and distant abstraction. We suggest that much of the pensive, abstracted, and self-involved appearance is due to the child's failure to visually focus directly on other people or to maintain eye contact. Once this contact develops, the child's facial expression seems to change; he appears more alert and responsive to external stimuli and, concurrently, less pensive and abstracted. (It would be instructive to compare the frequency and duration of eye contact in psychotic and normal children.) Not only did Frankie's facial expression change, but he began to watch alertly and giggle at the movements of the other children (particularly Billy) and to make brief verbal comments such as "Bi-lly down!" Frankie began to respond to our attempts to teach him to look at pictures, and he grunted and pointed as their names were given. Although slurred, his speech increased in frequency and complexity, and he was soon using phrases such as "Billy go out" or, referring to an infection on his face, "Booboo go down." Using the trading stamp catalogue and picture-word games, we taught Frankie to identify and verbalize single names of a great variety of objects. One of the significant occurrences was our observation that he responded well to pictures of tools. We purchased a set of plastic tools and Frankie began using them in his chacteristic slow manner. Working closely with him we were able to shape imitative sounds such as "ZZZ" when he handled the toy saw.

We reinforced and emphasized such sounds until he produced them at a high rate and then, through differential verbal reinforcement, began to develop closer approximations of words. For example, the "ZZZ" for the electric saw shaped up from "ZZZ" to "ZZZU" to "ZZZUW" to "ZZZAW" and finally to "SSSAW." Likewise, the word hammer was taught by repeating it in rhythm as he slowly hammered on the roof of the doll house. With each of Frankie's downswings, the therapist said, "ha!" and with the upswing, "mer." At first, Frankie's imitations were nearly grunts, "ah-uh!" as he swung in rhythm. Soon Frankie was steadily and rhythmically hammering while both he and the therapist sang "ha-mer!, ha-mer!" His physical involvement also grew and by the 100th session Frankie was using crayons, picture puzzles, clay, books, trucks, and play tools, and he was rolling a ball with the therapists. Frankie began to observe, sit near, and occasionally hug the other children. In general, his physical and verbal activity level had increased noticeably.

Frankie was not toilet trained and was having frequent bowel movements in his clothing as late as the 80th session. From the 80th session, we worked more directly on toilet training. In the 100th session he made his first successful signal, squirming around on the floor, and vaguely pointing to the bathroom. Although he continued to be incontinent at home for some time, he had fewer lapses in the group setting. His toilet training will be more fully discussed in Chapter 9.

100th Session

Freddie arrives first at 9:00 A.M., getting out of his car without difficulty and carrying a canvas flight bag that holds his snack and some favorite objects. Always slow on the stairs, Freddie is far behind his mother, walking slowly with a little smile on his face and making cooing sounds. Reaching the first landing, he coos loudly, does a little skipping dance, and then slowly proceeds the rest of the way. Greeted as he enters the room, Freddie vaguely, silently, smiles, and makes no response as his mother says "goodby," and kisses him. Walking to the center of the room, Freddie sets down his flight bag and rapidly hops side-ways to the window where he paces back and forth, continuing to make cooing sounds.

Freddie goes to the coat rack with Mrs. B but does not take off his jacket. Mrs. B encourages him and he manages to get one arm almost out. Freddie says nothing, but has maintained his little smile and cooing. As Freddie and Mrs. B return to the room Billy runs up the stairs ahead of his mother who admonishes him to be careful not to fall down. At the top he stops and says, woodenly, "Where's the rosebush?" and slowly goes back down stairs to his mother who urges him to go up by himself. Billy hesitates, starts, stops, and then rapidly dashes up the stairs where he passes Freddie's mother and returns her "hello," without slowing down. Inside the room Billy asks "Where's the rosebush?" "Rosebush?" Mrs. B replies. "Do you mean Mrs. __ ?" Billy does not answer but only smiles and walks slowly to the window near Freddie. Dr. G greets Billy who responds with a flat, mechanical, "Good morning." In response to our suggestion Billy says "Good morning, Freddie" and Freddie, smiling and cooing but not looking directly at him, walks over to Billy, hugs and briefly leans his head on him.

Billy, looking out the window, his arms at his sides with both hands rapidly fluttering, makes no further response to Freddie. The therapists maintain verbal reinforcement for Freddie and Billy for their "nice hello" and they began to get Billy verbally involved in commenting on how well Freddie did. Mrs. B notes that Freddie has done very well in many things including picture puzzles, one of which she holds out to Freddie. He smiles, takes the puzzle, smells it, mouths it, and seats himself at the table, working that and other puzzles for about the next 20 minutes, constantly surrounded by the verbal praise of the staff. Billy has thus far been uncommonly quiet but he suddenly laughs, becomes very excited and bounds across the room, out of the door, down the stairs and into the street. He had seen, from the window, Frankie and "Rosebush" arriving and, presumably, had gone down to meet them. Billy hesitates and then runs back in great agitation, saying "ooh, ooh, don't leave me. Don't leave me!" At the top of the stairs Billy sees "Rosebush" and in considerable excitement jumps in her lap, wrapping his long arms around her, laughs, waves his arms and legs and repeats "Ouch, oh, ouch. Rosebush has thorns?" After returning to the room he continues "Does Rosebush have thorns?" "They hurt. Do they stick you? Do they? Do thorns on Rosebush stick you? Does Rosebush hurt?"

While Dr. G and Billy are outside, Frankie is taken upstairs. He enters the room, is greeted by Mrs. B, grunts, "Good morning," and informs the therapist "Bi-lly down!" pointing vaguely to the floor. Mrs. B answers, trying to occasion further verbal responses and, amidst his giggles, Frankie replies, "Bi-lly OUT!" "Bi-lly DOWN!" "Gee DOWN!" the latter phrase referring to Dr. G's being outside with Billy. As Billy was being brought back into the room Mrs. B had already managed to seat Frankie next to Freddie, and engages him in drawing with crayons. The two boys sit there, both involved in their tasks, while the therapist talks with them, praising and, when necessary, assisting them. Working a piece into his puzzle correctly, Freddie says "Airplane," which is immediately reinforced by Mrs. B. Frankie joins in, naming "airplane," "chief's car" and "hammer" as he points to pictures in a trading stamp book. Frankie now sits in one therapist's lap and the two look at several books, pointing out pictures and naming them. This situation was surrounded by a constant but soft verbal stimulation by the staff, including immediate praise for the children's verbal responses and other appropriate behaviors. Freddie, who has been at the table for nearly a half hour, completes another puzzle and leaves. He walks over to his flight bag and takes out his mother's portable electric hair dryer, which he has insisted on bringing daily for two weeks. With the chord trailing behind him, Freddie carries the hair dryer around the room, occasionally mouthing it. He pauses at our table and then puts the dryer back in his flight bag. Freddie does not respond verbally to our questions, comments or show of interest. Slowly, never looking directly at us, and making no vocal sounds, he returns to the table and stands quietly. A few minutes later he takes the therapist's index finger and, using it as a pointer, indicates pictures and waits for the therapist to say the names.

Soon both Freddie and Frankie are pointing out and naming some of the objects. Billy and Mrs. B have a halting conversation about "school rules" and academic work such as reading and writing. Having brought about a sustained verbal response, Mrs. B then succeeds in getting Billy to print his name and to read a few lines from the book—all, of course, richly reinforced with verbal praise.

At about 9:45 the door bangs open and Mary enters, announcing her arrival by throwing her lunch bag across the room saying "I mad? Why I mad? Because I late?" Mary's face is rapidly contorting from wide, flashing grins to bizarre grimaces, and her hands, held up near her ears, flutter and wave about.

Billy and Frankie look up at Mary, while Freddie looks up but in the opposite direction toward the window. Billy tenses, begins saying "tss, tss, tss," and raps his fingers on the table. At a mutual signal the two therapists move to prevent an explosive reaction. Mrs. B walks slowly to Mary, quietly greets and helps her remove her jacket, and, in the process, turns her slightly so she will not be visually stimulated by, and stimulating to, the other children. Still talking soothingly, Mrs. B keeps Mary verbally engaged for several minutes. At the same time the other therapist has taken Billy's hand and gently stills it, while speaking softly: "Look at this picture, Billy, it's a lighthouse." Sketching rapidly with crayon, the therapist draws the lighthouse, a favorite subject for Billy. Still holding Billy's hand, the therapist coaxes him into pointing out where the "light" should go and "Where do the windows belong?" In a few moments Billy's attention has been redirected from Mary, he is more relaxed and engaged in helping to draw the picture.

As Billy focuses on the picture, Frankie, who has begun to giggle at Billy's finger-rapping, also becomes involved in pointing out parts of the lighthouse. By the time Mrs. B has calmed Mary and turns her to again face the table, the group is relaxed and quietly involved in socially appropriate verbal interaction—completely ignoring Mary's outburst. This, we thought, was a smoothly success-ful example of on-the-spot crisis-averting action. Our silent self-congratulation and self-satisfied nods to each other ended as a sharp scream pierced the room. In our concern to avert an explosion by controlling Mary, Billy, and Frankie, we had overlooked Freddie. At this scream Mary, saying, "He too noisy? He too noisy?" swings at his back with her left hand, missing only because Mrs. B pulls her back quickly and steers her in a wide arc around Freddie, who does not perceive the attack. Billy, absorbed with the lighthouse, only looks up briefly at Freddie and then back to the picture. Freddie, apparently because he is not further stimulated by either Billy or Mary, does not repeat the scream, but, with his little smile, returns to his favorite picture book. By the time Frankie, always far behind the action, has located the source of the scream all the children are relaxed and engaged in table activities. With no disruption to distract him Frankie too returned to the lighthouse picture.

For about 15 minutes the verbal, socially adaptive interaction continue. The children are not yet conversing but are verbally responding to each therapist and controlled enough to remain together actively participating in a socially adaptable manner for periods up to a half hour.

At about 10:05 the group moves into the playroom, with all children cooperating by carrying books. Freddie and Billy move to windows while Frankie slowly walks to the sandbox and sits in front of it. Mary tries to start the phonograph and begins her characteristic rocking, arms bent up at the elbows, hands fluttering about her shoulders, leggs stiff, back rounded forward and head down. Mrs. B interrupts her and moves her over to the sandbox, while Mary repeats, "I want a record? I want a record? I want a record?" Mrs. B explains the record player is broken (Mary had broken it the previous week) and she manages to engage Mary with toys in the sandbox, keeping up the constant verbal stimulation. Frankie, in the meantime, has started to handle the plastic tools near the sandbox.

Dr. G brings Freddie to the sandbox, starts him playing with a truck, and then goes to get Billy. Frankie, Freddie and Mary squat at the sandbox with Mary holding up the sand-filled toy pots and saying, "This food? This food? This food?" The two boys do not respond and Mrs. B explains that it is only "play food." Grimacing and gesturing, Mary becomes increasingly tense, shoving the pots under the noses of the two boys, who respond only by turning their heads away. Further agitated, Mary begins a gutteral, grunting laugh and suddenly throws sand into the boys' faces. Mrs. B stops her, gently holding her hand, saying, "We don't throw things." Wide-eyed and still grimacing, Mary relaxes, but, as soon as the therapist lets go Mary hits her in the face. Again Mrs. B holds her hand and says, "We don't hit." Billy and Dr. G have just returned and Billy immediately begins shouting, "Oh, oh, Mary's bad. Are you gonna hit her? Are you gonna spank her?" The therapist's response that "We don't ever hit children" seems to have no effect, and Billy became increasingly agitated and insistent, asking, "Will you spank her? Will you?" Finally the therapist replies, without sufficient thought to the possible consequences, "You want us to spank her!" Agitated and hanging on the therapist's arm, Billy grins broadly into his face, shouting, "Yes, oh yes! Please do! Oh please, please do!" The agitation and noise level increase and the next 20 minutes are explosive. Billy insists loudly that we will spank Mary, despite all our disclaimers and efforts to quiet him.

Mary protects her head, cringes and sobs, "You gonna hit me? You gonna hit me?"

Therapist: "No Mary. We never hit you. You don't have to be afraid."

Billy, loudly while bounding, laughing and clapping his hands in front of Mary: "Yes, oh yes! Oh yes, they are! Yes. Yes. Yes! They're gonna hit you!"

Mary, louder: "You gonna hit me?"

Therapist, gently: "No, Mary . . ."

Billy, wildly agitated: "Yes, they are! They are! They are gonna hit you!"

Mary, now screaming: "You gonna hit me! YOU GONNA HIT ME! YOU GONNA HIT ME! YOU HIT ME? YOU HIT ME? SHIT ASS! SHIT ASS!"

Frankie now giggles wildly while Freddie starts to screech out the window. Billy, agitated, goes through his whole repertoire of "forbidden acts," bounding around the room, giggling uncontrollably, rattling doors and yelling "There's a rosebush in the hall, there's a rosebush in the hall! Help, police. They're beating Mary!" Careening around the room he knocks over a pile of cardboard blocks. Giggling and shouting, he throws them around the room.

When the therapist moves toward him, Billy jumps upon the snack table, to the radiator, stamps up and down, and shouts, "Hey, hey, look at me!" Finally he leaps to his perch on the windowsill where he claws at the heavy screen and, still giggling wildly, shouts out the window, "Help, police! Help, police! They're beating Mary!" Freddie in the meantime has thrown several toys out of the window, but is no longer screeching.

After about 20 minutes the children quiet down. Staff calms Mary and Billy by holding them physically and quietly repeating, "We don't hit." Frankie continues giggling for a few moments after Billy has calmed but with no further stimulation he too quiets. Freddie has been standing quietly at his window for about 15 minutes, no longer a contributor to the upset. When the children are calm for a few minutes, the therapists engage them in picking up and straightening the room and setting the snack table. Freddie picks up a building block but only mouths it, finally dropping it. Mary, repeating "What's that? what's that?" picks up quite a few objects. Billy, still tense, gingerly using only his finger tips, spends nearly five minutes picking up and putting away a single block. Frankie silently puts a few toys into the sandbox where they belong.

Under Mrs. B's direction Frankie and Mary set the snack table and wash their hands. "Snack time" is announced. Freddie snatches the cookies and has to be restrained. He runs off but, when ignored, returns, and is immediately rewarded with verbal praise and cookies.

The four children and two therapists sit together at snack, the therapists talking quietly, directing the children to socially appropriate behavior and immediately reinforcing them with verbal praise. Snack time is calm and orderly for about five minutes during which Billy drinks his juice, but, as usual does not eat cookies. Frankie eats and drinks slowly and points at each child, grunting each name for which the therapist rewards him. Freddie has brought salted crackers for his snack, refuses to eat them and asks quite clearly "Cookie?" He is immediately given a cookie and verbal praise.

For about seven minutes, while both therapists are involved in reinforcing and further stimulating verbal responses of Frankie, Freddie and Billy, Mary is ignored briefly, a lapse which leads to the next series of upsets. Mary responds with her repertoire of attention-getting behavior: spitting up her chocolate cookie on the table and nearest person, putting cookies into her juice, throwing the soggy contents into a therapist's face and then laughing wildly while being physically controlled by the therapist. Billy leaves the table, raps his fingers on the windowsill for a few moments and then returns to Mrs. B who is still holding Mary, grabs her right arm and says "Its a pretty arm." Both therapists ignore this behavior but Frankie giggles and points at Billy who becomes increasingly tense.

Dr. G engages Mary and Frankie in clearing up while Mrs. B, with Billy hanging on, grinning, babbling, caressing her arm, walks with difficulty across the room. After helping to clear up the snack table Frankie moves slowly around the room, sits on the floor, squirms silently and points vaguely in the direction of the bathroom. This is the first time he signals successfully his need to go to the bathroom. Over the previous ten sessions Mrs. B has worked with Frankie, trying to toilet train him and has succeeded in getting him at least to signal to her after he has had a bowel movement. In those ten sessions he has soiled himself at least four times. This first successful signal was immediately reinforced with praise.

It is now 11:00, past time for the group's after-snack walk. Mary goes into the bathroom and plays with water in the sink. The general clearing up and the end of the snack period is a cue for Freddie, who runs to the door and screeches loudly. Billy is still pawing Mrs. B's arm and Frankie still giggling at him when Mary suddenly comes out of the bathroom with her pants down. Billy sees her and leaps away from Mrs. B yelling, "Woo Woo! Woo Woo!", and runs to the window where he raps his fingers and laughs wildly. Frankie giggles. Freddie, ignored as he screams at the door, pauses, then says clearly "Door!" Dr. G immediately opens the door, lavishly praises Freddie and, calming Billy and

Frankie, leads the three boys out while Mrs. B dresses Mary. The walk around several blocks is orderly and quiet with no upsets or other incidents. Freddie smiles silently, Frankie points correctly when asked and says appropriately, "Car," and "train." Billy verbalizes little, except to answer all questions with "yes." Mary skips and grimaces, flutters her hands and occasionally asks "What's that?", or "It's too noisy?" This is one of the best controlled walks we have had so far.

A few moments after returning, for no apparent reason Mary kicks Frankie and pokes her fingers into Freddie's eyes. Frankie sheds tears silently, and Freddie screeches, careens around the room screaming and flapping his arms for several seconds. At this Mary slides to the floor against the wall, pulls up her knees, covers her head and sobs "Why he crying?" "WHY HE CRYING?" When Freddie stops, Mary is still sobbing and shrieking. Again the therapist settles and soothes the children and, when all is calm, gathers them together for a story reading that holds them quietly for nearly 10 minutes after which they rock in the boat while the therapists sing.

The children are relaxed and the session continues quietly for the next 10 or 15 minutes. Billy, Frankie, and Freddie play at the sandbox and Dr. G tries to get Billy to use various toys. For the first time Billy uses a toy hammer and pounding bench and actually pushes a truck a few inches along the floor. Frankie uses his plastic tools, "repairing" the large doll house, making buzzing, cutting, hammering noises. Freddie holds a truck in his lap, makes crooning sounds and occasionally hugs Frankie or puts his head against Dr. G and croons. The therapist continues verbalizing and reinforcing the cooperative play and verbal responses of the children.

Mrs. B, meanwhile, sits with Mary and the two of them roll clay and have some brief verbal interaction. It is now nearly noon and the children have been engaged in cooperative social interaction for approximately half an hour. When Freddie's mother arrives, she finds all the children quiet and busily engaged. Mary runs to her, hugs her, calling her "Mommy" and smiling at her. Freddie leaves without incident and his mother, obviously pleased, remarks that we must have had a "very good day." The other three children also leave quietly and under good control, with no further upsets.

THE FOCAL GROUP

In addition to serving therapeutic goals, the first 100 sessions were to serve as a period of observation and assessment of the children's deficit and surplus behavior. During that time too we were to create a workable, consistent framework and schedule within which the program could operate. Reviewing the daily notes and intensive interviews with parents, it was clear that the children had shown demonstrable behavioral gains. It was not known, of course, whether the children would have made those gains regardless of their involvement in the program. It was clear, however, that Frankie and Freddie's increased speech, Billy's more coherent and extended conversation, Mary's generally better control and fewer tearful episodes, Frankie's near mastery of toilet training, and all the children's increased use of toys and other objects strongly suggested that changes had occurred in the program in just a five month period.

In the fall the program was enlarged, groups reshuffled and schedules changed. The larger number of children necessitated a change in group structure and scheduling. Accordingly, Billy and Mary, both verbal, were moved into an afternoon group with several children who had been dropped from public school because of bizarre, aggressive and other disturbed behavior. Frankie and Freddie, non-verbal, remained together and were joined by Cathy and Gerry, two autistic children who had no communicative speech. In the next section we shall introduce Cathy and Gerry and from that point on the morning group will serve as our main focus, illustrating the various attempts we made from 1963 through 1967.

We will periodically refer to Billy and Mary because they have already been introduced, and we will also later introduce new children who were added to the morning program.

CATHY

History

The early development of both Cathy and Gerry was like that already described for autistic children. Six years old when she began in our program, Cathy had been evaluated at several clinics, and earlier reports noted her "... grossly disordered behavior ... hyperactivity, lack of judgment, temper tantrums, failure to be toiled trained, inability to understand directions and refusal to chew solid food ..., (solitary) play with household objects such as spoons, toothpaste and cosmetics rather than toys ..., unable to use language for communicative purposes ..." (She is) "in a world of her own" most of the time ..., she amuses herself with a soup ladle ... (looking) at it for long periods, making a sound such as "Ee," as she is waving the ladle or looking at her reflection in it. She often moves her body back and forth as she does this. Her day is usually spent in running, jumping or climbing aimlessly. She loves to hear records and could spend hours doing this. She is not interested in dolls and does not show any interest in such things as riding a tricycle. Other children refuse to play with her."

At the time of that evaluation Cathy (age 5) was too uncooperative for formal testing. Based on observations and interviews with parents, the examiner indicated that Cathy was a "psychotic child." A year later the parents consulted a child psychiatrist who diagnosed Cathy as autistic and referred her to our program. Cathy was nearly six years of age and, as described by her parents, her conduct at home included many deficit and surplus behaviors such as bizarre mannerisms, toe walking, severe tantrums, stereotyped behavior, lack of speech, no socialization. The behavior deficits described by the parents were also observed and verified by our own staff during Cathy's first few months in our program. At six, Cathy remained an aloof little girl who rarely interacted or responded even minimally to others. On those rare occasions when she did respond briefly, her response was almost always totally inappropriate.

Although Cathy reportedly had used one or two simple words as early as six months of age, communicative language had not yet developed at six years. Cathy still did not respond to verbal stimuli, was not able to hold meaningful conversations and had a limited vocabulary which was used rarely and inappropriately, and consisted of repeating fragments from television commercials, sometimes for hours.

Cathy ate well enough to meet nutritional needs. When younger she had taken a bottle well, gained weight, but refused to eat any solids except one particular brand of infant cereal. At age six, when she began in our program, her diet consisted almost entirely of strained baby foods but, in addition, she had learned to eat pancakes, macaroni, meatballs and hot dogs. At age six, toilet training was incomplete with both enuresis and uncontrolled bowel movements during the day. Because Cathy did not give any signal, she frequently soiled herself.

Cathy was not aware of normal dangers and was apt to walk in front of moving cars and get herself into other dangerous situations. At home Cathy wandered through the neighborhood, entered any house and rummaged through boxes, cabinets or drawers, frequently taking and eventually losing objects.

Cathy also had many aggressive tantrums. Generally hyperactive, she engaged in much apparently non-directed physical activity; she ran, jumped, climbed, screamed, and engaged in violent head-shaking and constant toe-walking. This general pattern of hyperactive behavior was in considerable contrast to a quiet aloofness which she also revealed, consisting of holding dolls while crooning TV commercials.

The hyperactivity became intensified whenever there was even mild frustration; it consisted of severe tantrums, screaming, kicking people, throwing herself on the floor, throwing objects around, smashing, knocking over objects, and, in general, violently destroying her environment for unrelieved periods, sometimes as long as two or three hours. The tantrums occurred several times daily in any situation where there was some frustration. They happened in church, stores and other public places as well as at home, and her parents had found no way of handling them.

Cathy's gross motor coordination appeared good; she could easily run, jump and hop on her toes. She was not adept in small muscle coordination, however, and except for her dolls or an object she was about to throw, she seldom grasped anything. Unable to dress herself, Cathy had to be dressed completely by her parents.

Cathy would line up several dolls along a windowsill. Selecting one doll which she held against her face, she would spin, bob and prance in front of the dolls and frequently hum or croon bits of television commercials. Because the line of dolls was spotlighted by a living room lamp, and flanked by the window curtains, the whole situation resembled some bizarre fantasy of a stage production. While watching the dolls spotlighted on the "stage," Cathy did the performing; in some confabulated manner she and the dolls were at one, both performers and audience, completely aloof from the rest of the world.

Cathy's days routinely began at 5:30 A.M. when she awakened. She remained quietly in bed until about 6:00 when, by using characteristic gestures to her parents, she demanded her radio be turned on. For the next hour Cathy remained in bed with the radio playing, while she lined up dolls and repeated commercials. Sometimes she fell asleep again until about 7 o'clock: when her mother attempted to rouse her, Cathy fought and screamed. Bathing and dressing were always problems and her mother had to perform the entire task. Breakfast invariably consisted of a muffin, butter, milk (the only liquid she would drink) and strained baby foods. It was not until after beginning in our program that Cathy's eating increased in variety to include breakfast cereals and other foods.

For the rest of the morning Cathy usually stayed in the house, playing with the dolls and kitchen ladles in her stereotyped manner. There was usually no difficulty or upset though occasionally she did something particularly annoying. One Christmas, for example, she pulled down the freshly decorated Christmas tree causing a shower of glittering ornaments and fluttering tinsel. On the occasional morning Cathy went out she was aloof, ignoring other children. Her mother had to keep careful track of Cathy outside because of her tendency to wander and enter houses.

The rest of Cathy's day consisted of lunch, more solitary and stereotypical playing with dolls and ladles, dinner (which was usually brief, and uneventful) and two or three hours of aloof, stereotyped play during which she shared the living room with parents and sibling, but did not share in any activities. Her day ended when she went to bed without protest. Cathy fell asleep quickly, slept well, apparently without nightmares or terrors.

Thus, Cathy moved through a typical day in a fixed, repetitive way, aloof, isolated, and not varying her schedule or behavior in any significant manner. Because of her frequent and severe tantrums she could not be taken to public places. Once, for example, when taken grocery shopping, she ran through the store, knocking articles from shelves, tipping over shopping carts, screaming and kicking and behaving so violently aggressive that the store manager requested she not be brought back.

Although Cathy's older sister was concerned and interested, she did not spend much time with Cathy because the child failed to respond and the older girl found little satisfaction in playing with her. At six years of age, then, Cathy was a physically robust girl with many severe behavior deficits. She was apart from the world of other people and responded to it only when that world intruded upon the narrow limits of her own. In those instances her reaction was immediate and violent, so much so that other people rejected her, thereby further limiting her reality contacts.

Initial Behavior in the Program

Well-proportioned and pretty with excellent large-muscle motor coordination, Cathy was the most insistently aloof child we had ever seen. She behaved in a single-directed, unswerving fashion that admitted no distractions from whatever the specific single object of her intense focus might be. This determined exclusion of her immediate world became evident in her first two days with us. On her initial day Cathy entered carrying a small doll. In the first "verbal" hour she remained aloof, spinning in a small circle while holding the doll against the bridge of her nose and crooning bits of TV commercials. Attempts to stimulate her verbally failed. After the first hour we took the children into the playroom where, seeing an assortment of dolls on a shelf, Cathy rushed over to them and devoted the next hour and a half to holding them, spinning, rocking, all the while repeating rapidly the name of a well-advertised doll. "Penny Bright, Penny Bright, Penny Bright, etc." Cathy ignored all verbal stimuli, did not join in any activities, but remained aloof and focused on the dolls. Her physical activity for the first full two and a half hours was limited to two tiny circular areas. When she left, the staff felt that Cathy had hardly perceived them, the children or anything else but the dolls during her first session.

The next day Cathy came down the hall quickly and directly and went into the verbal session room without guidance by the staff, then immediately and unhesitatingly walked through it to the playroom door, opened it, entered, and went straight to the dolls. This was obviously purposeful behavior, carried out with a directness which allowed no waste action. Despite her apparent lack of perception of surroundings the previous day, she had very quickly, in only one trial, learned the path to the first room, through it into the playroom, and directly to the doll shelf. Because we were attempting to maintain a program structure and teach a schedule to the children, we decided to limit Cathy to the first room with the rest of the children, and not let her into the playroom at that time. Thus, when Cathy walked into the playroom, we went in and brought her out. The following description is taken from the notes written on that day:

> I took Cathy's hand, led her out of the playroom explaining it was not yet time to go there, and closed the adjoining door. When I let go of her hand she immediately went back into the playroom and to the dolls. I again went in, gently explained we could play with the dolls later, and again led her out, only to have Cathy rush back in as soon as I had let go of her hand. Each time I explained the limits and brought her out, she immediately rushed back in. Throughout all of this Cathy appeared oblivious of me and my attempts at explaining. I spoke directly to her, loudly, but did not stimulate even a minimal response. Cathy did not actively resist being brought out each time, she simply seemed to ignore it. On the seventh repetition, I brought her out as before, but this time continued to hold her hand. Cathy, still held by the hand, turned back toward the playroom and began walking toward it. Because I held her hand and was standing still, Cathy could not proceed any further than the combined lengths of our arms but, when she reached the point where she could no longer make physical progress, Cathy continued to walk. As if on a treadmill, Cathy, remaining in one place, continued pumping her legs, facing the playroom, and soon began to gently slip on the tile floor.
>
> Slowly, gently, still firmly held by the hand, walking all the while without even breaking stride, Cathy began to slide down on the floor onto her right side. There she remained for the next two minutes, like a little fallen wind-up soldier with legs still pumping ineffectually against the air, making no progress. The fact that she was lying down on her side, her hand still firmly held by mine, and total lack of movement toward her goal, seemed to make no impression on her, as if there were simply no vestibular or proprioceptive feedback. Like the wind-up soldier she might have continued walking until she "ran down" or was fatigued and, after two minutes of no change in her behavior, I picked her up, set her on her still pumping feet and, like the mechanical toy, she moved off toward the playroom as soon as her pumping feet made contact with the floor. Throughout this Cathy's total behavior suggested that she was responding only to the playroom as a goal, and she seemed totally impervious to the presence of the therapist, her changed

bodily orientation from vertical to horizontal, and her lack of movement toward the goal.

During her first 100 sessions Cathy's marked aloofness continued. However, as the program became more structured and our stimulation of the children was intensified, Cathy began to make brief contacts with other people. For example, instead of ignoring snack, she began to sit with the other children for as long as five minutes. At times she played briefly with other children, although in a primitive manner. Her speech too began to refer to objects and events in the room whereas, previously it had been limited entirely to commercials. However, despite this increase in the number and duration of her contacts with other people during her first 100 sessions, they were characterized by hyperactivity and aggressive behavior. She was reacting more frequently to other people, which was a positive development, but her response to others became increasingly violent, which was a negative development. Cathy's violent outbursts continued throughout her first 100 sessions, reaching their peak about midway through her second 100 sessions. For example, a child turning on the overhead light would immediately precipitate a violent reaction in her. If another child, particularly Gerry, looked at her, pointed and called out her name, Cathy responded, again, with wild, screaming rage. Any change in routine, any unexpected development, would stimulate similar reactions.

In addition, it was observed toward the end of her first 100 sessions, that many of Cathy's violent outbursts were apparently becoming self-stimulated. This development was extremely interesting, for it suggested a more complex interaction with the environment than Cathy had previously shown. Previously she had tended to ignore almost all of her immediate environment, but gradually began to react violently and directly to specific stimuli. Now it appeared that Cathy was beginning to manipulate the environment and then respond equally violently to the conditions she had created. For example, after she started to develop communicative speech, she would push her dolls into the hands of a therapist and, in great agitation, crying, and bouncing from foot to foot, would scream, "Take the babies, take the babies, take the babies!" If the therapist did not comply, Cathy persisted into a total loss of control. However, if the therapist did take the dolls, Cathy immediately threw herself on the floor screaming, "No, no, no take the babies," again precipitating a violent episode.

Similarly, during snack time Cathy frequently demanded the therapist to say "please," or "hold hands" or some other action. If the therapist complied, Cathy immediately screamed, "No please, no please," or "No hand, no hand," knocked over the snack table with its juice and cookies, threw chairs, and dashed around the room. If the therapist did not comply, Cathy's reaction was the same except she now screamed "Say please! " instead of "No please!"

Such violent reactions, therefore, occurred not only in reaction to frustration, but also when we called attention to or rewarded her. Cathy might be sitting at the snack table being extremely cooperative, and controlled; if, at that point, we presented our stock verbal reinforcement, she might accept it and continue the good behavior, or she might immediately react violently with the same table-upsetting reaction as described above. Her response was largely unpredictable (she kept us on a variable schedule) and we were hard-pressed to specify the conditions under which she would react violently or peacefully. Toward the end of her first 100 sessions it was clear that Cathy's behavior seemed to fall into three general categories:

1. Although she had at first been continuously aloof, she now remained aloof from the others only a little more than half of the time, playing in her private way with her dolls. Her verbalizing to the dolls became more varied and complex, and she could also be drawn more easily from the stereotyped play.
2. Nearly all of her remaining time was spent in tantrums or aggressive battling with others. It appeared that when she did respond to others, it was almost always with violence.
3. Her third general kind of behavior, which accounted for only a very small but slowly increasing portion of time, consisted of minimal cooperative interaction. Such cooperative playing with other children—sometimes just sitting together—was rare and sporadic but was at least beginning to emerge.

During her first 100 sessions Cathy's verbalizing was almost totally limited to the contents of three or four radio and TV commercials ("Penny Bright," "The National Safety Council," and "Fantasy Furniture,"), usually repeated while holding one or more dolls against her nose and spinning and dancing high up on her toes. Her voice was rapid, the words tumbling out without pause, and her whole body was in action. At such times we could not interrupt her easily as she continued the activity regardless of external verbal stimulation. Only direct physical intervention interrupted her stream of commercials, invariably causing violence. There was no doubt that Cathy had attended to and learned those commercials, even to the point of changing pitch, loudness and clarity of voice to imitate appropriately background speech in one of the singing commercials.

In terms of behavioral deficits, Cathy lacked: (1) toilet training, (2) communicative speech, (3) relating to persons, (4) ordinary use of objects, (5) academic learning, (6) normal variety of foods, (7) the ability to dress herself and take care of her own toilet needs, (8) attention to normal age-appropriate stimuli.

Her surplus behavior included: (1) constant toe walking, (2) spinning, (3) stereotyped repetition of commercials, (4) violent, destructive tantrums.

GERRY

History

Gerry's early development was slow and characterized by obvious behavioral deficits. He sat up at 11 months but did not walk until 20 months. At age six and a half, Gerry still had no communicative speech and most of his vocalizing consisted of loud, shrill screeching and screaming.

His parents became increasingly concerned as they observed that in addition to slow motor and verbal development he was also far behind other children in social development. Try as they might, they were not able to bring about approach behavior in this child, and he became more aloof. In general, he showed no awareness of or concern for other people, but remained intensely absorbed in an activity to the exclusion of all else and regardless of whether he interfered with anyone else. At mealtimes, for example, intent upon eating, Gerry would grab food from the other plates; when stopped, he would scream violently and have a severe tantrum. The entire area of social behavior, his general responsiveness and his relationships to other people constituted a large and major area of deficit behavior.

Gerry invariably seemed involved in some destructive preoccupation such as pulling dolls apart, tearing books, or destroying whatever he could grasp. When he was frustrated, this intense absorption in destruction became even more exaggerated and led to full-blown tantrums in public as well as at home. Throwing, smashing, kicking, and vigorous tearing of objects would occur, accompanied by loud, high-pitched screaming and physical attacks on other people. This behavior was obviously effective in keeping people away from him, further limiting Gerry's lack of normal, age-appropriate social experience, thereby deepening and perpetuating his already severe deficits.

Put into nursery school at the age of four and a half, Gerry lasted only two days. A year later, he was enrolled at a different school, completing the academic year in a small class of ten. Gerry was greatly disruptive, aloof, and had such severe tantrums when approached that the teacher tended simply to leave him alone.

The following year, at six and a half and under the guidance of a child clinic, Gerry was enrolled in kindergarten where he remained for nearly two weeks. This schooling ended one day when Gerry screamed, threw toys, attacked children and teacher, and became completely uncontrollable. For the next several days, he remained upset, even having difficulty sleeping at nights. It was at this point that the parents were told not to bring Gerry back to school and were referred to our program.

Gerry's typical days upon beginning in our program were much the same as they had been over the past year. He awoke without difficulty, after a generally restful night which, however, had been interrupted at least once apparently by nightmares, causing him to awaken and scream. In the morning he was docile, although noisy, allowing his mother to dress him without resistance. Although his mother reported that Gerry was able to help dress himself, she did it for him in the morning to save time. Gerry's behavior at breakfast was much the same as at other mealtimes. If the whole family were present, he became more stimulated and difficult to control, and frequently had a tantrum. At times when only his father had breakfast with him, Gerry appeared to maintain better control. His choice of foods varied over time but like everything else with Gerry seemed exaggerated and overplayed.

After breakfast, while other children were being readied for school, Gerry usually wandered around, aloof from other people, and spending this time in solitary, destructive play, often accompanied by loud shrieks. He had to be stopped frequently from activities such as tearing the couch cover, breaking the TV or phonograph, or tearing books, toys or other things. Later, when it was time for him to leave for school, Gerry willingly entered the car but once underway became dangerously unmanageable and almost wild. After school there was another equally disquieting automobile trip home.

At lunch the mealtime behavior described above was repeated and after lunch he continued his usual solitary, aloof, destructive and noisy behavior. When left alone, Gerry was merely destructive and noisy but when frustrated, i.e., if prevented from breaking something, he went into a tantrum, becoming *intensively* noisy and destructive. His tearing apart of objects helped to drive away other children especially when the toys he destroyed were theirs. The common complaint of his older siblings that their younger brother had broken some of their personal objects was heard repeatedly and was a major irritant in the family. Gerry became increasingly upset when prevented from completing his destruction of something belonging to another, and this upset, in turn, seemed to bring about increased destructiveness. The family's efforts at reducing his destructiveness had failed, and each year he seemed increasingly destructive.

Our first impression of six and a half year old Gerry was that of the most tense, tightly wound up and potentially explosive little boy we had ever seen. Everything about his behavior suggested tremendous tension—his rapid, uneven walk, his nearly constant tightly grotesque hand motions and other mannerisms, his rapid, loud repetitive and inappropriate speech, his high-pitched and loud screaming, his repetitive, almost studied destruction of objects such as dolls, and even his tantrums which all characterized an intensity and total body tautness that seemed to fatigue people who were only observing him. Gerry moved through his world rapidly, intensely, noisily and destructively, frequently encountering, attacking, and often destroying obstacles in his way. His world did not include other people, except as tools to be occasionally used or as obstacles to be attacked.

Initial Behavior in the Program

During his first 20 weeks in the program, Gerry, a well-proportioned six and a half year old boy, seemed well-coordinated and had no difficulty moving physically through his environment. He easily avoided obstacles, seldom tripped, and rarely lost his balance or injured himself because of motor discoordination or lack of attention. He ran easily, jumped, grasped objects with either or both hands and his "throwing arm" was magnificent! However, despite his apparent good balance and motor ability he did not play appropriately with toys or use common objects in appropriate ways. For example, he was capable of manipulating the light switches, but would not do so either when asked or on his own initiative when the room was dark. Gerry did frequently play with the light switches, turning lights on and off repeatedly, but without reference to lighting needs or staff requests. In another realm, although Gerry nearly always picked up small, colorful material such as checkers, crayons or clay, he thoroughly mouthed or licked them. This was particularly true of clay, which he mouthed with as much lip-smacking intensity, as another child might an ice cream cone. Later, when his verbalizing had increased, Gerry would frequently scream, "Not poison, not poison!" as he continued to avidly lick the material.

Both paper objects and complex mechanisms such as phonographs, were approached by him in a highly destructive manner. With tenacious persistence Gerry devoted a large part of each session to tearing the heads and limbs from dolls, perservering with the sturdier ones until he succeeded. This dismembering extended to pictures too, which he would tear across, separating the head or limbs from the body. Although most frequent in his use of human and human-like forms, his destructive behavior would encompass any material available, such as furniture covers, clothing, drapes, etc.

Another general approach to objects was quite simple and direct; he threw them. This behavior included any objects of any material and was limited only by size and weight. Trucks, cars, blocks, boxes, books, phonograph records, etc. were thrown around the room. If an object such as a tricycle, table or chair were too large to throw, Gerry, screaming, simply knocked it over onto the floor with a great clatter.

Thus, when he began in our program Gerry's apparently good motor manipulative ability was limited in use to moving him destructively through his world. It was obvious that while he had developed a facility for tearing and teasing things apart, he had failed to acquire the socially appropriate, adaptive use of objects. Here, then, was both an area of severe social-behavior deficit as well as an area of surplus inappropriate behavior.

In general, Gerry's activity level was high and he was constantly in motion. Physically tense and rigid, Gerry displayed his many grotesque mannerisms and posturing, particularly when he was agitated. All of his behavior was intense, and even his vocalizing was high pitched, loud, and nearly constant, consisting of inarticulate screams and repeated, loud shrieking, simple phrases, such as "Gerry arm broken!" The only time Gerry was quiet was when he was absorbed in tearing apart dolls, following which he frequently began screaming.

Generally aloof, Gerry moved through his first four weeks in the program paying little attention to anyone. When intruded upon, such as when prevented from throwing some particularly dangerous object, Gerry characteristically attacked the arm of the restraining therapist by hitting, biting and pinching it. This behavior occurred during his first session and continued, becoming even more frequent and intense.

Also during those first four weeks, he frequently engaged in severe head-banging, which usually followed even mild frustration. He either banged his head against the wall or his forehead down on a table. Later, his head-banging was always followed by a statement such as "Gerry head broken." Verbalizing was limited to a small range of words and under only a few conditions. The first words uttered by Gerry during his very first session were "Oh, Goddammit," which he repeated loudly, shrilly and rapidly but without any apparent appropriate reference to the activities occurring around him. He verbalized little, seldom appropriately and, during his first three months most of his verbal behavior was focused on his destruction of dolls. After tearing a doll apart, for example, Gerry would look at his own hand hanging limply at the wrist, and rapidly shriek "Gerry arm broken, Gerry arm broken!"

During his first month he did not speak directly to anyone. Unlike Cathy, Gerry was not observed speaking to objects. Gerry's most frequently-used phrases were "Arm (head, eye, hand, wrist, etc.) broken," "No, no, no!," "Help!," "Oh, Goddammit!" and "Fire!" Obviously, verbalizing was another area of major behavior deficit.

Gerry could not be drawn into any of the activities such as verbalizing, playing, painting or drawing, which required his specific attention for more than a few seconds. The only activities which held him for a few minutes were: destroying dolls, eating snack, running in the gym. The first two would keep him occupied for three or four minutes at a time, while the latter was good for as long as ten minutes. Thus his attention span for controlled, skill activities was extremely short. He literally would not stay still long enough to be worked with.

In summary then during his first nearly three months Gerry remained a loud, shrill, tense and apparently fearful little boy moving rapidly through his environment, aloof from other people except when he attacked them for interfering. He spent his time in the program constantly circling the edge of the room, screeching, throwing and knocking things over, pausing long enough to tear the head and limbs from some hapless doll or tear apart a book or some other breakable object. He exhibited constantly tense and grotesque mannerisms, still posturing, frequent and severe head-banging, and limited, inappropriate verbalizing.

Gerry's aloofness continued as he devoted most of his time to his destructiveness, rapidly aimless activity and noise. After about the first five weeks, however, he seemed to begin responding to some of the careful strategies applied by the staff. For example, under carefully-prepared conditions, he played with Frankie for some five minutes, rolling a ball or pushing a toy truck. Likewise, equally careful planning and effort seemed successful in teaching Gerry to put dolls back together and to construct rather than destroy creations in clay, blocks and interlocking plastic forms. With structuring and step-by-step reinforcement of the constructive and cooperative behavior by his 100th session (approximately five months) Gerry was able to devote as long as a half hour to looking quietly at pictures in books and some fifteen minutes, under immediate staff supervision, to constructing in clay or blocks. By the 100th session his severe head–banging had disappeared and his direct verbal contacts had increased. For example, while he had previously ignored everyone except to attack, he was now calling every therapist, male or female, "mommy" and was correctly using the names of the children, often calling to them to play.

As the program became more structured and our stimulation of the children was intensified, Gerry made more frequent brief contacts with other people. However, like Cathy, Gerry's response to other people became increasingly aggressive as it became more frequent. Thus, he was in more frequent and severe aggressive conflict with the therapists as well as the other children. Since the same process was occurring concurrently but more slowly in Cathy, these two children came into frequent conflict, resulting in wild, destructive and abusive battles. By Gerry's 100th session he had developed a consistent behavior of screaming Cathy's name at her, which never failed to elicit her full rage which might last for hours. By Gerry's 125th session (Cathy's 150th), the two children were almost continually involved in raging battle, a state of affairs which continued for many months, and about which more will be said later.

Thus, by Gerry's 100th session it was clear that his major behavioral deficits could be summarized as: (1) general deficit in appropriate social responses across the entire spectrum of social behavior, (2) poorly developed and generally non-communicative speech, (3) lack of appropriate playing with toys and manipulation of common objects, (4) lack of attention span for more than a few moments. His surplus maladaptive behavior consisted of: (1) marked hyperactivity, (2) generalized aggressive and destructive behavior, (3) loud, high-pitched and nearly constant screeching and screaming, (4) severely aggressive tantrum behavior when provoked, for example, by frustration.

CHAPTER 6

Shaping Complex Social Behavior

THE FIRST YEAR: DIFFERENTIAL REINFORCEMENT

The first part of the program was directed at increasing the rate and variety of behavior and developing effective reinforcers. Over the next 100 sessions, as the focal group continued to be stimulated and reinforced for more active and social behavior, the children began to move around more, to pick up and use objects, to make more noise, and to come into increased contact with each other and the therapists. Their original severe deficits, particularly the constant aloofness, were reduced. In fact, the children were now responding at such a high rate that they were characterized more by surplus than deficit behavior. The staff's attempts to increase response rate may have been carried out too zealously perhaps with the result that all behavior, even that not particularly adaptive, had been reinforced. Further, whereas previously the behavior of one child seldom affected another, now that the children were operating at higher behavioral rates there existed greater probability for contact between them and greater conflict.

Clearly, response rates had increased as planned. However, reinforcement may have been provided too lavishly without proper response differentiation so that the apparently pre-potent maladaptive surplus behavior was also reinforced and consequently increased in frequency. Cathy and Gerry, as noted, became almost constantly violently reactive to each other.

The sessions became livelier with all four children active in both adaptive and maladaptive ways. Faced with the vastly increased and more complex and conflicting array of behavior, the therapists now had to perform in a more selective fashion, differentially reinforcing only the more adaptive behavior. Whereas previously they had to be reactive to all behavior so as to move in quickly and reinforce it, the staff now faced the constant task of rapidly assessing behavior and sorting out what was to be reinforced and what was to be ignored. Thus, the already active role of the staff increased, demanding not only immediate reactions but also adding the process of selectivity in order to maintain differential reinforcement. When a child behaved, the implicit question for the staff was, "Does that behavior fit into the learning sequence? Is it adaptive or not? Should it be strengthened or weakened?"

The demands made upon the staff were great. Within a total non-hurried, calm, controlled approach, each therapist had to remain constantly alert and reactive, continuously and rapidly assess behavior and immediately act on their assessments. They had to be aware not only of themselves and the children, but of all the complexities of possible interactions among and between variables such as children, staff, objects and even time. In this approach, then, the therapist must make rapid-fire decisions concerning his handling of every situation, and every decision must be rational and fully justifiable. There must be good reason for everything the therapist does because he is accountable for all of his reactions.

The major goal now was to strengthen adaptive behavior and weaken maladaptive behavior through careful differential application of the reinforcers developed earlier. This differential reinforcement was aimed not only at the group as a whole, but was individually geared to insure that the responses reinforced were appropriate to the planned learning sequences for each child. For example, with Frankie, the child with the most severe deficits, any approach or assertive behavior was reinforced, including vocal sounds, physical manipulation and even aggressively assertive behavior. For Gerry, loud screeching and aggressive behavior were already existing surpluses and, therefore, not reinforced. Because the therapists' role was so complex, directive and highly active, we began here to more pointedly appreciate some of the limitations imposed by use of a group setting.

There were several other problems in the effective application of differential reinforcement. One of the most basic was that the only available effective reinforcers required that the therapist be immediately near the child in order to reinforce him. Many good opportunities to reinforce adaptive behavior were lost because the therapist happened to be across the room at the time. We thus had to develop reinforcers that did not require immediate physical proximity, but were useful at a distance. Obviously we had to bring the children under verbal control. Our attempts to do so will be discussed later in this chapter.

A second problem involved the increasing interference of the conflict behavior. For example, because Cathy and Gerry's frequent lengthy outbursts thoroughly disrupted the sessions, the opportunities for developing alternative adaptive responses were severely curtailed. Thus, aggressive surplus behavior had to be diminished before significant acquisition of alternative adaptive behavior could occur.

The next problem in administering effective differential reinforcement (which began at this time but did not reach its peak until the following year) involved uncontrolled sources of unintentional reinforcement, including:

1. *Other children:* When Cathy, for example, behaved in some grossly disruptive manner, Frankie went into lengthy gales of giggling which reinforced Cathy's behavior. Gerry's aggressively provoking behavior was apparently reinforced by Cathy's violent reactions. Freddie's screeching was reinforced by the other children's immediate withdrawal from him, and poor Frankie's few halting attempts at assertive behavior were immediately punished by all three children, while his aloofness was reinforced by their leaving him alone. Despite the best intentions and plans of the staff, the children themselves provided much unwanted reinforcement. Teaching the children to ignore the disruptive behavior of others was a task gradually achieved. In fact, it later became a stock response for Gerry to warn an intruding child that "If you don't stop it I will 'nore you," which he then carried out quite well.

2. *Social imitation and vicarious reinforcement:* Planned into the program as aids in teaching adaptive behavior, social imitation and vicarious reinforcement seemed to also unintentionally contribute to reinforcing undesirable behavior. Freddie began to imitate some of Cathy's disruptive behavior, while Cathy picked up Frankie's uncontrolled giggling. In addition, it appeared that reinforcement of subdued, quiet behavior for Gerry and Cathy was also inappropriately vicariously reinforcing for Frankie, who should have been learning more overt assertion. Gerry, in turn, already too reactive, seemed to become even more stimulated and uncontrolled when Frankie or Freddie were being urged into more activity.

3. *The automatically reinforcing framework of the overall situation:* Many cues in the group room acquired reinforcing value, so much so that simply coming into the room eventually seemed to be reinforcing. One result which became increasingly true as the program continued was that the use of *simple extinction*, the non-reinforcement of undesirable behavior, could not be relied upon. Thus, if a child engaged in some undesirable behavior, even if the staff and other children ignored him and withheld reinforcement, the child could find reinforcement from many less intrusive, subtle sources not readily controlled. Immediately following an upset assiduously ignored by all, Cathy, for example, might nevertheless be reinforced by simply coming across her favorite doll lying on the floor where she had thrown it. It

appeared that so much effort had been and continued to be devoted to the development of reinforcers that even undesirable responses were being reinforced through an automatic, reinforcing framework, a concept like Skinner's "web of reinforcement."

In summary, the children had developed high response rates, as had been sought in the first part of the program, and the staff now turned to the task of differential reinforcement, of actively selecting out those behaviors to be reinforced and those to be weakened through non-reinforcement. From here on, only *adaptive* behavior was to be reinforced, and increasingly social behavior would gradually be shaped. Several difficulties, however, soon became apparent: (1) the demand on staff for attention, constant evaluation, decision-making and immediate rational reactions became increasingly high and complex; (2) many opportunities for reinforcement of acceptable behavior were lost because the reinforcers thus far developed required immediate physical contiguity of the therapist and child; (3) increasingly aggressive and conflict behavior interfered with the development of adaptive alternative behavior; (4) in spite of the staff's attempts to structure carefully, there were at least three important sources of uncontrolled reinforcement which served to maintain maladaptive behavior: (a) the children's behavior toward each other, (b) the operation of social imitation and vicarious reinforcement and, (c) the "automatic reinforcing framework."

Thus, it became apparent that selective or differential reinforcement aimed at shaping social behavior of severely autistic/psychotic children is a task mired in complex contingencies. The therapists were aware of some of those contingencies, such as sources of uncontrolled reinforcement, and some attempts were made to control them. Even with this awareness and attempted control, much and perhaps even most escaped us. One wonders about therapists, unaware of such contingencies, ascribing to psychodynamics behaviors that might in fact be stimulated and reinforced unintentionally. Some of the more obvious are the therapists who see children in offices so visually stimulating with books, typewriters, hanging pictures and so on, that a child's specific behavior might be as much stimulated by his fleeting glance at a colorful painting as by the incisive remarks of his therapist. Even more obvious is the therapist who keeps an open box of candy or cookies easily accessible to the child. The child is then free to reinforce any behavior, adaptive or not, that might have preceded his self-reinforcement.

The second major phase of the program, differential reinforcement, was under way in the second year, with all of its demands, complexities and unexpected contingencies.

SNACK TIME AND THE
DEVELOPMENT OF VERBAL REINFORCERS

As noted in the previous section, it had become necessary to develop effective reinforcers which could be used *at a distance*, without requiring immediate physical (i.e., tactual) contact. Obviously, what was required was the development of *verbal* reinforcers. It should be apparent, however, from earlier descriptions that verbal behavior constituted a major deficit, verbal stimuli were obviously not of reinforcing value, and we can infer that verbal mediators were not employed by the children. Thus far in the program, the children had become increasingly familiar with verbal stimulation and some positive value had presumably already been attached to verbal stimuli simply through repeated association with earlier reinforcers such as toys, pictures and food. However, there had been no systematic attempt to teach or directly develop the reinforcing value of verbal stimuli. Thus, at this point a third goal was focused on: *the active development of verbal reinforcers*. If verbal reinforcers could be developed, then a powerful reinforcing tool would be available to the therapists that presumably would accelerate the group's social learning.

Moreover, because they are of obvious generalized importance in our highly verbal life, verbal reinforcers may be the most important for children. For autistic children, as noted, a verbal reward such as a kind word or a bit of praise had no effect. Somehow these non-verbal, aloof children, functioning outside the normal, human verbal framework, had to be started along a sequence which would enable them eventually to respond to and even give verbal reinforcement. Verbalizing had to become an important part of their lives—not only their own verbalizing, but also that of other people.

In addition to verbalization, the children needed to learn other skills such as playing games, and basic social conduct like simple cooperation or remaining near someone without conflict. Although the children at this point, were no longer completely aloof, they were still lacking most of the acceptable social behaviors expected of children of their ages and a great deal of learning along many varied behavior dimensions had to be accomplished. Just as earlier successful attempts had been made to teach children to sit down and to look at pictures or use puzzles, even if only for a few moments, the children now had to be taught a variety of different behaviors that were at a higher level of social development.

The staff now had many directions of focus and their task became increasingly complex. It was necessary simultaneously to still stimulate higher response rates for some of the children, seek and develop useful reinforcers, and watch and reinforce all positive social behavior. In addition, physical training was necessary to overcome motor coordination deficits and speech had to be shaped. Thus, the staff had to focus in many different directions, and had to create many situations in which desired behaviors would occur so that they could be reinforced. In planning this phase of the program toward the end of the first year it was important to create a relatively simple social situation that could be the basis for social and academic behavior later—i.e., simply sitting together at a table. Table behavior is obviously common to mealtimes, school and work. These children, however, had little training in it; Cathy simply refused to sit near anyone else and others remained seated only for brief moments while engaged in activities like puzzles. They had not learned how to remain together for any appreciable period of time as a small social group interacting and cooperating with each other. In order to develop table behavior a snack table was set up, and snack time became a regular part of the daily schedule and an important learning situation. The snack table always remained in the same place and at first was used only for snacks. Snack time occurred at a fixed, predictable time and place, and we attempted to make it clearly differentiated from the rest of the activities. Thus, table behavior had to come under the control of clearly defined discriminative stimuli. During the three-hour daily program, the snack which was brought by the children supplemented by our supply of cookies and juice, was available *only* during snack time and only at the snack table. Children (and staff) were not allowed food under any other circumstances. If a child did not have snack during snack time, he was not allowed to have it later.

The first time snack was announced the children characteristically ignored it though the two therapists seated themselves at the table, obviously "enjoying" eating. On the second day, Frankie, the most docile child, was led to the table and put in his chair where he remained but without eating. Within a few minutes Freddie, responding to his name, turned and looked at the snack table, and began approaching slowly. When within arm's reach the therapist put a small bit of cookie in Freddie's mouth and, from that point on, Freddie remained near or kept returning to the table during snack time. Several sessions more were required before Freddie sat for more than two minutes. By the time Cathy and Gerry joined the group, Freddie and Frankie were well accustomed to the snack period and were able to remain at the table reinforced by food for as long as 10 minutes. Gerry learned quickly to approach the table and sit but became so excited that he seldom remained for more than two or three minutes. Cathy was most resistive. At first she ignored snack time, then began literally bouncing past the table. With immediate food reinforcement she successively approached, touched and sat in a chair. Like Gerry, however, she did not remain long at the table.

No more than two weeks (10 sessions) were required to shape up approach and sitting behavior. Once that was developed, all but Frankie began to approach the table, attempt to grab cookies and then run off to the other end of the room. When this occurred, the food was quickly taken away from them. The children were allowed to eat all they wanted as long as they remained near the table.

Getting the four children to sit together was only a first step in approximating more social behavior. They tended to snatch food, rapidly devour it, and quickly leave the table. They rocked, displayed bizarre mannerisms, screeched, screamed, spilled juice, spat and regurgitated food. As the therapists began structuring more limits, that is withholding the food until acceptable behavior occurred, the children became more frequently frustrated, and severe tantrum behavior increased.

By making cookies and juice contingent upon acceptable behavior, the therapists controlled the situation and, over a period of one year, gradually lengthened the time the children remained at the table from zero, to more than 20 minutes. It easily could have been increased more but because of the schedule a limit of approximately 20 minutes was set and maintained.

Food in the form of bits of cookies and sips of juice was used by the therapists as the primary reinforcer, but always contingent upon the behavior of the child. Working with four children at a time and relying upon the reinforcing value of the sweets, the therapists gradually lengthened snack time and also improved significantly the children's social behavior. The children learned to remain together for longer periods without conflict, to eat with some decorum, to trade and share snacks, and to use and respond to speech. Thus, not only simple cooperative social behavior but verbal behavior too was gradually shaped during snack time. It was relatively easy to shape up words, such as "more," "please" and, later, phrases such as "May I have a cookie?" As snack time continued, the first halting conversations occurred. In addition to those more obvious behaviors, the therapists also worked to build even more basic responses, such as attention, eye contact and reduction of bizarre behavior.

Although still periodically disrupted by upsets, snack time developed into a pleasant and relatively relaxed island in an otherwise often hectic morning, providing a significant period of sustained, controlled and cooperative social behavior. Eventually, from that base of well established social behavior, attempts were made to generalize the social behavior to other aspects of the program. Thus, gradually as always, the children were required to wash their hands before snack, to perform small chores like getting out the cups, setting the table and, eventually, to help in cleaning up—thereby extending the cooperative social behavior shaped up in snack time to activities both before and after it.

Teaching the children to wash their hands, set the table and in other ways prepare for snack time was relatively easy to accomplish, since these behaviors were part of a sequence leading to eventual food reinforcement. Teaching them to clean up after snack was considerably more difficult, but, with persistence and the eventual development of verbal reinforcers, this too was accomplished. The total time devoted to preparation, eating and clean-up began to approach a half hour of sustained, controlled, cooperative behavior. As the program continued and the children developed the more basic social behaviors of sitting together and cooperating without conflict, snack time was gradually shifted into a more sophisticated verbal session where the children eventually did a good deal of talking. Most significant in this respect was the gradual emergence in the second year of the focal group of real, though simple, conversations, which entailed attentive listening as well as talking, and some sustained conversational focus. By the end of the first year of the focal group, snack time was firmly established, behavior was controlled and cooperative during snack time, and already beginning to generalize to contiguous parts of the program. Snack time was also well on its way to focusing the verbal conversations that developed in the second year.

SHIFTING FROM PRIMARY TO SECONDARY REINFORCEMENT

Thus, from the development of snack time an aura of relatively calm and controlled behavior began to extend to activities occurring both immediately before and after snack. As will be described in a later section, this generalization of table behavior became the basis for further programs such as the development of academic "school." It was reasoned that if the food presented at snack time did serve as a primary reinforcer, then any stimuli presented regularly immediately prior to the food would soon begin to acquire secondary reinforcing value. Verbal reinforcers were completely lacking for these children and it seemed consistent to expect that the regular presentation of verbal praise, followed immediately by food and contingent upon acceptable behavior of the children would have two results: a direct strengthening of the social behavior by the primary reward, food, and the acquisition of secondary reinforcing value by the verbal praise.

From the initiation of snack time, the presentation of a food reward for some specified behavior was always immediately preceded by one of two phrases, "good job" or "good work," both of which had earlier been impressed upon us by one of our teachers, Dr. Abraham Blum in his own work with children. When Gerry, for example, approached the snack table he was told, "Good job, Gerry," and immediately given a bit of cookie or sip of juice. Presumably the food reinforcement not only strengthened the social behaviors such as sitting at the table but *it also imparted secondary reinforcing value to the therapist's immediately preceding verbal phrases*. In this way too as the therapists gradually engaged in more conversation, the entire complex social situation was strengthened by the primary reinforcement of food, and the varied cues of snack time presumably developed secondary reinforcing value. In this manner, we attempted to attach secondary reinforcing value to the table and chairs, the group situation and to verbal stimuli, particularly the phrases "good work" and "good job."

If these varied social stimuli did in fact acquire secondary reinforcing value then they should be successful in strengthening new behavior without the primary reinforcer of food. The children, we predicted, would soon sit together at the table, not for food reward, but because sitting together had become a learned behavior under stimulus control and would be sustained by the secondary reinforcement of the varied physical and verbal cues. Likewise, the phrases "good work" and "good job," having acquired secondary reinforcing value, would also be effective reinforcers. Thus, the group's reinforcement level, as it were, was shifted from the level of primary reinforcers (food) to the level of secondary reinforcers (verbal praise, and social cooperation). This shift was seen as a significant development toward moving the children to a more social level of behavior. This direct development of secondary reinforcers also was designed to create a sustaining reinforcing framework. That is, the table-and-chair situation, even without food, would be an automatic, always-present secondary reinforcer, and would provide important discriminative stimuli for appropriate social behavior. Furthermore, the table-and-chair setting and the social group atmosphere could serve as a basic and highly reinforcing social situation. Thus, after snack was over and the table cleaned, the children were asked to remain at it to play with games, puzzles, clay, painting, etc., such activities presumably being reinforced not only by the value of the toys and art supplies, but by the secondary reinforcement of the table-and-chair situational cues. Controlled, cooperative, appropriate behavior was coming under stimulus control of the table-and-chair situation.

In addition, once the secondary reinforcing value of verbal praise was established, a child could be reinforced verbally immediately, even though the therapist might be across the room. Previously, when a child made a desirable social response, the therapist could reinforce it *only if he happened to be immediately near the child*. Now, however, with verbal reinforcers, the therapist had a new reinforcing tool which greatly enlarged his ability to strengthen social behaviors—he could now *reinforce at a distance*.

With this extremely important development of secondary reinforcers the entire group shifted to a more verbal and social level of operation. There was less need for direct physical manipulation of the children, and the use of mildly noxious stimulation was also decreased as the new secondary reinforcers were increasingly applied. The therapists now possessed a wider array of useful reinforcers as well as more freedom in applying them to more varied situations. The children began not only to respond to the verbal reinforcers, but to actually use them. When praised, they often repeated the praise in a rote fashion. Gradually, however, they began to apply spontaneously the verbal praise to other children, and at times even to the staff. This application not only indicated a growth in language usage, but suggested awareness and social responsiveness. Occasionally, however, their use of verbal praise was not helpful. For example, when Cathy began a tantrum, Gerry sometimes contributed a cheery, "Good job, Cathy!", which of course sent Cathy into an even deeper tantrum.

THE SECOND YEAR: SCHOOL TIME, AND GENERALIZING SOCIAL RESPONSES

By the end of the first year of the focal group, there had been several important developments. First, the higher response rate and the identification and development of simple reinforcers had been accomplished. Secondly, there had been put into effect the differential reinforcement of social behavior. Thirdly, the "table-and-chair" setting had reached a 20-minute duration and could now be used as the basis for further social learning. Approximately 12 months after the focal group began, the children's new ability to remain seated together in social situations was used as the basis for "school time" which was gradually developed over the next two years.

At the same time that all these developments were occurring, the children were becoming increasingly alert, responsive, active, and, as noted earlier, increasingly inclined to aggressive conflict. The conflict behavior grew, reaching a peak about the middle of the second year. The surplus aggressive behavior was obviously interfering with the continued development of adaptive behavioral alternatives. Accordingly, it was decided to focus specifically on the reduction of this interfering surplus which included such actions as assaults on children and staff, destruction of objects, self-injury and a wide range of tantrums.

The staff began to plan appropriate strategies. It became apparent that the aggressive reactions varied among the children, and strategies effective with one child would not necessarily work with another. Thus, throughout approximately the focal group's second year, the focus was on: (1) continuing to strengthen adaptive social behavior, (2) the development of academic school, and (3) a specific effort to reduce maladaptive aggressive surplus behavior. The staff experimented with a variety of strategies and eventually did succeed in bringing this behavior under control.

In summary, the focal group's first six months was focused primarily on increasing general response rates, and identifying simple reinforcers. The next half year began to stress the direct reinforcement of simple social responses, capitalizing on the increased response rate and using the reinforcers previously identified and developed. One of the major social settings initiated during this first year was snack time in which much of the social learning was achieved. In addition to the direct reinforcement of social behavior during snack time and the use of primary food reward, this setting provided the basis for the development of secondary reinforcers and, in particular, verbal reinforcers. By the end of the first year i.e., September 1963-June 1964, the children were behaving at a far higher rate than they had started, were behaving in more socially appropriate ways, and had learned to maintain themsleves for approximately 20 minutes during snack time.

As that first year continued, the reliance upon the removal of noxious stimulation as a reinforcer was decreased while food as a primary reinforcer and various secondary reinforcers became more important. Thus, that first year was one in which basic goals were sought, simple social behaviors begun and reinforcement tools developed, all of which would be used later in developing higher levels of adaptive behavior.

The second year—September 1964-June 1965—saw an intensified effort at shaping social and verbal behavior through both primary and secondary reinforcement and a utilization of the basic behaviors and reinforcers previously developed. Thus, in this second year, snack time became the basis for developing school time; the secondary reinforcers developed during snack time were used to strengthen behaviors during school. The range of learning social behaviors increased and attempts were made to generalize the newly-learned social behaviors to wider aspects of the world, i.e., taking walks into town, going into stores, visiting parks and playgrounds. Also in this second year the staff and children came to grips with the children's fantastically high degree of aggressive behavior.

By the end of the second year the children had reached a far higher and more stable level of social behavior, and their aggressive behavior was under far better control. We now will turn to a more detailed discussion of that second year, focusing on the development of school time, the control of aggressive behavior, and attempts to generalize the newly acquired behavior.

DEVELOPMENT OF ACADEMIC BEHAVIOR

Our general goal was to bring the children up to as normal a behavioral level as possible, including an academic one. In our culture school is one of the most common and important social experiences for children, who often begin nursery school at three or four years of age and may continue through grammar and high school, college and the university for 20 or 25 years. Even the child who stops after high school has devoted some 13 years to formal education, and the high school drop-out, the "failure," has had as much as nine or ten years of school experience! The social, physical and academic experiences encountered in school form a major portion of the socialization of normal children who devote 13 or more years in preparation for their adult worlds. Although the total impact of the institution "school" on the shaping of permanent behavior in children is at present incalculable, it is reasonable to assume that its effect is of major importance in shaping whatever our society labels as normal or desirable behavior. Without academic experience, a child in our culture would hardly be normal. He would not only exhibit gross academic deficits, but would also be socially deficient. His verbal behavior, social cooperation, general awareness of the world around him and, perhaps even motor skills, would presumably be deficient. Thus, deprivation of the school experience or some comparable tutorial system would practically insure his development into an academically and socially deficient person, and perhaps still aggressively infantile in many ways. In short, deprivation of school would produce a noticeably abnormal or, perhaps, subnormal adult, who might even be incapable of supporting and caring for himself.

What of the severely disturbed child? Probably most and perhaps nearly all autistic and severely psychotic children are *deliberately* and *systematically* excluded from this important social and academic experience. The schools as they now exist cannot tolerate such children, though the rationale they give is that the child cannot tolerate school! Maintaining the myths that schools teach primarily the three R's and not social behavior, and that psychotic children are "too ill" to learn the three R's, the conclusion is inevitably drawn: School is no place for psychotic children. Rather, they belong in the clinic and the hospital with their psychotherapeutic treatment. The practical and rather inhumane result is that the school abdicates responsibility and the hospital assumes it. Thus, while the school deliberately withdraws one of the most relevant learning frameworks for these children, the hospital imposes one of the least relevant.

Our society therefore imposes a double assault on the psychotic child: (1) we deny him his opportunity to experience school by making no provision for him, thereby insuring severe behavioral deficits as he grows older, (2) labelling him "ill," we deliver him to the clinic or hospital, where his deficits are probably reinforced. Certainly traditional psychotherapy is no substitute for school.

Denied the crucial experience of school and either ignored or carefully coached in the irrelevancies of psychodynamics, the psychotic child is forced by the deliberately imposed contingencies of society to maintain his psychotic behavior. Then, after two, three or four years of irrelevant and deficit-reinforcing "treatment," the child is considered incurable and delivered up to the state hospital where the final assurances of maintaining psychotic behavior are systematically imposed. The inevitable result is complete justification of a self-fulfilling prophecy as the child psychotic does, in fact, become the adult psychotic.

Thus, the psychotic child has to overcome not only his deficit and surplus behavior, but the mistreatment and barriers of an ignorantly bureaucratic society. The task is difficult and seldom accomplished. Society's mistreatment and the barriers it erects are major factors in maintaining the children's maladaptive behavior. If that behavior is to be changed, those social contingencies must also be changed.

If our focal group of autistic children were to move eventually into the "normal" world, they would have to learn at least some basic academic material. Thus, we initiated school time which had two major goals: (1) to develop academic behavior in autistic children, and (2) to demonstrate, particularly to the local school systems, that even the most severely disturbed children are amenable to academic approaches.

The focal group had been functioning for just under a year when our academic program began. For students, we had our original four children who were obviously "too ill" to profit from teaching in academics. They were aloof, unresponsive, showed many severe deficit and surplus behaviors. None had communicative speech, two had no speech at all. None could read, write or demonstrate any other academic skill. They exhibited no interaction, communication, cooperation or even simple and basic social skills such as sitting near each other.

Unlike normal school sessions of approximately six or more hours daily, these children had only two and a half hours of a daily program. Thus, in its first year the focal group received less than half of the scheduled time of the normal school child, (the equivalent of approximately four months). By the beginning of the second year, however, we believed that sufficient social learning had occurred to enable the children to have increased academic programming.

The development of school time was based on the previous development of snack time. Through the use of primary food reinforcement at snack time the children had learned to remain seated together at the table and to remain generally cooperative. They had begun to learn the value of verbal reinforcers, beginning with Dr. Blum's two standard phrases, "good job" and "good work," and gradually increasing to a greater number and variety of verbal reinforcers in the form of praise. By the end of the first year the children's ability to remain seated together at snack time was slowly generalized and extended into other activities. This was accomplished simply by having the children clean up after snack time and, instead of moving them off immediately into a free-play situation in another section of the room, encouraging them to remain at the table and play with puzzles, games, clay, crayons and other quiet pre-academic activities. The newly-developed verbal reinforcers were used to reward and maintain this behavior and, gradually, the pre-academic period grew to some 10 or 15 minutes in time. For example, Frankie, the most compliant child, easily remained, looking at pictures and interacting with the therapists by pointing and grunting. Gerry, too, stayed at the pre-academic table, using clay. Although he generally mouthed and chewed it, he eventually learned to mold simple shapes representing such things as animals and cooking utentils.

Freddie also learned easily to work on puzzles and to look at pictures at this pre-academic session. When specific attention was paid to them, each of these three children interacted with the therapists. Cathy did not remain long at the table after snack, but pranced off alone to play with her dolls. She did, however, manage to remain for very brief periods of two or three minutes, as long as she was being engaged by a therapist.

The children began to learn to remain together at the table and to participate in various pre-school or school readiness activities. The assumption was that their behavior was sustained by the acquired secondary reinforcing value of the table-and-chair setting and did not require primary food reinforcement. Thus, the learned snack-time behavior which had been reinforced with food now generalized to the pre-academic setting and was presumably also sustained by the growing framework of automatic, built-in reinforcers.

In the last week of October, soon after the focal group's second year began, the academic setting was formally initiated. This new aspect of the program had to be introduced slowly and orderly and in such a way as to minimize its newness. The children, we had come to learn, characteristically rejected anything new, especially sudden changes.

The initiation of the academic setting was accomplished first by preparing the children by telling them a few days ahead that school time would begin and secondly by utilizing only highly familiar settings, objects and activities. On Wednesday and Thursday, the children were informed that school time would begin on the next Monday, and they were shown the corner in which it would be set up. On Friday, they were again told and were invited to help move the two small tables and benches into the school corner. Cathy did help for a few moments, but none of the others participated. Before leaving on Friday, the children were again reminded of school time on Monday, shown where it would be, and again that it would occur immediately following snack. The announcements had been made quietly, carefully, and always when the children appeared well relaxed and not on the verge of upset. There were no negative reactions to those announcements.

On Monday, after snack was over, school time was simply announced,and the children were asked to "come and sit in school." An attempt had been made to maximize the generalization from the familiar pre-academic sessions to this new school time. The tables and chairs were the same type as those used at snack; the matching games, books, crayons and paper were all familiar; the children had all previously made chalkmarks on the small blackboard; their familiar Group Worker was teacher; and the entire setting was in a familiar corner of their room. Thus, the various elements of school time were familiar to the children; their combination in a given time and place labelled "school time" was new. However, if our previous judgments about what the children had learned and grown to accept were correct, there should have been positive transfer to the new situation, and children should not have had much difficulty in accepting the new setting.

On that first day of "school," Cathy refused to join and Gerry and Freddie left after only two minutes. Frankie, of course, would remain for a very long time wherever he was put. However, it had been decided to end the school session when any two of the four children left the situation.

During the first two weeks, the major problems were in defining the limits surrounding school. That is, the school setting, (tables, chairs, blackboard, etc.) was to be used only during school time and only for school activities. Further, during school time toys were not allowed into school, and the phonograph or other distractors could not be used in the other parts of the room. If a child did not wish to attend school he could leave the situation, but he could not distract the others during school. Obviously, with these children this structure could not simply be posted as a set of rules, but had to be physically and verbally reinforced. Cathy, for example, demanded to have the phonograph playing all through the school session, to bring her dolls, and to lie across the top of the children's desks or under the benches. These behaviors had to be corrected repeatedly and much reinforcement given for the more appropriate responses.

The children were given simple tasks, all well within their ability. They were asked to repeat words, phrases, letters, and numbers, point out letters on the chalkboard, listen to stories, and answer very simple questions. Immediate verbal reinforcement was given for their appropriate responses and particularly for their attentive behavior. Gradually the little class began to shape up. Within two months they had achieved a duration that ranged in one week, from three to 20 minutes.

Following is a description of a school session during the fifth week (Nov. 1964). This session lasted 12 minutes, with Cathy having left after only seven minutes. It should be pointed out that aggressive and wild tantrum behavior had been steadily increasing since the beginning of the program, and school time was initiated during a period of intense, prolonged and nearly constant aggressive behavior.

The children were called to school after clearing up the snack area. Cathy, Gerry and Frankie moved to their seats, but Freddie screeching, ran to his toy airplane. The Group Worker began school with a roll call, having each child go to the blackboard, point to his name and say it aloud, for which verbal reinforcement, which had been built up earlier, was immediately given. Freddie joined the group at this point bringing his airplane and had a mild upset when it was gently taken from him. While the Group Worker briefly soothed Freddie, Cathy ran off, got her dolls, and brought them to school. She made no protest when they were set aside on their accustomed shelf. All the children were able to go to the chalkboard easily, point to and say their names, but Cathy refused to go back to her seat. She was ignored. After lying on top of her table for a moment, she returned to her seat. The Group Worker gained their attention with a story book, holding it up so the colored pictures were clearly in view. After reading the story she pointed to each picture and asked the group simple questions ("Who is this?" "What is she doing?" etc.). The children raised their hands, were called upon and praised verbally when they answered. In response to the question, "Is this the red ball?" Freddie inexplicably answered "Nineteen."

Gerry had remained excited but relatively quiet. He rapidly shook and waved his hands, rocked back and forth, and did not respond when his name was called.

After seven minutes, Cathy ran over to the phonograph, but was prevented from turning it on by the other Group Worker. Frustrated, Cathy threw a doll but was quickly quieted.

The class continued as the teacher lead the three remaining children in simple vocal exercises such as "My name is _____ ." The class ended as each child in turn went to the blackboard and carried out verbal instructions to draw large circles, wavy lines, etc. When they were back in their seats, sitting quietly and attentively, the class was dismissed.

In subsequent weeks, the Group Worker-teacher, continued to reinforce longer periods of appropriate and attentive behavior, including responding verbally to stimuli, carrying out simple instructions, using crayons and pencils, drawing figures on the chalkboard, using books, looking at pictures, and singing songs.

Consistent with our use of structure a regular sequence was established. School was opened with the roll call requiring active response. A weather report followed during which the children observed through the window and reported the prevailing weather conditions. (This was the basis for a later more involved daily "orientation" exercise in which the children were taught to observe the conditions around them and properly orient themselves; i.e., each day they reported the year, month and day, identified children present and absent, carefully noted the weather conditions, the time of day, discussed what they had done yesterday, planned to do today and suggested what they might do tomorrow). After the weather report were stories, questions, etc.

During the nearly ten months from late October 1964, to early fall 1965, school time had reached a fairly regular 30 minutes daily. At that point we judged the children had acquired a sufficient repertoire of attentive and coopera-

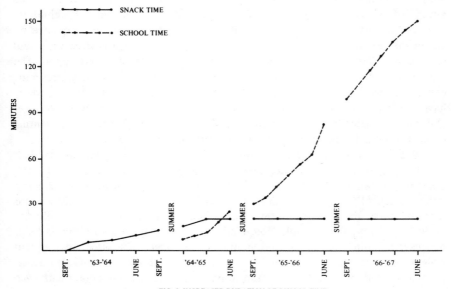

FIG. 2 INCREASED DURATION OF SCHOOL TIME

tive behavior to increase the school duration even more. Accordingly, a brief recess was initiated, followed by a second daily school session of about 10 minute's duration. From then on, both school sessions were gradually increased, though the duration of recess remained fairly constant. By December 1965 the children had two daily school sessions, totalling about 40 minutes, and the duration of school sessions sharply increased, as can be seen in Figure 2. In other words, once the basic repertoire of attentive and cooperative behaviors had been reasonably well established, the duration of daily school sessions could be more rapidly increased.

THE THIRD YEAR: ACADEMICS IN EARNEST

With the acquisition of reasonably long attentive behavior by the children, the school could now focus on teaching basic academic skills, such as reading, arithmetic, and specific content areas. The group worker who had been acting as teacher was trained as an R.N., and her knowledge of teaching material and methods was soon no longer adequate to meet the new academic goals which had been set for the children. Accordingly, a state certified elementary school teacher was hired.

Consistent with our usual procedures, the new teacher was introduced gradually with each part of the sequence known to the children. Specifically, the advent of the new teacher was explained to and discussed with the children. Considerable care was taken to describe clearly the steps in the sequence by which the teacher was to replace the group worker who, it was stressed, would still be with the children during the morning recess and every afternoon. The teacher joined the class in December 1965, first observing, gradually becoming active and, by January 1966, assuming the role of teacher. (The group worker, having left that class, now focused her attention on a new group of younger children to teach them basic socializing and prepare them for their own eventual entry into school sessions, much as she had with the focal group).

When the teacher began in January 1966, the children had made their transition from snack to school time. They had also been introduced to pre-academic material and skills (e.g., books, chalkboard, identification of some letters, etc.). Although school time duration had increased to two daily sessions totalling now about 45 minutes, each session still included many behavior problems. Cathy, for example, frequently insisted on lying across the desks or benches, moaning, humming and pounding her heels. She also had frequent violent blow-ups. Freddie often shrieked, flapped, threw toys and ran away. Frankie giggled excessively and often stubbornly refused to cooperate with even the simplest request. Gerry became wildly excited and often bit and severely scratched himself. Much of the teacher's time was devoted to reducing the disruptive behavior. One effective strategy was the use of relaxation training, which had been initiated in the fall of 1965, about two months before the teacher began.

The teacher was given two major tasks: (1) to accelerate the development of an interacting, functioning group, i.e., to continue shaping attentive and cooperative behavior and reduce the disruptive individual episodes, and (2) to bring about acquisition of academic behavior.

The teacher used simple materials and activities to create a variety of brief learning settings that required active response by the children and provided immediate rewards. These settings were also designed to provide many built-in reinforcers to support attending behavior while the teacher directly reinforced specific academic target behaviors. The weather and calendar exercises, as described above, are examples. Also, two sets of children's name cards were made, each child's name was taped to his desk, while the teacher retained the other set of name cards. At first, the children were required only to go to their own desks, which they knew by position, point to their name card and say their name aloud. Later, each child was given all four name cards and asked to match the correct one from the four with his own name taped to his desk. The exercise therefore required inspection of the cards and correct matching. Based on recognition the children gradually learned to select their own name from the card pile, and also to select correctly the names of the other children. Roll call could then be varied in a number of ways, all necessitating active responses that were immediately rewarded. The teacher might hold up one name card at a time and ask, "Is this person present?" The children took turns playing teacher and calling the roll, reading each name from the card or simply distributing the cards appropriately. Once they had learned to recognize the various names, they used the name cards to learn to recognize and later print the letters, which led to phonics.

In addition to name cards, the children also had cards with common words like "door," "desk," "window," etc. that were at first taped to the appropriate place in the room. Holding up a card the teacher would instruct a child to "Put the pencil on the _____ " and the child would be immediately rewarded if he correctly carried out the task. The rewards were primarily social and verbal rewards, which had been developed earlier in the program.

Another variety of learning situations was created by using appealing objects, such as small, colorful plastic or metal cars, airplanes, boats, houses, animals, or dolls. One of the most successful groupings was a small barn, several fences and a variety of plastic animals. Set up on the table, the barnyard held the children's attention for relatively long periods. At first, the children focused on simply identifying the animals ("Find the cow."), and then discussing characteristics ("Where do we get our milk?") and comparing them with other animals ("Which animal likes to swim in water? From which animal do we get the eggs we eat for breakfast?, etc."). After becoming familiar with the animals and labelling the barn and fence, the children were taught a variety of relational and color concepts. For example, they practiced instructions to "Put the horse *in* (behind, next to) the barn; ". . . the chicken on the box; Find the white (brown) cow, etc." Size relations were taught by having the children select "big" and "small" animals, rank them as big, bigger, biggest, or small, smaller, smallest, etc.

As their familiarity grew, they became able to match the toy animals with the name of the animal printed on a card and, eventually, the teacher could hold up an animal-name card and instruct, "Freddy, put the _____ in front of the fence, etc." As with the earlier name cards, recognition of animal names led to identification of letters and work in phonics.

Number concepts were also introduced through the barnyard setting, as the teacher instructed "Put one (two, three, etc.) duck in the pond;" "How many cows are there?, etc.)." These exercises led to counting, use of number cards and simple arithmetic. For example, later in that spring (1966) in a particularly effective counting exercise, a bowl of pennies would be placed on the table and each child in turn was allowed to keep as many pennies as he could count in sequence, without error.

By February 1966, the children were beginning to print their own names and to use a common textbook. Over the next four months, more traditional academic materials like textbooks and flannel boards were being used. The class continued to work on phonics, printing, use of common phrases ("good morning," "we like," etc.), differences and similarities (hot-cold, big-small, etc.), number concepts, simple arithmetic and reading.

Teaching was further carried out through use of a variety of ordinary settings. Daily walks in the city gradually developed into expeditions to stores, playgrounds or the zoo, and soon children were going on bus rides. These activities occurred in the afternoons and were not part of the academic period.

Throughout the school sessions, small-step sequences were carried out; much individual attention was given to the children and immediate and lavish reinforcement was provided for each bit of appropriate behavior.

After working with the academic portion of the program for five months (end of May 1966), the teacher had succeeded in increasing the duration of school time to an hour and a half. Within these sessions the children were more consistently working together. Whereas it had been originally necessary to separate the children, their tables were now placed together and they faced one another around them. The children were reading from pre-primer books (*Alice and Jerry Basic Reading Program*, Row-Peterson & Co.) and by June were well into lower first-grade reading material. They were also now able to work independently and could be given seat work consisting of brief programmed sequences while the teacher worked with other children.

By May 1966, the four children had learned to remain together cooperatively in school sessions totalling one and a half hours daily. The increased attentiveness and social cooperation which so obviously occurred during those five months were direct continuations of the earlier basic teaching processes that had been carried out by the group worker and the rest of the staff. It should be pointed out too that while the teacher worked with the children for an hour and a half, the three hours remaining in the daily program also involved social learning situations with the staff.

To illustrate, a typical day began at 8:45 A.M., with the four children of the focal group meeting together in the playroom with the four children in the younger group and the staff for both groups. This was an approximately 15-minute transition period in which social behaviors such as "good morning" and cooperative play across age groups were strengthened. After all the children had arrived and had had time to greet each other and play some quiet table games (drawing, Lotto, which entailed matching pictures and words, picture puzzles, clay), the younger children and their staff moved to their group room while the focal group prepared to begin their school session. They put away the toys, had a brief relaxation exercise period, and went to the school corner, where the various academic activities were carried out. After approximately one hour of school, a 20 or 30 minute recess began, which included running, shouting, ball-throwing games in the gymnasium, and, again, was with the younger children. Snack time and another relaxation period followed after which the two groups divided, with the focal group returning to school for approximately half an hour.

At about 11:00 A.M., school ended, and approximately 45 minutes of varied activities such as the expeditions followed. Time was flexible and increased or decreased according to the particular activities that day. About noon, all children had lunch together, another 15 to 30 minute play period, relaxation and they then made preparations to leave. Parents came for their children at about 12:30 or 12:45. (After the children left, the afternoon groups came, with staggered arrival times, and included public school children who joined our afternoon social learning programs.)

Thus, by May and June 1966, the focal group had increased its daily program duration to four hours (8:45 to 12:45) out of which one hour and 30 minutes were specifically spent in the academic school time.

School time added a true academic dimension to a previously essentially social-learning program. The teacher, continuing the shaping of social, cooperative behavior, helped to bring about an interactive, social group, in which clearly demonstrable academic achievement occurred. The clear emergence of a group and the demonstrable academic achievement, along with the major reduction of disruptive surplus behavior, were the major developments of the focal group's third year.

The remainder of the third year (July and August 1966) was spent in our annual six-week summer camp. The development of the summer programs will be discussed in Chapter 8.

SUMMARY

Approximately the first six months of the focal group (October 1963 through April 1964) were directed at the development of program structure, identification of deficit and surplus behavior, identification and development of effective reinforcers and increasing the rate and variety of behavior. The next half year (May through October 1964) began to stress the direct reinforcement of simple social responses, capitalizing on the increased response rate and using the reinforcers previously identified and developed. Efforts were made to more selectively, differentially reinforce adaptive social behavior. A major social setting initiated during this first year was snack time during which early social learning was achieved. In addition to the direct reinforcement of social behavior during snack time and the use of primary food reward, this setting provided the basis for the development of secondary generalized reinforcers and, in particular, verbal reinforcers. By the end of the first year (October 1963 through September 1964) a clear program structure had been established, the children were behaving at a far higher rate and variety than that with which they had started, were behaving in more socially appropriate ways, and had learned to maintain themselves for approximately 20 minutes during snack time.

As that first year continued, the reliance upon the removal of noxious stimulation as a reinforcer was decreased, while food as a primary reward and various secondary reinforcers became more important. That first year was one in which basic goals were sought, simple social behaviors were begun and reinforcement tools developed, all of which would be used later in developing higher levels of adaptive behavior.

The second year (September 1964 through August 1965) saw an intensified effort at shaping social and verbal behavior through primary and secondary reinforcement and a utilization of the basic reinforcers and behaviors previously developed. In this second year, snack time was used as the basis for developing school time; the secondary reinforcers developed during snack time were used to strengthen behaviors during school; the range of learning social behaviors increased and attempts were made to generalize the newly-learned social behaviors to wider aspects of the world, such as taking walks into town, going into stores, visiting parks and playgrounds. Also in the second year, the staff and children came to grips with the children's high degree of aggressive behavior. By the end of the second year, the children had developed to a higher and more stable level of social behavior, their aggressive behavior was under somewhat better control, and school time had been initiated.

The first portion of the third year (September through December 1965) involved a continued developing of school time with the daily duration increasing to more than a half hour. In addition, differential reinforcement of other social behavior was continued, and attempts were continued to control the children's aggressive behavior.

In January 1966, school time became more academic as a certified teacher began to conduct the class. By May and June 1966, there were two daily academic school sessions totalling one hour and 30 minutes. The children were far more attentive, interactive as a true social group, and had made demonstrable academic gains. Overall, the program had expanded in time, in academic achievement and in greater contact with more children.

Summer camp followed in July and August 1966.

In the foregoing discussions, various strategies to control aggressive behavior have been frequently mentioned. These were carried out simultaneously with other parts of the program already discussed. However, because they constitute approaches to essentially one problem, aggressive behavior, they will be discussed together as a unit rather than chronologically as they actually occurred in the program. The next chapter will be devoted to control of aggressive and tantrum behavior.

CHAPTER 7

Control of Aggressive and Tantrum Behavior

We shall use the term "aggressive behavior" to include physical assaults on oneself or others, damaging objects, throwing objects inappropriately, yelling, screaming, name-calling, or swearing at someone or something. "Tantrum behavior" refers to any loud behavior in response to frustration, including the classic tantrum of throwing oneself to the floor, kicking, and screaming. In our focal group, aggressive and tantrum behavior ranged from mild, brief reactions of a single child to severe, prolonged reactions of all four children simultaneously. Because of the wide range in intensity, number of children involved, behaviors and situations, control techniques employed by the staff had to be varied; no single approach could effectively control such a broad variety of situations.

As the children became more responsive to each other, aggressive and tantrum behavior increased markedly, reaching its highest level of intensity and duration midway into the second year. Gerry and Cathy were almost constantly embattled, Frankie did a great deal of giggling and passive-resisting, and Freddie devoted considerable time to screeching, running, grabbing things from others and throwing objects out the windows.

The same development of high aggressive behavior was noted in children in other groups, and its emergence seemed to be a natural consequence of two factors: (1) the increased general response rate which had been deliberately developed, and (2) the failure on our part to predict increased aggression and thus build in controlling contingencies. With more careful planning and less zealous reinforcement of *all* behavior initially, we might have mitigated the unintended reinforcement of aggressive behavior, thereby reducing though not avoiding the later problem.

Several parents had noted that their children were more active and aggressive at home and were becoming concerned with the unbelievably wild sessions they had witnessed in our program. As long as the children maintained this high level of aggressive behavior both in our program and at home their learning of adaptive social behavior would be curtailed. It was important, therefore, to bring this behavior under control.

In our attempts to control and reduce aggressive behavior we had several methods, each of which appeared effective for a specific kind of condition. These approaches (in the sequence in which they were attempted) were: (1) extinction, (2) physical restraint, (3) repetition and reinforcement of verbal rules, (4) removal from the situation and social isolation (i.e., time out from reinforcement), (5) suspension from school, (6) programmed relaxation and reciprocal inhibition. The basic approach of reinforcing all adaptive alternative responses was maintained but, while effective in shaping adaptive behavior, it did not reduce significantly the aggressive behavior.

EXTINCTION

The first approach was based on the concept of *extinction*, the weakening of a response through its non-reinforced repetition. Extinction was attempted by ignoring aggressive behavior and engaging the other children in activities so that they too would ignore the upset child.

The use of simple extinction was of limited value with these severely disturbed children and seemed effective only in the few instances of mild tantrums and low-keyed aggression such as yelling, perfunctorily throwing non-dangerous objects, or swearing at people. (Our basic rule for these behaviors became "Ignore it, don't reinforce it.")

However, because these children rarely exhibited such mildly aggressive behavior (their outbursts were immediate and major), ignoring them had no observed effect on the behavior. Trying to ignore a child who is going through a loud, violent, destructive and dangerous rampage is ludicrous and even harmful, and did not seem effective for several reasons. Most obviously, while we withheld social approval and recognition, these were probably not the major reinforcers at all. It appeared that once a severe episode began it was perpetuated not because of possible social approval and recognition, but through the self-stimulating effect of the tantrum itself. It was noted repeatedly and consistently that a child in a rage did things that stimulated him to further excitement and aggression. Upon tearing off a doll's head, for example, Gerry immediately became excited, and proceeded to tear the arms and legs, leading to even more excitement, aggression and loss of control. Cathy might begin to calm down during a tantrum, but if she threw one last object that made a great deal of noise, she was immediately stimulated to more screaming and destruction. Freddie was stimulated by his own screeching and reinforced by his own success in throwing things out the window. Frankie was greatly stimulated by all noises and tantrums, including his own giggling.

The more severe, aggressive outbursts seemed to be self-perpetuating, stimulated and reinforced by their own effects. Withholding of approval by the therapists was irrelevant in this situation, and probably not even perceived by the enraged child! Thus, withholding recognition and approval for excessively aggressive behavior did not weaken the behavior apparently because social approval by the therapists did not constitute the effective reinforcement for severe aggressive behavior.

PHYSICAL RESTRAINT, REPETITION AND
REINFORCEMENT OF VERBAL "RULES"

Because extinction worked only for mild tantrums and aggressive behavior, it became necessary to develop techniques to control the more severe behavior. We inferred that severe aggressive behavior occurred at a high level because the behavior had been overlearned and therefore was highly resistant to extinction—that is, very little reinforcement was required to maintain it. Effective extinction procedures require high control over the reinforcers. In our group, however, the many occurrences of uncontrolled reinforcement made it difficult to specify and control the effective reinforcers for aggressive behavior, precluding the successful use of extinction procedures.

The fact that aggressive behavior was increasing suggested not only its resistance to extinction, but also the existence of contingencies in the group that reinforced aggressive behavior. One source of reinforcement might have been the reactions of the children, such as Frankie's giggling, Freddie's screaming, Gerry's shouting, and Cathy's tantrums. In addition, the immediate effects of aggressive behavior (higher noise and activity levels) might have also stimulated further upset. Events moved quickly and at times, despite our alertness, a child's aggressive behavior might have been reinforced by his success in achieving some goal. In a wildly aggressive outburst, a child might succeed in grabbing a fistful of cake or a toy from another child, or escape from some demanding situation. His occasional successes constituted a variable reinforcement schedule.

In our group setting it was not possible to eliminate all potential and actual reinforcers for aggressive behavior or to avoid partial reinforcement. Our efforts seemed to have resulted in a variable ratio reinforcement schedule that strengthened the undesirable behavior. In addition, the stimuli that occasioned the aggressive responses were far too varied for effective control—a child might burst into a long, severely aggressive response when his name was called, or because a loud fire engine screamed by, or because he dropped a toy, or another child touched him, or innumerable other possible occurrences.

In the group situation, with its many uncontrolled variables, neither the stimuli occasioning aggressive behavior nor the reinforcing stimuli that maintained the aggressive behavior could be adequately controlled. It became clear, therefore, that aggressive behavior was bound to occur and be reinforced and under these conditions aggressive behavior would continue to increase. Since we could control neither the eliciting nor occasioning stimuli, nor the effective reinforcers for aggressive behavior, our attempts to reduce that behavior would have to focus on the behavior itself. It appeared that the only way to prevent the reinforcement of aggressive behavior in our situation was to intervene physically and prevent the occurrence or continuation of aggressive behavior. This entailed brief and carefully contingent physical restraint. The use of restraint is in direct opposition to the currently more common catharsis idea that aggressive behavior can be reduced through evocation of that behavior. In our view, however, allowing the aggressive behavior probably had at least three major negative results: (1) it interfered with the learning of alternative adaptive responses by the entire group and by the child who was engaged in the aggressive behavior; (2) the repeated and prolonged occurrence of aggressive behavior afforded much sheer practice of that behavior, making the child increasingly proficient at it; (3) the more that behavior occurred, the greater was the probability of its unplanned variable reinforcement. There were then several good reasons for *not* allowing aggressive behavior to occur. Had we used strong punishment such as electric shock the behavior would have been allowed to occur, followed immediately by the punishment contingency. However, we believed that punishment was probably of greater harm than help and, therefore, was not to be used. Thus, we could find no justification for allowing the severely aggressive behavior to continue.

Restraint of the child occurred as soon as an aggressive episode began and it varied with the intensity of the episode. For example, minor episodes were ignored and invariably stopped quickly. For a more intense or prolonged reaction, a staff member moved in and held the child lightly, but firmly. If a child had begun kicking, biting, scratching, or in some other manner attacked another person, the therapist quickly moved in and held the child's arms and his legs if necessary. As staff controlled the child physically, they repeated phrases, such as "We don't kick," "We don't bite," or whatever verbal admonishment was appropriate to the particular behavior. When restrained in this manner, the children at first became frustrated, and their aggressive behavior intensified. They fought harder, screamed louder, and the staff "hung on" more doggedly. The therapist was in such close contact with the child that he could discern subtle changes in the child's muscular tension. As the child began to relax, the therapist attempted to reinforce the relaxation response by using the previously taught verbal reinforcers of praise followed immediately by decreasing his own restraint of the child. For example, he would repeat, "That's it, good job, settle down." At first, if the therapist loosened his physical control, and particularly if he let go completely, the child re-erupted, forcing the therapist to move in again, exert physical control, and repeat the process of differentially restraining and admonishing the aggressive behavior and reinforcing the more controlled, more relaxed alternatives.

By his close contact in holding, looking at, and listening to the child, the therapist perceived and responded immediately to many cues. As the child relaxed, so too did the therapist, and as the child tensed, the therapist increased his restraint. The restraint itself was accomplished by holding the wrists lightly or, if the child were kicking, by holding him at arm's length away from the therapist. (The therapists soon became adept at not only controlling the child, but simultaneously protecting themselves. For a child who kicked severely, we often removed his shoes or instructed the parent to have him wear sneakers).

There are three essential factors in this approach: (1) the restraint of aggressive behavior to prevent its occurrence, (2) intervening in the ongoing behavior and forcing at least some of the child's attention on the therapist, (3) reinforcing the alternative relaxed or controlled behavior through verbal reinforcement and through cessation of the noxious stimulus restraint. As long as the child maintained his severely aggressive behavior, noxious restraint continued. As soon as he began to relax, he was verbally reinforced, and the noxious restraint was decreased. The increase or decrease of noxious restraint could thus be controlled by the child. The occurrence, intensity and duration of noxious restraint waxed and waned as an *immediate* consequence of the child's own behavior. It was not long before the children began relaxing more quickly and for longer duration.

As the children gained control over their aggressive behavior, an interesting sequence was noted. At first the children did not seem to respond to either the restraint or the admonishments. They generally made so much noise that the therapist's voice was masked, and they also showed a "frustration effect" of increased rage when restrained. Eventually, however, they began to slow down, perhaps at first only from fatigue. As they did, the therapist could be heard more easily as he presented verbal reinforcement and began to decrease the noxious restraint. The child immediately launched again into his loud aggressive behavior, only to be quickly restrained again. As this approach continued it was noted that the children began to respond more quickly to the variations in the therapist's degree of restraint and to repeat the verbal admonition, "We don't kick," etc. This echoing was of the same intensity as the rest of his behavior—loud, insistent, and screaming—and it seemed ludicrous to see a therapist controlling a child who screamed continually, "We don't kick" all the while kicking hard and fast.

Gradually, the children began to refrain from the aggressive behavior as they continued repeating the behavior rule. At first, their control was brief but at least had occurred. A child could be seen standing rigidly alone, hands clenched, shouting "We don't throw! we don't throw!", only to quickly lose control and begin throwing things around the room as he continued screaming. The children gradually delayed the aggressive behavior for longer periods as they loudly repeated the rules. This obvious, overt verbal repetition of rules gradually diminished to a whisper, then to silent mouthings of the phrases, and, finally, dropped out altogether, while their control over the behavior remained.

Presumably, the children had learned subvocal verbal control, and no longer needed the externally imposed control or their own loud verbal commands. This process seemed to be one of internalizing, of bringing overt aggressive behavior under verbal stimulus control. They had apparently learned to tell themselves to slow down, not to kick and so on, and then to bring the tantrum under control. Essentially this procedure generated response-produced cues which were then gradually faded. The children were obviously learning to check aggressive behavior which had first come under the external control of the therapist and subsequently under the vocal and implicit verbal stimulus control of the child himself; i.e. they were developing self-control.

REMOVAL FROM THE REINFORCEMENT SITUATION AND SOCIAL ISOLATION

Although the use of physical restraint and repetition of behavior rules appeared to bring much of the most severe aggressive behavior under control, there were still numerous daily episodes, some lasting 15 or more minutes. By the end of the second year, though these episodes continued to occur at a high rate, they were less severe in intensity and duration, and the three-hour, intense tantrum was now rare. The milder episodes had come under greater verbal control, and a child would now often calm down by himself or in response to the therapist's verbal command. Physical restraint was rarely needed any longer.

By the end of the second year, the children were generally more responsive to social reinforcement, and another method of teaching self-control was attempted. This consisted of removing the child from the room and having him stand in the hall with a therapist until he had calmed down. Used during the third year of the program, it replaced physical restraint, which no longer appeared appropriate at the children's new, higher level of verbal and social behavior. Removing a child from the room was always done after the child had been told to settle down, warned about having to leave, if he did not and then continued to disrupt the group. The child had to remain in the hall with the therapist until he quieted and clearly verbalized that he would remain under control when he returned to the room.

The children responded in various ways to the "social isolation" technique. It did not have the desired effects on Frankie nor on Mary and Billy, who were not at that time in the focal group. The latter two merely continued their agitated talking in the hall, while Frankie became extremely resistive, lying down in the hall and refusing to look up, speak, or move for long periods. Cathy and Gerry appeared to settle fairly quickly once taken into the hall, while Freddy's behavior appeared unaffected. Thus, it seemed that removal from the situation as we carried it out was generally not useful, appearing to work only for Cathy and Gerry and even then with questionable efficiency.

As this approach was continued, the number of upset episodes began to increase, particularly for Cathy and Gerry in the focal group, and Billy in the older group. We began to suspect that social isolation from the room might actually constitute a reinforcing contingency. This suspicion seemed confirmed one day when Cathy began an obviously forced screaming and a fake tantrum, a loud, but poor attempt to stimulate loss of control—accomplished in an alert and controlled manner. After perhaps 20 seconds she suddenly stopped, looked directly at a therapist and in a conversational tone said "OK, now you can take me into the hall." The therapist laughed, as did Cathy, who then wandered off to play with some toys. From then on Cathy was taken from the room for a walk in the hall or to see another room only as a *reward* for good social behavior. For her, removal from the room as a negative condition, was no longer utilized.

Billy's reaction was equally interesting. When taken into the hall he continued to giggle and remained excited. As with Cathy, removal for him seemed to serve as a reinforcer to increase rather than decrease his wild behavior. Upon taking a closer look at the situation it became clear that while Billy was in the hall, he maintained a constant, insistent verbal chattering with the therapist. Two conditions of social isolation therefore became apparent: (1) removal from the room immediately followed some proscribed behavior, and (2) while in the

hall, the children had the complete attention of a therapist. The whole procedure consequently resulted in increased attention to the child and thus
actually constituted reinforcement of disruptive behavior. For Cathy, as seen
above, removal from the room became a positive reinforcing contingency, a
reward for sustained, interactive social behavior. Cathy's rewarding excursions
from the room led to special, individual activities including, for example, piano
lessons.

For Billy, like Cathy, removal from the room resulted in a reinforcing
period of attention. We decided to continue the procedure but to reduce its
positive reinforcing value by eliminating all attention to Billy while in the hall
until he quieted. The first and *only* time we employed it with Billy, he
responded with such a severe and unpredicted reaction that the entire exchange
is reported here, as this writer had recorded it just minutes after its occurrence.

> Bad day for Billy. Extremely active—leaping around—giggling inces-
> santly—swinging on __'s hair—kissing, sucking, hitting, hanging on the
> arms—general severe and bizarre behavior. Verbal commands to no
> avail—repeated instructions to settle down had no effect. Finally, set
> limit—if he continued, we would remove him from room. Billy's reac-
> tion was to become more excited, leap around and shout, "Oh boy, Oh
> boy, Oh boy, yes." After several more minutes of this I took Billy from
> room. He remained excited, talked rapidly, grinning and gesturing. In
> the hall I told him: "Billy, from now on when you have to be brought
> out here because you won't control yourself, I'm going to bring you
> out here and ignore you. I won't talk to you out here; I won't pay any
> attention to you out here; I won't even look at you out here." Billy's
> reaction was immediate, and a marked change in behavior occurred. His
> loud giggling and active gesturing stopped abruptly. He was silent for a
> moment and then, with increasing agitation said, "Oh no. You won't
> talk to me? You'll ignore me? Oh no! Don't ignore me!"
>
> I explained that he would be taken out of the room and ignored
> when he lost control and did not obey the school rules, particularly
> those pertaining to safety. Billy's strong reaction continued, and he said
> he would henceforth obey all rules.
>
> In a few minutes he had settled down and we returned to the room
> where Billy maintained excellent control for the remainder of the day.

From that episode on, Billy's previously characteristic wild behavior was
under better verbal control. When he began to act aggressively he needed only to
be reminded gently of the particular limits or school rules involved, and he
brought himself under control. The prospect of being taken into the hall and

ignored obviously was so noxious that merely being reminded of it stimulated his own efforts at control. His peak of wild, aggressive, bizarre behavior ended with that brief conversation in the hall, and his own control increased. No other child had shown such dramatic reaction and sudden behavior change and the intensity and completeness of his reaction had been quite unpredicted. (Following that incident Billy, like Cathy, began a series of individual "trips" from the room as reinforcement for desirable behavior.

Thus, the third strategy in controlling aggressive behavior, removal from the group, generally did not have the desired effect. Perhaps if a social isolation room had been available where the child could remain safely alone, removed from the stimulation of the group, this technique might have had more consistent results. As it was, in our situation it appeared to reinforce rather than weaken the immediately preceding behavior, probably because it resulted in increased individual attention. The observation that our removal technique seemed to be reinforcing for some of the children led us to abandon its negative use and to employ it as a reward for positive behavior. Only with Billy was there any reduction of the disturbed behavior, and that was only after "removal" became more clearly structured as "social isolation."

In summary, within the limits of our situation, removal of a child from the room did succeed in (1) reducing the immediate disruptive stimulation of the rest of the group, but (2) also seemed to be reinforcing for the child removed because of the increased individual attention. Removal, then, may be an effective technique when it involves brief social isolation. From our observations, however, even social isolation would appear to be effective only with those children who had developed to a fairly high social level. It would be expected that isolation would have had no effects on the children in our focal group when they first began in the program. In fact, it apparently had been a reinforcing situation for them at that time.

Removal from the situation, then, while effectively removing the disruptive influence on the rest of the group, was not a generally effective technique for weakening undesirable behavior. It is suggested that it might have effective application when coupled with social isolation, and then only with children who have developed to a social-interactive level.

"SUSPENSION" FROM SCHOOL AS "TIME-OUT" FROM REINFORCEMENT

During the second year's summer camp, removal from the situation was carried even further, and one child—Billy—was sent home on two occasions. In the third and fourth years, sending children home was used on six occasions, mostly with the public school children in summer camp. It must be emphasized that as a teaching technique it was used sparingly, only under very carefully planned and controlled conditions, and only for behavior which resisted modification by other means. It appeared to be a very powerful technique, never requiring more than two applications to stop otherwise resistive behavior, such as running away, hitting other children and staff and deliberately disrupting group sessions. This technique will be discussed in detail in the chapter on summer camp.

PROGRAMMED RELAXATION AND RECIPROCAL INHIBITION

As the third year began, it was apparent that the children had gained considerable control over their aggressive outbursts. The staff's interruption of aggressive behavior through physical restraint and strong positive reinforcement of appropriate behavior seemed to have checked most of the severe aggressive behavior, and the violent two-or-three-hour screaming battles were no longer occurring. Aggressive upsets still happened daily, but they were milder and shorter than previously. By the beginning of the third year, the children were enjoying more conflict-free periods during the course of each day and the group sessions, now five hours long included a greater proportion of appropriate behavior and activities, such as school, playing, snack time and daily trips into town. The children were more controlled, social, verbal, and far less aggressive.

Curiously, while each daily session spent less time in upsets, there seemed to be no decline in the number of upsets. In fact, the records show the number of episodes had actually slightly increased. The recorded increase in frequency of aggressive behavior during the first year has already been discussed as a result of our active intervention with the children. However, our attempts to deal with aggressive behavior during the second year did not result in any appreciable decrease of the mean daily frequency of aggressive episodes though these episodes did become shorter and less intense. The observations suggested that our attempts to decrease aggressive behavior may have resulted in a reduction of the duration and intensity but not the frequency of the aggressive behaviors. It appeared that the children were learning how to control and reduce their outbursts *once the outbursts had started*, but were still not capable of preventing the onset of aggressive outbursts.

Taking a closer look at this, we concluded that the aggressive behavior itself was occasioned by specific stimuli in the group situation. That is, there was always some apparent stimulus preceding the aggressive behavior—a suddenly broken crayon, spilled juice, a loud noise, teasing or hitting by another child, a sudden change in routine, and so on. The child's resultant screaming rage was his characteristic and successful way of removing the stimuli. Thus, the screaming rage was reinforced because it successfully removed aversive stimulation presented by other people. Many everyday stimuli are apparently highly aversive for autistic children and they developed an exceedingly effective technique of "screaming away" any aversive stimulus. This would result in the effective negative reinforcement of the screaming or aggressive behavior, making it overlearned and highly probable following aversive stimulation.

In our group situation many stimuli neutral to normal children appeared aversive to the autistic children. They reacted with their characteristic rages that sometimes lasted for hours. Gradually, control over the aggressive behavior was established. When aggressive behavior occurred we reinforced the children's vocalizing ("We don't hit," etc.) and their other attempts at self-control. Their own aggressive behavior presumably became the discriminative stimuli that occasioned their control responses. Their own outbursts thus came to occasion their own attempts to control those outbursts! Their own aggressive behavior had become the effective discriminative stimulus in the presence of which the operant control responses had been repeatedly reinforced by the staff. Aggressive behavior, as we had hoped, was coming under the children's own stimulus control, and the aggressive outbursts decreased in duration.

Despite the children's growing control, they were still reacting to the same aversive stimuli. Their reactions were less intense and of shorter duration, but still occurred at the same frequency. The outbursts lasted only 10 or 15 minutes, but were nevertheless disruptive and constituted maladaptive surplus behavior. Children who react with violence to stimuli neutral for most obviously cannot function in normal social situations. Even one such reaction weekly (there were 10 weekly in our group) would be a major disruptive occurrence in most schools.

We had apparently succeeded in bringing about the children's own control of already-occurring aggressive reactions, but had not succeeded in preventing those reactions from occurring in the first place. Our next task, therefore, was to reduce the *frequency* of occurrence of the outbursts.

We observed that the aggressive upsets occurred at any time of day and were associated with discernible stimuli to which the children reacted immediately and violently. The stimuli varied among the children. Cathy reacted with extreme violence whenever Gerry pointed at her and raucously called her name, whenever a staff member said "no" to some demand, and under many other specifiable conditions. Gerry reacted to broken objects and any interference with his ongoing activity. Billy was stimulated by granulated sugar, stones, bare arms and any signs of distress in other children. Freddie was upset when intruded upon. Mary responded to any real or imagined threatening gesture, however mild; and Frankie was stimulated by any other child's gamboling around the room. Thus, for each child except for Frankie certain stimuli would result in immediate, loud, destructive, and aggressive behavior.

We were fairly confident that the children would continue to strengthen their ability to control their outbursts once the outbursts had begun. However, to teach the children not to react so violently in the first place was a problem of a different order. The stimuli that provoked their upsets were common in social situations, and could not therefore be removed or easily controlled. Thus, we could not eliminate the reaction by removing the discriminative or eliciting stimuli. Furthermore, the behavior seemed too well-developed and so quick in occurring that when the discriminative or eliciting stimuli appeared, the children reacted instantly and maximally. The immediate reaction seemed to be elicited rather than occasioned. If so, then the upset response was basically respondent rather than operant and would require approaches other than the manipulation of subsequent response-contingent reinforcers.

The following assumptions were made:

1. Aggressive, upset behavior of long duration, i.e., tantrums, constituted operant behavior.
2. This operant behavior had been shaped through both positive reinforcement (when a tantrum succeeded in getting something for the child) and negative reinforcement (when a tantrum resulted in cessation of aversive stimuli such as "intrusion" on the child by other people).
3. Such tantrum behavior could be controlled and reduced through manipulation of the subsequent reinforcers, i.e., differential reinforcement of adaptive behavior.
4. Through such differential reinforcement, aggressive tantrum behavior was already coming under stimulus control, and the tantrum behavior itself had become the effective discriminative stimulus that occasioned the newly learned verbal and motor control.
5. The operant tantrum was in turn occasioned by internal discriminative stimuli of a conditioned emotional reaction.
6. The conditioned emotional reaction, consisting of the usual sympathetic arousal-emergency reactions, was a respondent elicited by specifiable stimuli in the environment.
7. A large variety of previously neutral stimuli had become conditioned stimuli, eliciting the conditioned emotional response.

Based on these assumptions we concluded that the children's aggressive upset or tantrum behavior occurred as follows:

A conditioned stimulus, (screaming, a broken toy, human intrusion, etc.) established in the child's previous conditioning history would elicit an immediate conditioned emotional reaction consisting of the usual autonomic reactions that prepare the body for action. Thus, the child would presumably experience immediate increase in heart rate, respiration, muscular tension, and so on.

This complex of internal physiological reactions then constituted discriminative stimuli for screaming, kicking, throwing, etc. That is, these operant behaviors had been repeatedly reinforced in the past in the presence of the emotional reaction. Therefore, whenever aroused emotionally, the child became aggressive. The tantrum itself constituted an *operant*, and it could and did come under stimulus control through careful manipulation of subsequent reinforcing contingencies. However, *the original emotional response which occasioned the tantrum was in itself respondent and was not weakened by* subsequent differential reinforcement of adaptive behavior; it had to be approached through a deconditioning process. The bond between conditioned stimuli and conditioned response had to be somehow weakened. If that could be done, then the emotional reaction would not be so easily and frequently elicited and the tantrum behavior would not be so frequently occasioned.

Thus, whereas we previously believed that specifiable group stimuli occasioned the tantrums, we came to perceive an important intermediate step: environmental stimuli *elicited* the emotional response which in turn *occasioned* the tantrum behavior. That intermediate step, a product of *respondent conditioning*, was not affected by differential operant reinforcement of adaptive behavior. This analysis would, we believed, explain why the manipulation of subsequent operant reinforcers seemed effective in reducing the duration and intensity but not the *frequency* of upsets. While duration and intensity of upset depended upon operant conditioning, their frequency was occasioned by an emotional reaction which depended upon respondent conditioning.

Having made these assumptions regarding an internal emotional reaction, we began to consider the use of *systematic desensitization* as a therapeutic approach to weakening the variety of emotion-eliciting conditioned stimuli. Systematic desensitization has been extensively used by Joseph Wolpe (1958, 1969) in treating neurotic adults. Wolpe attempted to inhibit anxiety responses through the principle of *reciprocal inhibition*. The client is seen to behave maladaptively because of strong conditioned anxiety responses to a range of common stimuli, and the treatment is directed to weakening the bond between the conditioned stimuli and the all-too-frequent anxiety responses. The therapist attempts to weaken that bond through reciprocal inhibition by causing a patient, in the presence of the anxiety-provoking stimuli, to make a response which is incompatible with anxiety.

Eysenck and Rachman (1965) observed that the success of reciprocal inhibition therapy depends upon carefully selecting and manipulating the appropriate inhibitory response, the most commonly employed being muscular relaxation as described in Jacobson's (1938) classic work.

Wolpe's approach involves essentially three steps: (1) *diagnoses*, in which the patient is carefully interviewed and tested to determine the hierarchy of anxiety-arousing stimuli and to identify those stimuli as precisely as possible; (2) *relaxation training*, in which the patient is carefully trained to relax his body on command and to maintain that state of relaxation; (3) *desensitization*, in which the anxiety-arousal stimuli are presented while the patient maintains his relaxed state. Beginning with the least arousing stimuli in the hierarchy and progressing over several sessions to the most arousing, the patient is taught to maintain his relaxed state in the presence of the anxiety-arousing stimuli.

The patient cannot be simultaneously relaxed and anxious because the two responses are *incompatible*; and the stronger of the two will weaken or dampen the other. In the desensitization process the learned relaxation is pre-potent over the first few, low-arousal value stimuli in the hierarchy and thus anxiety, as a response to those stimuli, is progressively weakened. As the tendency to relax becomes stronger, it progressively inhibits anxiety responses to stronger stimuli. Thus, the therapist moves his patient along the anxiety-evoking hierarchy by progressively weakening the anxiety responses to stronger stimuli.

Reciprocal inhibition was developed for treating adult neurotics and is generally not considered useful for psychotic conditions. Wolpe[1], for example, assumes that schizophrenia derives from an "abnormal organic state" rather than from a core of learned maladaptive behavior and he therefore excludes psychotics from this treatment. Eysenck and Rachman (1965) noted that reciprocal inhibition might alleviate "neurotic habit patterns" in some psychotics, but, because they are less accessible and cooperative than neurotics, generally cannot be approached through behavior therapy. In contrast to these assertions, Cowden and Ford (1962) reported successfully desensitizing phobic behavior in one hospitalized adult schizophrenic and compulsive behavior in another.

While most work utilizing reciprocal inhibition has been with adult neurotics, it has been reported used with children by Mowrer and Mowrer, (1938), Wolpe (1958), White (1959), and Walton (1961). Most of this work, however, has been limited to treatment of phobias and eneuresis and, except for those two conditions, there has been little systematic investigation of reciprocal inhibition with children. There seems to be a general acceptance of the idea that children, particularly young ones, cannot be approached with a sophisticated technique that demands cooperation by the patient. Eysenck and Rachman for example

[1] Personal communication

noted, "For obvious reasons, it is not possible to use relaxation with many children, especially young ones" (1965, p. 210).

When we decided to use reciprocal inhibition with the autistic children, we were surprised to find that other investigators had apparently not done so previously. It appeared that because the theoretical predictions had been made that reciprocal inhibition could not be effective with psychotics or children (and certainly not with psychotic children!), no one had seriously investigated its use with psychotic children. However, having observed our group of psychotic children for two years, we believed that they were amenable to relaxation training and, previous opinions to the contrary, we decided to investigate the technique. The results of our exploratory study of reciprocal inhibition with psychotic children were reported in an earlier paper (Graziano and Kean, 1967, 1968) and the following is a somewhat more detailed presentation.

The main objective in the use of reciprocal inhibition was to control the inferred conditioned emotional response and thereby reduce the frequency of the occasioned overt "upset" high excitement reaction pattern. As in Wolpe's approach, there would be three steps in our investigation of reciprocal inhibition with psychotic children. First, we had already carefully observed the environmental conditions under which the upset reactions occurred and had defined and ranked them for each child. Step two involved training the children to relax on command. The third step was the initiation of planned sequences of desensitization in which the least arousing stimuli in each child's hierarchy would be presented while the child was instructed to relax. Thus, by moving through the hierarchy we would presumably reciprocally inhibit each child's upset reactions.

RELAXATION TRAINING

Having already observed, recorded and ranked the apparent conditions under which each child reacted with upset behavior we moved to the second step, relaxation training, and were immediately confronted with problems involving the cooperation of the children. Although they had developed fairly good verbal behavior and were generally more cooperative, they still could not be relied upon to cooperate easily with the rather involved verbal explanations and instructions to relax. In fact, it became apparent that the children did not know the meaning of the word "relax" or have any behavioral referent for the concept. Consequently, in training we could not assume that the children "understood," were "motivated" to achieve goals of improved behavior through relaxation, or would cooperate willingly. In other words, none of those conditions essential for work with adult neurotics could be assumed to exist for our children.

The training sessions would have to (1) assume minimum cooperation by the children (2) de-emphasize abstractions, and (3) focus on a specific and concrete behavioral level, with a great deal of practice and reinforcement. We had in effect to teach the children that the verbal label "relax" referred to changes in muscular tension. They had to perceive clearly and react to even subtle variations in bodily states. In short, they had to experience and learn behavioral referents for the idea "relaxation." The general approach involved (1) reducing as much as possible the stimuli associated with hyperactive behavior, (2) making the children physically comfortable and muscularly "loose" or flaccid, (3) detecting the occurrence of muscular relaxation, and (4) reinforcing the relaxation responses. Verbal reinforcers such as the phrases "Good work" and "Good job" laboriously taught to the children earlier in the program were to be used as the major reinforcers for the appropriate behavior. It was also assumed that the experience of relaxation would itself be pleasant and reinforcing, thus adding its own reinforcing value.

A specific area of the room was selected and for three days prior to the initiation of relaxation training the children were told about "relax time" and shown the "quiet spot" where the training would occur. Characteristically, they asked no questions nor exhibited any reaction to the announcements. The first training session was announced simply: "O.K. kids, now its relax time." The lights were turned out, and the children were led to the "quiet spot" and instructed to lie down on a clearly defined blanket on the floor. The therapist gently, quietly, and in a soft, almost "lullaby" cadence, told them, ". . . Close your eyes, now, just like when you're in bed, nice and comfortable. That's it, eyes closed. Breathe slow and easy, slow and easy, that's it, good job, nice and easy, nice and slow, nice and relaxed, good job, calm, slow, easy, relaxed. That's right. That's it. Real good, real relaxed!" The therapist continued her quiet instructions to breathe easily and be calm, settled and relaxed. After two minutes of quiet cooperation, Cathy got up and walked away. The therapist then ended the training session, and the children resumed their usual program.

The training sessions occurred once daily, always following snack time, and just prior to resuming the academic session. The children continued to experience relaxation not only lying down, but gradually also sitting and standing. The therapist continued her soothing, quiet instructions and paired the gentle manipulation of arms, legs and necks, with the verbal instructions to relax. Any sign of approximating relaxed behavior was given immediate verbal reinforcement and, eventually, the children learned to relax on verbal instruction alone.

Freddie, Gerry and Frankie cooperated quite well, rarely missing a training session, and gradually increasing the duration of their periods of relaxation. Cathy, on the other hand, attended the first three sessions, and then only 15 of the next 83. While the three other children cooperated, Cathy went off by herself and played with dolls. Frequently the therapist asked her to join the group, but did not persist when Cathy refused.

The training sessions continued until all four children reached the previously-specified criterion of five consecutive sessions in which the child was cooperative, quiet, and visibly "loosening" and relaxing on instruction. These criteria were reached in 25, 32 and 43 sessions by Gerry, Frankie and Freddie, respectively. Cathy re-joined the relaxation training in the 87th session, attended most of the remaining sessions and achieved criterion on the 94th; furthermore, she cooperated in all subsequent sessions.

Daily relaxation-training sessions became a regular part of the program from November 1965 to June 1966. With time off for the winter holidays, 21 weeks of training were carried out, spanning 105 sessions (five per week) and totalling 14.8 hours. This total training time distributes to only 42 minutes each week for all four children and only *10.5 minutes per week* per child for direct training. It is clear that even these grossly psychotic children can be taught to relax on instruction, and with an amazingly small investment of therapist's time! Further, their new ability improved with practice. The duration of relaxation sessions lengthened from a mean of 4.4 minutes for the first ten sessions to 12.7 minutes for the last ten. The children's cooperation, involvement and apparent enjoyment visibly increased, and they were now easily reporting their bodily states of relaxation or tension.

DESENSITIZATION SEQUENCES

When the four children had reached our criterion of relaxation, we were ready for the next phase, systematic desensitization, which involved invoking relaxation and then systematically arranging sequences in which originally arousing stimuli were presented and reciprocally inhibited by the relaxation response. Desensitization was the major goal of this endeavor which sought to determine whether relaxation could dampen the conditioned emotional reaction and thereby decrease the incidence of overt upset responses. It had already been observed that the relaxation training sessions themselves were almost completely free from upset reactions. In fact, there were only three upsets during the entire 94 training sessions! The children appeared to be more relaxed, were verbally reporting so, and an aura of relaxation seemed to develop, extending in time perhaps 30 to 45 minutes after the training session was over. It appeared that relaxation training was in fact antagonistic to excitement and was successfully dampening it.

An interesting finding was that the relaxation and calm that prevailed during the relaxation training sessions apparently extended beyond the sessions themselves. There was a wholly unpredicted and marked decrement of the generalized excitement or "upset" behavior throughout the entire day! Thus, by the time they had learned to relax on instruction and were ready for the next step, systematic desensitization, the children were emitting so few high excitement responses that systematic desensitization did not seem necessary. Through the relaxation training, there apparently had occurred an "unsystematic" desensitization that effectively inhibited the generalized high excitement responses.

Figure 3 shows the frequency of upset responses recorded during a 125 day baseline period. When relaxation training began a sharp increase in upset behavior soon occurred. Similar increases occurred whenever we focused for the first time on altering some behavior and they might be interpreted as a "frustration effect." As can be seen, soon after the third child reached relaxation criterion, there was a sharp drop in frequency of upset responses. Following Cathy's achievement of the criterion, the curve continues downward, and remains at a very low, near-zero level throughout the entire fourth year.

Thus, after achieving the criterion for relaxation, the children showed a marked decline in excitement responses throughout each entire day. The relaxation response was observed to occur in many situations and frequently the children spontaneously practiced relaxation. During the fourth year, one frequently heard a child calmly telling another child to "relax," or "take it easy,"

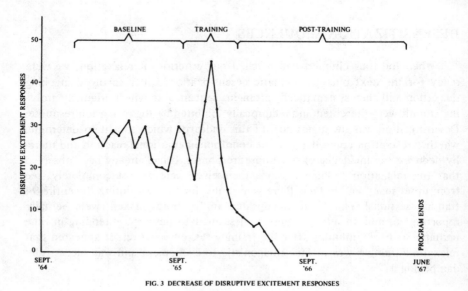

FIG. 3 DECREASE OF DISRUPTIVE EXCITEMENT RESPONSES

and thereby help to control each other. One such incident occurred during the fourth year involving Cathy and Gerry who had previously battled and roared furiously with each other. The group had been out for a walk in the park. On returning, they had taken a short-cut that necessitated crouching through an opening in a hedge. As they approached the opening, Gerry pulled back and stopped, saying, "I'm afraid. I'm afraid to go through that hedge." Cathy, who had been in front of him, came back and said, "It's o.k. Gerry. Just relax and then you won't be afraid." She took his hand, and the two of them slipped quietly through the hedge together.

Relaxation also appeared to generalize to situations at home. Parents frequently reported that the children were beginning to appropriately tell their siblings and parents to "relax" and "take it easy." Thus, it appears that considerable generalization did occur. During the fourth year of the program, relaxation sessions had been built into the schedule, and occurred three times daily. This was done to (1) train new children more quickly in relaxation, (2) provide repeated practice and reinforcement of the skill for all children, (3) "slow down" and relax the children at crucial points in the program. It was observed that new children readily entered the "relax times," cooperated well, and quickly learned to relax themselves. The results strongly indicate that psychotic children, contrary to previous opinion, can be taught physical relaxation. The training can be achieved efficiently in small group settings with only a small expenditure of time per child. As planned, the relaxation responses came under the control of many stimuli, including verbal instructions of the staff and later of the children themselves. Further, the ability to relax seems to increase with practice and reinforcement. Thus, "programmed relaxation" (Graziano and Kean, 1967) appears to be a feasible therapeutic technique with psychotic children.

The most significant hypothesis generated by this exploratory project is that carefully structured and programmed training in physical relaxation without formal desensitization sequences effects a significant decrement in the generalized response of high excitement, and the resulting relaxation generalizes beyond the training situation. This exploratory project thus suggests that relaxation training appears to bring about a major, constructive, modification of behavior. It may be that systematic desensitization is necessary to modify specific patterns such as phobias, but the generalized excitement response of psychotic and other severely disturbed children might be effectively modified simply by general training in relaxation.

Hopefully, this hypothesis will be tested by others under better control conditions. If supported, programmed relaxation training without desensitization training might be a significant therapeutic technique with hyperactive children. It is also an uncomplicated, parsimonious technique, applicable in small groups, requiring little investment of time, and easily taught to and used by persons other than highly trained psychotherapists.

SUMMARY

Aggressive and tantrum behavior increased markedly toward the end of the first year, presumably because of the deliberately developed general response rate and our failure to predict increased aggression and initiate controlling contingencies from the beginning. Certainly aggressive and tantrum behavior is common and severe among psychotic children, and is an area of major disruptive behavioral surplus that must be brought under control.

Because the aggressive and tantrum behavior was varied and occurred under so many different conditions, our attempts to bring it under control also varied. Throughout the development of "strategies" or techniques of control, there were three consistent, basic, ideas: (1) the continual shaping of increasingly complex alternative adaptive social behaviors, (2) prevention and interruption of aggressive behavior in order to avoid unintentional reinforcement and sheer "practice" of aggressive behavior, and (3) the goal of bringing aggressive and tantrum behavior under stimulus control, i.e., under the children's own internalized or self-control.

As the children continued to develop from their non-responsive to increasingly verbal and interactive levels, the techniques used to teach control of aggressive and tantrum behavior were likewise assessed and changed. At first, *extinction*, the non-reinforcement of aggressive and tantrum behavior, was attempted, and found apparently effective with mild outbursts, but not with the more severe occurrences.

The second systematic approach was that of physical restraint, coupled with reinforcement of verbal rules, or imposed limits. This consisted of gently but firmly restraining the child and reinforcing all of his approximations of control by relaxing our restraint, while presenting previously-learned verbal reinforcers. The children were observed to mimic the admonitions, such as "We don't hit people," and they eventually apparently internalized that verbal control.

The carefully-planned use of restraint and verbal control appeared to decrease the intensity and duration of aggressive outbursts, but their frequency of occurrence remained high. Attempting to reduce their frequency, we initiated a modified social-isolation approach, i.e., removing the child from the room. This technique did succeed in immediately removing the disruptive influence of the child, but it also seemed to constitute a reinforcement for the child's disruptive behavior. It appeared effective only with Billy and only after it had been made to more closely approximate true social isolation. For other children, removal from the room (and the attendent individual attention of the therapist) was of such obvious reinforcing value that it was soon used as one of the many rewards for a variety of adaptive social behavior. Thus, removal from the social situation was not a generally effective technique as used by us, but, as Billy's reaction suggests, might very well be effective if social isolation is actually employed. Even then, we suggest, it would be effective only with those children who had developed to a fairly high social level.

The next approach involved sending a child home when he was disruptive or abusive. Used only eight times and then under carefully controlled conditions, it appears to have been one of the most powerful techniques with very resistive behavior.

By the beginning of the third year, the children had achieved a fair degree of control over the duration and intensity of aggressive behavior, but the frequency remained high. It was reasoned that while operant approaches seemed to modify the duration and intensity of emitted "upset" or "high excitement" behavior, respondent approaches were necessary to reduce the inferred internal emotional reaction which *occasioned* the operant, upset behavior. Thus, to decrease the frequency of upsets, we had to first weaken a conditioned emotional response. Programmed relaxation based on reciprical inhibition therapy was investigated. The results suggest that training in general relaxation without specific desensitization sequences may be an effective and potentially important therapeutic technique with hyperactive children.

The third year ended with our annual summer camp. Rather than discuss each year's camp separately, the overall development of camp will be discussed in a single chapter.

CHAPTER 8

Summer Camp

INTRODUCTION

Summer camp, as an extension of the regular program, was based on the same assumptions and approaches. It began with 15 children the first summer and by the fourth summer had expanded to more than 60. The facilities were enlarged and use was made of a large, old, city-owned beach-side building and a new, small grammar school.

The expansion of summer camp resulted from attempts to provide mental health services to children from poverty families. As in most cities, mental health services were not available to the poor, but our attempts to develop appropriate services had not struck responsive local chords from 1963 through 1965. The following year (when poverty programs had become politically acceptable) the public schools became interested in our old proposal to include poverty level children in summer camp. This chapter will focus on the last two years of summer camp which involved the expansion of behaviorally-oriented mental health approaches to emotionally disturbed, poverty level children.

PROGRAM OBJECTIVES

In addition to providing continued programming for the regularly enrolled children, the summer camp program had several goals aimed at demonstrating some of the ways in which the schools might utilize their resources to help poverty level children. Summer vacation was seen as an opportunity to utilize the schools' facilities and personnel to: (1) give emotionally disturbed, poverty

177

level children an enjoyable summer, (2) help them learn more adaptive behavior, (3) train teachers, college students and adult non-professionals, (4) select and train high school students from the poverty areas to work as mental health or educational aides, and (5) demonstrate special programs and techniques for disturbed children that could be adopted for programs in the schools themselves.

THE CHILDREN

The 17 grammar schools in the city's disadvantaged areas yielded a population of over 2000 kindergarten through third-grade children (five to ten years old). Working closely with teachers, principals, school psychologists and social workers, and trying to select equally among boys, girls, and withdrawn and aggressive behavior, we identified those who were clearly the most seriously disturbed. The homes of the children selected from each school were visited and the project discussed with the parents, whose written permission was required. When a parent could not be located or refused permission, the next-ranked child was considered. In this manner, the 36 most disturbed children out of a population of 2000 children were selected. They comprised a very highly select sample of the most disturbed children in the school system. The following table shows the categories of children selected in the last two years of camp:

Table 4. Poverty Children Accepted in Summer Camp, 1966 & 1967

		Boys	Girls	Totals
1966	Aggressive	12	9	21
	Withdrawn	9	6	15
1967	Aggressive	12	7	19
	Withdrawn	10	7	17
	Totals	43	29	72

STRUCTURE: GROUP ASSIGNMENTS

Each of the final two years of summer camp included 36 poverty level children and 20-25 others, most of whom had been enrolled in the regular program. The structure and approaches were the same both years although the setting changed from an old building at the beach to a new grammar school building. The children enrolled each year were divided into six groups of equal size. In order to give balance to the groups, each child's placement was determined by his chronological age, sex, and behavior problems (i.e., whether he was aggressive or withdrawn). Each group also had a team of summer trainees composed of one teacher as a group leader, one college student and one high school student as aides. The team and its group remained together for the duration of the camp.

Each group was assigned its own room or home base where most of the direct behavior modification was carried out. The groups functioned independently most of the day, but came together at various planned points. The frequency and duration of the interactions between groups increased as camp continued and the children were better able to tolerate larger groups and less immediate attention and control by staff.

The camp was planned to provide consistent, predictable structure and high automatic reinforcement. Within that structure of groups, schedule and sequence, the staff utilized specific activities and materials designed to focus the children's behavior and foster pro-social, cooperative behavior. This entire structure was organized to maximize stimulation and reinforcement of increasingly social, adaptive behavior.

OVERALL SEQUENCE

The eight-week camp project was divided into five periods:

1. Initial week of staff orientation
2. First two weeks—establishing the reinforcing value of camp
3. Second two weeks—providing structure and alternative adaptive behavior.
4. Third two weeks—consolidating gains.
5. Final week—evaluating and report writing.

Each period had an essential focus and was designed as a foundation for the next period.

INITIAL WEEK OF STAFF ORIENTATION

The focus of the initial week was to orient the 20 new summer staff. In group meetings we explained our basic assumptions and approaches, and we discussed the children and their backgrounds. Intensive large-group discussions were carried on during the initial two days, covering primarily behavioral theory and hypothetical examples.

On the third day, the discussion became more concrete and specific, outlining the overall time-scheduling of camp activities. By the fourth day, the staff had already become acquainted with each other and staff teams were formed. Each teacher selected a college student and a high school student as aides, and the aides selected the teacher they wished to work with. Several groups formed spontaneously and overlaps or conflicts were rare.

For the remainder of the fourth, fifth, and sixth days, each team worked together in its assigned room, planning a detailed schedule of activities and reading all available reports about the children assigned to it. They developed coherent, integrated, and highly detailed programs within the general theoretical and practical structure that had been presented and discussed during the first three days. After working out their programs they then selected appropriate supplies, and prepared their rooms.

By the end of the initial week, approximately 30 staff, including 20 novices became acquainted with one another, learned basic concepts of behavior modification, formed teams, developed programs, arranged and equipped their rooms, and were ready for the children assigned to them. In addition, specific duties were assigned, such as being responsible for records, coordinating transportation, allocating bus duty schedules, caring for equipment, distributing snacks, and supervising lunches.

THE FIRST TWO WEEKS: ESTABLISHING
THE REINFORCING VALUE OF CAMP

Objectives for the first two weeks included establishing structure, becoming acquainted and smoothing out administrative difficulties and details that invariably cropped up. The major goal, however, was to maximize the reinforcing value of camp. It was necessary to create a consistent framework with a variety of built-in, automatic reinforcers, Skinner's "web of reinforcement." We aimed at maximizing as quickly as possible the reinforcing value of all aspects of camp so that when a child arrived in the morning he would be reinforced immediately by the many visual, auditory and other stimuli which abound in any situation.

In short, our aim was to devote the first two weeks to making the camp overwhelmingly enjoyable and positive for the children. We hoped to accomplish this through continued giving, including two snacks and a lunch, the use of toys, games and recreational equipment, pleasant and stimulating activities and a friendly, highly supportive, reinforcing, and non-punitive approach by the staff who had been selected, among other things, for their ability to relate to children without resorting to anger, punishment, ridicule or other types of aversive control.

There were three major reasons for stressing the development of high positive reinforcing value of camp, the most obvious being to increase the enjoyment and pleasure of these children who were deprived in so many ways. Secondly, these children had developed suspiciousness, apathy and even intense hostility toward school, teachers and other authority figures. Camp hopefully would be made so reinforcing that it would overcome their suspicion and rejection of anything remotely school-like. Attendance was always a problem in public school for these children. By maximizing the positive reinforcing value of camp, we would presumably increase the probability of their willing daily attendance.

Thirdly, as camp progressed, we would systematically increase the demands made on the children. New limits would be set, requiring adaptive, cooperative behavior, and a refusal to accept their characteristic impulsive, destructive or withdrawn conduct. For the first time some of the children were going to be faced with firm and consistent "no's," and with continued attempts to teach adaptive alternatives. It was predicted that they would become frustrated, begin to actively retreat from some aspects of camp, and an approach-avoidance conflict would develop; the tendency to attend would be strong, yet because camp was becoming increasingly frustrating the children might tend to stay away. In the growing approach-avoidance conflict we had to be sure that however high the avoidant gradient became, the approach gradient was always higher. Thus, no matter how unpleasant, frustrating and anxiety-provoking the increased demands might become, the positive value of camp, developed during the first two weeks, would be greater, and the children would maintain their attendance over what was to become a period of struggle and frustration.

THE SECOND TWO WEEKS: INCREASING THE STRUCTURE, LIMITS ON BEHAVIOR, AND DEVELOPING ALTERNATIVE ADAPTIVE BEHAVIOR

By the end of the first two weeks the children and staff had been mutually oriented, the children had become accustomed to the schedule, and the positive value of camp had presumably been developed. We were ready to shift to our second two week's focus, to create individually-geared learning sequences to overcome surplus and deficit behavior. Having carefully observed the children for two weeks, the staff formulated behavioral goals for each child and, starting with the third week (sooner with some children), began reinforcing approximations toward those goals. We placed our emphasis on cooperative group activities, reinforcing both individuals and groups for progressively closer approximations of those cooperative, mutually benefitting, goals. Many goals, of course, were idiosyncratic, and varied among the children. One boy, for example, never spoke, and repeatedly engaged in the highly specific acts of throwing directly-aimed rocks into people's faces and leaping out of windows. A girl had to be taught how to eat without throwing up onto the table at every meal.

These two weeks saw limits imposed on children who had experienced few previous consistent limits. Aggressive behavior was not allowed—it was stopped and rewards were clearly withheld when undesirable behavior occurred. The children severely tested the limits and were frequently highly frustrated by the staff's firm stand. When one girl, for example, was prevented from injuring another, she launched into a severe attack on the staff member. This eight-year-old girl screamed, hit, kicked, scratched, swore with a sharply honed scatolgical succulence, and bit, frequently drawing blood. The staff member who attempted to physically control this motion of teeth and curses was the target of language and physical fury that was totally unchecked by any "ladylike" rules of combat (e.g., "I'll kick off your balls, mother-fucker!"). When this girl eventually learned that her outbursts did not gain what she wanted, the aggressive behavior disappeared. As one unsympathetic observer tartly remarked, "It's like bustin' a bronco," and so at times it seemed. (The above incident was further complicated because it had occurred in a public place and a group of people had gathered.)

Some children were surprised when they discovered that "we don't fight" or "play with guns" at camp, or that, while self-assertion and "standing up for your rights" with authorities were encouraged, we did not want them to tell teachers to "go fuck yourself." The children called each other and staff "nigger," "Sambo," "whitey," "boy," "black crow," "white trash," "spic," "white crow," "paleface," "black buzzard," "greaser," "grease-ball," "cue-ball," "burr-head," "liver lips," and many other names which frequently precipitated battles. These exchanges were all between individuals and, despite the racial meanings, there were never battling groups of white versus black children.

The staff tried to teach the children that such language and goading only precipitated trouble. To a large extent we had here a clash of values between a poverty sub-culture and the prevailing larger culture. One of our major tasks in this regard was to curtail some of the children's asocial behavior (fighting, swearing, etc.) to help them succeed in school more easily, but yet not dampen their self-assertiveness or strong though misdirected enthusiasm. With respect to name-calling, swearing, and general clashing with authority, no punishment (e.g., time out from reinforcement) was given; alternative adaptive behavior was modeled and coached and, when performed, reinforced.

Despite the often intense frustration, conflict and statements of hatred and bitterness the children expressed as they responded to their new limits, attendance at camp during these two weeks was nearly 100 percent! The only absences recorded during that ten-day period for 36 children were three owing to illness. It seemed that regardless of how demanding we became, the children would not stay away!

During these two weeks, the basic approaches developed earlier with the psychotic children were employed, though on a more verbal level.

THE THIRD TWO WEEKS: CONSOLIDATION

The third two weeks constituted the consolidation period in which newly-learned behavior was further reinforced and strengthened. The children had already learned to value camp and, in the face of increasing demands, to maintain limits of self-control and of cooperation. They had been pushed, prodded and led into highly rewarded normal or adaptive behavior. By the end of the second two weeks through repeated experiences the children clearly knew what behavior was expected of them, what behavior would or would not be rewarded. Every child had begun to behave in adaptive, socially cooperative ways, but a few children were still maintaining some of their severe surplus behavior. These children, resistive to change, required a special approach that will be discussed later in this chapter.

In general, the third two weeks were a period of heightened social activity and greater cooperative and adaptive behavior. It was a smoothly-operating and highly pleasant time, the fruition, as it were, of all of our efforts. From the detailed notes of daily observations, it was clear that the children did show increased social behavior as predicted, and many of them had done so by the third week.

DAILY SCHEDULE AND ACTIVITIES

The daily schedule was the same for all groups, giving a workable uniformity to the structure. Within the approximate time periods, however, specific activities varied between groups. Each staff team moved its group through the time schedule and within that structure developed appropriate activities geared to that particular group. The activities were designed so that social learning and reinforcement could be best carried out.

In order to utilize all contact with the children, the daily program began not with their arrival at camp, but with their boarding the busses to come to camp. The daily schedule is outlined below, and will be discussed in the following sections.

1. Riding the bus to camp
2. Arrival time
3. Indoor activities
4. Snack time
5. Indoor or playground activities
6. Lunch
7. Dance or puppet shows
8. Beach activity
9. Snack
10. Leaving time
11. Riding the bus home

Riding the Bus

We had been cautioned that one of the vexing problems that these children presented at school was poor attendance. Many of the children had no adult direction or care in the morning, and some parents actively aided the child in his truancy. We therefore expected uncertain attendance and a high rate of program drop-outs. To avoid this, we aggressively insisted that the children attend camp and we brought them in by bus.

The children were bussed to camp from all over the city. They met at their neighborhood school—a convenient and familiar place—in each target area. Our three busses had assigned routes, covering about six schools and picking up 17 children. Riding each bus was the driver, a male teacher in charge of the children on that bus, and a high school or college girl as an assistant. A male and female staff was assigned to each bus in case any special contingencies occurred. None did.

When the bus arrived at an assigned stop, each child climbed aboard and his name was checked off the attendance list. If a child were missing, the teacher left the bus in charge of the driver and aide, and made a careful search of the bus stop area. He walked around the school building, looking in to the windows, trees, cars and other possible hiding places, and he checked other children in the area. When fully satisfied that the child was not there, the teacher then went to the child's home.

The teachers found themselves knocking on doors asking for children, being confronted sometimes by empty apartments that had been lived in just the day before, and by apartments with six or more pre-school children who were there alone all day. They encountered parents who were cooperative, sullen, hostile, actively abusive, or apathetic. In one apartment the teacher was told to wait while the girl was beaten by her father. In another apartment the teacher, while looking directly at the mother and the grinning child he was seeking, was told the boy was not at home. The teachers encountered garbage-strewn kitchens and disorderly apartments, still reekingly alcoholic from the night before. They stepped into apartments with no intact windows, no heating system, and no bathroom. Having nowhere else to go, one family lived in a partly-demolished building which was giving way to a new highway. The teachers stood in hallways with dead rats, urine odors, and small mounds of feces. They looked into some pitifully clean and spotless apartments, at tired mothers who apologized for the mess out there and looked weary of the struggle to keep the ever-threatening hallway from moving in.

Our middle class teachers stepped daily into a world they had never before known, and came away more knowledgeable, distressed and with perhaps a new measure of understanding. Riding the bus was a powerful experience for the teachers and college students.

For the children, the bus ride served other purposes. It was a transition period from home to camp, giving the children time to adjust themselves to the camp day. It helped to orient them each morning to the camp program and, at the end of the day, to re-orient them to returning home. Bettelheim (1950) has written of the importance of transition periods in his residential treatment program for emotionally disturbed children, and we have found the same importance in ours.

The rides also provided opportunity to become acquainted with staff and other children from different neighborhoods and strong summer friendships developed. The children also seemed to learn increased control of impulsive behavior while waiting for the bus. At times children had to wait for 15 or more minutes. At first, when the bus did not arrive within a few minutes, several children simply boarded other buses for different programs. Because neither the busses nor the programs were as structured as ours, the children usually went unnoticed until much later in the day. A number of children rode their bicycles to camp and some actually walked and hitch-hiked several miles! One boy, Albert, thinking his bus had missed him, rode several miles to camp on a bicycle. Quite late, Albert proudly pedaled in, having made it by himself all the way across the city. His friends crowded around excitedly, marveling about his accomplishment and one boy, in great surprise asked, "Hey man. What you doing? You ain't got no bike!" "Yeah, I do now," replied Albert, proudly, "The bus didn't come, so I *stold* it!"

As the summer progressed and the children learned that their bus was certain to arrive, they waited more patiently. They waited with children going to other programs, in groups of 20 or more. Significantly, there were never any serious behavior problems while these unsupervised groups of children waited.

The 30 to 45-minute bus ride to and from camp was viewed as a social-learning setting, as much a part of the program as any other activity. The staff utilized the time and physical boundaries of the bus to clearly state and teach behavioral limits and it required the children to control their frequently aggressive and destructive behavior. The children showed a gradual shift from overt physical conflicts to verbal interactions. As they became more argumentative and less pugilistic, their development of more socially adaptive behavior increased.

Nevertheless, difficulties existed, some involving parents as well as children. One child had hardly settled into her seat on the bus one day when her father, inebriated, climbed on board, cursed and threatened the driver for having "forgotten" to pick up his daughter. He did not see her just a few feet from him, as usual sitting quietly while the other children silently stared at her. Another difficulty was parents reacting to the teachers on the bus as representatives of an enemy system and blaming them for the intolerable conditions.

Some of the middle class parents of the regularly enrolled children also presented problems. One mother objected to her child's riding the bus with "those others." This mother stormed into camp one day, complaining that her son had been hit by one of "them." She also complained bitterly that it was unfair to require her to pay for camp enrollment while "those others" were allowed in "free" (i.e., on a federal grant). This issue later became a major factor in the program's demise.

A problem did in fact develop involving the interaction between the autistic children regularly enrolled in the program and the poverty level children enrolled only for the summer. The autistic children were included on the busses to provide another age-appropriate experience for them. However, they could not tolerate the aggressive, teasing behavior of some of the public school children, who quickly discovered that they could easily stimulate fearful reactions in them. Gerry, for example, became fearfully agitated when some boys pointed their fingers at him and shouted, "Blam, Blam! You're dead! I shot you," and he was immediately marked as a target for their aggressive behavior.

To help and protect Gerry, the teacher enlisted the aid of George, the toughest boy or "top-man" on the bus. George readily accepted the role of helper, protector and friend to Gerry and he showed a great deal of responsibility and gentleness in helping the autistic child. He sat with Gerry, pointed out sights through the window, protected him from other boys, and reassured him the shooting was make-believe. Within a few days the other boys stopped their aggressive teasing, and Gerry had learned to tolerate the "shooting."

The teacher had used several bits of knowledge to foster cooperative, concerned behavior in place of aggressive behavior and to teach the autistic child to tolerate teasing more easily. Believing that if George cooperated the other children would too, he obtained George's help. Underlying his belief was the teacher's assumption that George was a boy for whom some gentleness and love was powerfully reinforcing, but who lived in a family characterized by toughness and rejection. This toughest of boys was thus very gentle when the right conditions were arranged. Those conditions included not only the opportunity itself as well as the teacher's rewards for consideration and gentleness, but also his preserving the face-saving stance of the "tough-guy." Thus, the teacher did not interfere when, in protecting Gerry, George told the other boys, "You be nice to him or I'll bust your mother-fuckin' heads." In this one command, George summed it all up; he could be simultaneously kind and gentle and rough and tough.

Despite the early difficulties, the daily bus rides remained an integral, highly important and successful part of the program.

Arrival Time

While several staff members rode the busses, the remaining staff waited at the camp, putting rooms and materials in order and planning the day's activities.

Facing the first day of camp, and the expected arrival of more than 50 highly disturbed children (36 poverty level children and 20 regularly enrolled), the staff's one-week orientation period suddenly appeared wholly insufficient. The staff gathered in small groups, having last minute conferences, to reassure one another. The busses were late on that first day, and many children had not arrived. Some had gone to the wrong camp and were returned later in the day. Others had not been located by the staff, who had spent considerable time checking home addresses.

When they did arrive, the children were orderly and fairly quiet. The withdrawn children said and did little, and the aggressive children seemed to be watching, waiting, and sizing up the situation. If not too willingly cooperative on that first day, the children were not openly aggressive or destructive either and the staff wondered whether some of the children were in fact really disturbed. Over the next few days it became evident that many of the children had been on their best behavior. Here appeared to be the same phenomenon noted frequently in public schools and in our own program for psychotic children—that disturbed children, like normal ones, can control their behavior in new or unfamiliar situations.

It seems readily understandable that many children would be cautious, controlled and subdued in the strangeness of their first day at school. The normal child recognizes the situation as new, and he imposes his own developing behavioral controls and contains himself while he discovers the limits of the new situation. Every year, however, as on this first day of camp, we are intrigued by the fact that even psychotic children exhibit this controlled behavior during the first few days, suggesting that they not only perceive the surroundings as new, but are also able to apply control over their own disturbed behavior. This self-imposed control seems to be brought about by the change in environment and, by manipulating the environment, we should be able to maximize and sustain the child's emotional control.

As noted above, the children's "good" behavior quickly changed and over the first week there was growing confusion and commotion around arrival time. As the busses rolled in, sometimes all three at once, the staff gathered around to take charge of the children in their groups. The children came boiling off the busses, many eluding the gathered staff, and they scattered in several directions, screaming streaks across the camp. There were children swinging in trees, running in and out of the buildings, scattering toys. There was laughing, crying, shouting. Children fought and played and many staff, particularly the high school students, were drawn into the wild physical activity which tended to reinforce rather than control the exuberant disobedience, activity and aggressive destruction which seemed to explode upon camp with the opening of each bus door. With this commotion as their daily introduction to camp, it was no wonder that the children continued their loud, uncontrolled behavior for several more hours, refusing to settle down or become involved in other activities.

Arrival time constituted a transition period during which the children and most staff first met for the day. Because the tone and tempo of this period apparently had a major effect in setting the tone for the entire day, it was important to smooth out things quickly and create conditions that would move the children into the rest of the program. Accordingly, during the first two weeks staff worked to organize and structure arrival time. The goals were to create a framework whereby the children came into a quiet, well-ordered situation conducive to cooperative, constructive and adaptive behavior. It should be emphasized that we were not attempting to reduce exuberance or enthusiasm or to reduce noise per se. Orderly, sheer obedience was not our goal. Rather, staff tried to reduce uncontrolled stimulation that seemed to lead to severe disorganization of behavior, such as psychotic gesturing and posturing, severe aggressive attacks, destruction of objects, and intense withdrawal.

When the busses arrived, the children, eager to get off, were first quieted. Then, as a reinforcement for their controlled behavior, the bus door was opened. As each child came off the bus and his name was checked off the attendance sheet, he was taken by a staff member of his group and engaged immediately in relatively calm activity, such as strolling, just sitting at a bench, talking, or utilizing toys conducive to quiet play. When a staff member received two children from the busses, the three of them went inside to their own room and began indoor activities, such as arts and crafts. Thus, each child had a brief orderly transition period out doors during which he had the attention of one staff. He was then eased into the indoor situation and by the time other children arrived was quietly engaged in highly reinforcing activities. The later arrivals could consequently also be given individual attention to get them started. Most often, the second and third children arriving would simply enter into whatever activity was already started. By approximately 9:30, all the children had been eased into the day's program and were actively engaged in their rooms.

Snack Time

Scheduled for approximately 10:00 A.M., snack time followed the indoor-activity period and consisted of generous pastries and large amounts of fruit juice. Snack time served essentially the same functions for the poverty children as it did for the psychotic children, providing an "inherently" reinforcing social learning situation. The reinforcing value of food to a hungry child is basic. Many of the poverty children had had no breakfasts and this snack was their first food in 17 hours! Nearly all the children eagerly accepted snack and quickly learned acceptable, controlled and adaptive behavior during snack time.

For a few children, however, snack and lunch were difficult times. Some rushed to the food, grabbed from others and fought over it. One little girl would stuff a large doughnut or half a sandwich into her mouth and add the other half before swallowing the first. She ate with eye-protruding, gasping wolfishness, with both hands darting to snatch all food within reach. She seemed to lose contact with other people and to focus only on the food. This voracious behavior was also accompanied by a soft crying. Immediately following her rapid eating, she threw up, causing further agitation and more vomiting. Her behavior was changed by the third week by gradually convincing her of the abundance of food every day and by controlling her rate of ingestion. Her food was divided into small, bite-size pieces, and set before a staff member, while her plate remained empty. With all of her food in sight but controlled by the staff member, she was given a small bit at a time and only after she had chewed and swallowed the previous one.

During snacks and lunches, staff encouraged a soft, conversational atmosphere. They encouraged sharing, cooperating, assisting in preparation and clean-up and maintaining a quiet, orderly, and pleasant situation. The assumptions here were that food was a primary reinforcer, would thus "hold" the children and whatever behavior occurred during that time would be reinforced and learned. The staff guided the children to increasingly social behavior and reinforced such behavior with both food and verbal reward. For many of these children these eating situations, closely directed by the staff, provided their longest periods of "normal" adaptive behavior, and they sometimes conducted themselves appropriately for as long as a half hour.

According to our theoretical rationale, the best way to develop adaptive behavior in disturbed children is to arrange environmental conditions in which they can observe and practice adaptive behavior and be immediately reinforced for it. These children must have the actual experience of behaving normally. It is not sufficient to have only insight psychotherapy or to encourage cathartic acting out. If we want the emotionally disturbed child to behave in a normal fashion, then we must help him *practice* normal behavior and immediately reinforce it. The child will learn much more by *doing* than by talking about it, or, as is more typical in psychotherapy, talking all around it. In this respect, snack and lunch were used for staff-controlled, reinforced practice of normal adaptive social behavior.

Indoor Activities

Snack time lasted approximately a half hour at the end of which the children were encouraged to help clear the table and prepare for the next hour of activities, which continued to approximately 11:30. This period of indoor activities included table games, arts and crafts, reading, story telling, and some academic work in arithmetic and reading. Like the other periods, it was used to guide and reinforce adaptive social behaviors. It was more important that the children learn how to cooperate, stop fighting, and forego tantrums than acquire new skills in games or arts and crafts. In the same way that we used food to reinforce socially adaptive behaviors we also used pleasing, interesting activities as secondary reinforcement to support further social learning. The fact that the indoor activities immediately followed snack time and took place at the same table helped to generalize the reinforcing value of the food to the later indoor activities.

The children and staff engaged in the indoor activities for one hour daily. It was essential that the games and projects used be of high interest and sufficient reinforcing value to hold the children long enough to allow practice of adaptive social behavior. Much trial and error was required for the staff to determine which activities were useful in simultaneously (1) maintaining the children's attention and (2) providing opportunities to practice socially adaptive behaviors which the staff could reinforce. While some activities apparently had high interest value, they could at the same time interfere with social learning. During evaluation week at the end of camp, the staff evaluated all the indoor activities and indicated the following as most successful in maintaining attention and teaching adaptive behaviors: reading stories, play-acting, building with blocks, checkers, relaxation, kitchen-playhouse, dolls, puzzles, and a variety of arts and crafts, and especially Bingo.

Because of the great popularity of Bingo, a few comments are in order. Bingo seemed almost made to order for the children and appealed to them for several reasons. First, it is an extremely simple game with few intellectual demands and is therefore well within the abilities of the children. Even the least attentive child was able to follow the play. When a mistake was made, the staff could readily see it and quietly direct the child to correct it. Secondly, Bingo is made up of many parts, consisting of cards with columns of numbers and letter headings and small plastic or wooden pieces with numbers and letters on them. It is played in a group and requires verbal interchange, paying attention to the "caller," and searching their cards. As the children's cards neared completion, they experienced anticipatory excitement, which they expressed in their giggles and jokes. Finally, there is the pleasure of winning. The winner clearly identifies himself by calling out loudly, "Bingo!" and thereby gains the attention and even envy, of the others. To add still another dimension, the children could win with any one of a variety of different patterns. Finally, the children thoroughly enjoyed taking their turn as "caller," and thereby become the center of attention, the one to whom everyone listens attentively. Bingo provided a good deal of varied stimulation and reinforcement, but always within the framework of a basically simple, low-demand task.

Bingo was most enjoyed by the eight-to-ten-year-old psychotic children. It successfully held their attention and supported adaptive, cooperative and relaxed social behavior for as long as an hour.

As the camp progressed, snacks, lunch and indoor activities were all planned to increase social involvement. During the first week it was difficult to sustain any interaction or cooperation at meals. After the second week, visiting at mealtimes between groups was initiated by combining two groups at snack time. Further in the summer, more groups were brought together and for longer periods of time with a decrease in staff supervision.

The indoor activities also became increasingly cooperative, developing from highly structured and strictly individual tasks to group tasks, such as painting large wall murals and decorating rooms.

Playground Activity

Daily, from approximately 11:30 to 12:30, the children moved outdoors for playground games where physical activity was encouraged. Like all the games and activities in the camp, those here were geared to gradually increase cooperation.

Lunch

Lunch was provided from about 12:30 to 1:00 and had generally the same goals and structure as snack time.

Afternoon Activities

After lunch, the children devoted another half hour to activities such as taking walks, playing quietly, or working on indoor art projects.

The Beach

The children agreed that the most enjoyable activity was the daily two-hours at the beach where they ran, played, splashed in the water, dug in the sand, and some even began to learn to swim. The staff had to be extremely alert here because of the potential dangers at a seashore. The afternoon snack was had at the beach, and at about 3:30 the children boarded the busses for their return home.

Special Activities

Special activities, such as field trips, puppet shows, and dance classes were also included in the program, but not scheduled for any particular hour or day. The field trips ranged from walks to nearby parks to extended bus trips to museums, firehouses, a planetarium, bird sanctuary, a farm, an airport, a railroad station, a zoo, and a visit aboard a U.S. Navy destroyer docked at a local port. The children enjoyed all the trips and their social behavior noticeably improved as the weeks went by.

Although we had hoped to continue exploring the use of puppets in teaching adaptive behavior, the puppet shows were not available to us after the first year and we could not follow up the program we had begun. Nevertheless it might be fruitful to review that program. Assuming that (1) children learn by social imitation and vicarious reinforcement and that (2) puppets clearly represent humans, we attempted to utilize the children's obvious enjoyment of puppet shows to teach alternative, adaptive behavior. A professional puppeteer made hand puppets of White and Black children. The puppets were used in shows that had been written by the camp director and the puppeteer and depicted incidents presumably familiar to the children. For example, one show was about a boy who, denied something by his mother, had become very angry, and abusive. Other shows dealt with school situations. In each show, the child saw simple, alternative, adaptive behavior, that was reinforced by subsequent events. The assumption was that the children watching would also learn some of the alternative behaviors.

We did not test the hypothesis that children learn adaptive alternative behavior from puppet shows, but we did observe that the children enjoyed the shows and remained well controlled and attentive, while viewing them. At times, the children later verbalized the basic message of a particular show and, occasionally, actually tried out the alternatives which had been portrayed, saying that they were going to "do it the way Arnold (the puppet) did." These observations suggest some learning and transfer, but more valid confirmation will have to await controlled research.

DELAYED SECONDARY REINFORCEMENT

In addition to the many occasions of immediate primary and secondary reinforcement presented by staff throughout each day, there was also a system of delayed secondary reinforcement designed to extend newly-learned adaptive behaviors over longer time periods. Behavior goals just within the child's ability but seldom attained were specified and the child was urged to work for that goal. When he achieved it, lavish verbal praise was presented, and the child was brought to the camp director's office where the staff member bragged about the child. The camp director then added his own lavish verbal praise and, because the child had done such a good job, he was also allowed to choose any two toys from a box filled with hundreds of small plastic items. The lavish verbal praise, the special attention of going to the office, all backed up by the veritable treasure chest of toys through which he could dig and select, had its desired effect. The beaming child returned to his room with his prizes, obviously proud and just as obviously determined to win another trip to the office. Perceiving his winnings, the other children were also motivated to do a good job in order to be sent to the office and be given their own prize.

The office used by the camp director was the principal's office of the suburban school in which camp was held. The director was perceived by the children much like a principal who is the ultimate authority figure in the school. However, whereas the principal is frequently seen as the disciplinarian and someone to be avoided, in our camp, the reverse was true. The children were brought to the "principal's" office *only* after they had done "something good" and the principal therefore praised and rewarded them instead of punishing them. The children soon developed a competition to see who could be sent to the office most frequently. They also learned that they would *not* be brought to the office for disciplinary action. There was only one way to be sent to the office, and that was to be recognized by staff as having behaved very well.

The behaviors required for a trip to the office varied among children and over time. Several children for example were initially brought to the office for rewards simply for remaining in their rooms for a half hour without running away. Another child was brought in and rewarded when, instead of his usual mode of egress of jumping out the window, he voluntarily left the room by walking out the door. Other children were brought to the office because they had shared, cooperated, stopped screaming or fighting when told, verbalized well, rode the bus well, and so on. After their first trip to the office, they were eager to return again. Thus, children began to try to do well in some specified way for a half day in order to win a "half-day prize." They then tried for one-, two-, and three-day prizes. Several achieved one-week prizes, a few two-week prizes, and one girl earned a three-week prize. At each level, the required behavior was more social and complex, and the prizes increased accordingly to include books, paint sets, crayons, special pencils, plastic baseball bats, racing car sets and even fishing poles. The cost of the prizes was just under $1.30 per child for the entire six weeks, but the impact was that of offering a glittering treasure chest of fabulous value.

From observations of behavior and from the children's verbalizations, there is no doubt that this delayed secondary reinforcement was effective in quickly shaping much adaptive behavior. Interestingly, after gaining one or two prizes, the children apparently no longer worked for the material prize itself—several children in fact immediately gave away theirs to other children and, obviously, for other reinforcers. One child took his prizes home and ceremoniously gave them to his neighborhood friends, thereby gaining considerable social reinforcement. The effective reinforcement consisted of the entire web of recognition and verbal praise he gained both at camp and in his home neighborhood.

TIME-OUT FROM REINFORCEMENT:
TEMPORARY EXCLUSION FROM CAMP

Temporarily excluding a child from camp (time-out from reinforcement) was resorted to only when all other approaches had failed to stop particularly disruptive, aggressive or dangerous behavior such as setting fires, injuring others or destroying things. Although nearly all such behavior had come under control by the end of the third week, a few children still persisted in it. During the last two years of camp five children were temporarily excluded for particularly severe behavior.

This technique involved four factors:

1. Developing such a high positive value of camp that exclusion would constitute a powerful deprivation. This approach was not used during the first two weeks, but was adopted only after such high value had been developed.
2. Clearly structuring and articulating the particular behavioral limits, such as prohibiting throwing stones or setting fires, and carefully showing and reinforcing adaptive alternatives.
3. Enlisting the cooperation of the child's parents so that when sent home the child would not be compensated for the loss of camp that day. This was to be as complete a time-out from reinforcement as we could arrange.
4. Clearly specifying the consequences of breaking some specified behavioral limit (e.g., *"Today*, when you do that, we will send you home."), and carefully carrying it through. Two examples will be given:

After two weeks in camp, Billy, one of the autistic children, still persisted in running away from his group into the woods in spite of our presumably high reinforcement for staying with the group. At the start of the third week he was warned several times that if he could not stay with his group, he could not remain in camp. Two days later Billy was clearly informed, "The next time you run away from your group, we will send you right home." He laughed and immediately proceeded to test this new limit by running away into the woods.

Billy's mother, whose cooperation had been obtained through a telephone conversation a few days earlier, was called, drove to camp and took Billy home.

Billy was apparently quite pleased over the whole episode until he arrived home, found that he had to remain in the house and therefore could not go in his swimming pool, his favorite summer activity. The next day Billy returned to camp, again ran away, and again was sent home. No other repetitions were necessary over the next three years for Billy, as this particular behavior stopped and was replaced by more cooperative social behavior.

Ronald was a notoriously aggressive ten-year-old boy from a poverty home. He was well known throughout his school and neighborhood as the epitome of meanness and aggression. In fact, when teachers in several schools wished to describe a particularly aggressive child, they would frequently report, "He's a Ronald Baker." At the start of each new school year, teachers would ask each other, "Did you get any Ronald Bakers this year?" In camp, Ronald attacked staff and other children almost daily. His disruptive, aggressive behavior persisted after two weeks, although his cooperative social behavior had begun to increase. Essentially the same procedure used with Billy was followed and, when Ronald was finally told, "The next time you hit someone you are going home" he immediately struck several other children, making them cry. Ronald was not only sent home, but, because this incident had occurred at the end of the camp day, he was further informed that he had to remain at home the entire next day. Ronald laughed and bragged that he would not let us "push (him) around." The next morning, Ronald was at his bus stop, but was not allowed on the bus. After spending a rather lonely day at home, he returned the following day and did not fight for the remaining three weeks of camp.

This procedure was used with only seven children (eight times) in all four years and each time was successful in stopping the particular disruptive behavior that had been so resistive to change. It should be pointed out that public schools frequently exclude or expel children, but find little change in behavior. In fact, for many expulsion seems to be reinforcing, fortuitously removing them from an intolerable situation. For example, by being expelled, they do not have to resort to truancy. In our use of expulsion we were careful to utilize it only when we judged that exclusion from the program would constitute a *deprivation* rather than a *reinforcement*. In this we depended upon the success of the first two weeks in developing the high positive value of camp.

Here, then, is the essential difference between removal from our program and removal from public school. In the camp, much effort is devoted to the use of positive reinforcement and to making the program as positive, reinforcing and enjoyable as possible. Once that is achieved, even the most disruptive child will soon begin to respect *clearly stated* behavioral limits rather than suffer possible, temporary deprivation of the highly reinforcing program. In the usual school situation, little use is made of positive reinforcement, and most behavioral control is approached by use of aversive stimuli. It is no wonder then that many children, given an opportunity to stay home from school, actually welcome it. Some children may even persist in their disruptive behavior because they are periodically reinforced by being expelled. That is, the reinforcement for remaining away from school is greater than that for attending school.

CHAPTER 9

Active Therapeutic Roles for Parents

TRAINING PARENTS AS THERAPISTS

Prior to the beginning of our program nearly all of the children who were to become our focal group had been in treatment for at least three years, during which time the parents had become passive recipients of service. They had been taught no active therapeutic roles and had been given little practical advice on caring for their children at home. Their angers, failures, concern, and innumerable questions on how to respond to their children had not been dealt with by providing them with effective skills, but by group psychotherapy in which they explored their *feelings* about their relationships with their children. Given the psychodynamic focus of that earlier program the parents had been made to step several paces back from the objective reality of their children and to deal with verbal abstractions instead of the children themselves. This might have helped maintain the large gap that existed between parent and child.

When we initiated our program we hoped to change the parents' earlier passive roles into more active ones. Initially we rejected the notion that the parents needed psychotherapy. Rather, we assumed that they needed practical advice and skill training regarding interacting with their children. Presumably, some could learn to actively help train their children. In short, our intent was to develop a direct and cooperative working relationship with the parents, rather than the traditional client-therapist relationship.

However, early in 1963, we were uncertain of the extent to which the parents could and should assume therapeutic responsibility and we explored the co-therapist concept cautiously, sensitive to the implications of a shift in the parental roles. We expected the parents to be both capable and cooperative in observing and understanding their own and their children's behavior and of devoting sufficient time and effort to their children. We further assumed the importance of honestly sharing all relevant knowledge and ensuring that the parents knew what was happening to their children in the program. We in turn were to be kept informed of the children's behavior at home.

Thus, while the children were in the day-care program, parent meetings were held monthly, individually at first and later in parent-training groups. The major function of those meetings was to provide a picture of the child's behavior at home, and to help plan minor home programs to be carried out by the parents. A procedure evolved in which the parents focused on the two days preceding the meeting and reported in detail every event of those days from the moment the child awakened. In sessions that sometimes lasted four hours, the parents were taught to observe and record behavior. Using their reports we were able to specify problem behaviors, note the controlling stimulus conditions including parental and sibling reactions, and assess changes from one month to the next. As the problem behaviors were identified, the parents and interviewer together ranked them in priority and discussed how to deal with them at home, planning a variety of home programs.

Brief daily report sessions in person or by telephone were also held with parents who were actively working on the modification of some specific behavior at home. In addition, it was possible to note if therapeutic strategies in the day care program were having any effects at home and conversely to note effects of occurrences at home on the children's behavior in our program. For example, we noted increased verbalizing at home of phrases specifically taught in the program. Relaxation training was also seen to generalize from the program to home as was a variety of other program-specific teaching. Through this tracking of behavior it appeared that learning and generalization had occurred as we had hoped.

We had then two major sources of data: the highly detailed reports—both retrospective and concurrent—of parents, and the even more detailed daily observations by our staff. These two sets of data were compared regularly on specific points as well as general classes of behavior. In this way we could assess trends over time and also use the home data as a source of validation for our group work.

As we gained experience we became convinced that nearly all parents could operate as reliable and effective therapists and that it was the rare parent who could not. Consequently, our expectations about parents coming into the program after the initial two years were quite different from those we had held for the original parents. Whereas the parents of the focal group exercised only limited therapeutic roles such as carrying out specific and limited instructions at home, those parents entering later began with the clear understanding and acceptance of an active and responsible therapeutic role. There were four of those parents. For three days per week they were assigned to train in the children's groups in the same way as other staff, carrying out regular duties. Gradually, after mastering the general methods and styles of our approach, they were trained in specific techniques that applied directly to their own children, such as reinforcement procedures to shape discrimination, attention and verbal behavior, maintaining records, controlling reward schedules, and making judgments about criteria. The parents were trained not only to facilitate the acquisition of adaptive behavior in their children, but also to reduce maladaptive behavior, such as self-abusive, aggressive or grossly bizarre conduct. When the parent-trainees had attained a sufficient level of skill (usually within about four or five weeks) they began to carry out simple levels of programs at home. The most common home programs for the younger children involved reduction of hyperactivity and development of language which augmented the child's training in the daily groups. With the parents' growing skill, their home programs enlarged, they assumed greater responsibility in planning and monitoring them, while at the same time reducing their direct involvement in our daily groups. The children thus had a consistent, extensive program of training both in our daily groups and at home. The parents maintained at least weekly supervisory contact with our staff.

The remainder of this chapter will be devoted to three case descriptions arranged in increasing order of the degree of active therapeutic parental roles. All of the parents of children enrolled full time were interviewed regularly, individually and in groups, and instructed in a variety of home programs.

THREE CASE EXAMPLES

Frankie

An example of active parental involvement early in the program is the home training carried out for Frankie in 1963. When he entered our program at nine and a half years of age, Frankie and his parents had already spent some three or four years in psychodynamic group therapy. Frankie's behavior was primarily deficit. He lacked speech, bowel and bladder control, and social behavior generally. Frankie was tall and thin and walked with a stiff-limbed, toy-soldier gait. Sharply bent forward at the waist, his long arms hanging straight down, near the floor, stiff legs kicking out one after the other, he starchly marched along. Both neurological and psychodynamic explanations of this peculiar gait had previously been given, the latter being that it was a motor symptom of tightly repressed hostility—i.e., he was unable to express strong hostility because he feared losing control, attacking his father and being severely punished. Therefore he tightly controlled his hostility, became "completely bound up" and, as a result, literally could not unbend.

Because he was not yet toilet trained he had to be cared for much like an infant, with large diapers, specially-made training pants and large rubber or plastic pants. His special demands distressed his parents, caused considerable inconvenience, brought a good deal of intermittent punishment to Frankie and generally created tension in the family. It seemed that a good way to ease family tensions around Frankie would be to toilet train him.

The toilet training which was only one dimension in his program, was carried out both at home and school. His most probable times for urinating and defecating having been observed, Frankie was taken into the bathroom at those times and highly praised for success. When he made brief squirming motions just prior to defecating, the group worker or his mother (at home) immediately said "bathroom," took him to the toilet and praised any success, partial or complete. Frankie was also coached and rewarded for any appropriately-timed verbal approximations of the word "bathroom." The verbal praise Frankie received continued while he was taught to wash his hands.

On leaving the bathroom Frankie was led to some highly reinforcing activity, such as playing with his tools or the doll house, or, as it fortuitously happened often, to snack time or walks around the block. Thus, the entire chain of appropriate bathroom behavior—signalling, verbal approximations of "bathroom," use of the toilet, cleaning and handwashing—was strengthened by verbal praise for each segment of the chain and by a reinforcing activity immediately at the end. Each reinforced segment presumably became a discriminative stimulus for the next.

After ten days of training, Frankie's daily soiling decreased to about once per week and, within three more weeks, to zero. His signalling, verbalizing of "ba-room," use of the toilet, cleaning and hand washing, had been clearly established. Concurrent with his training in school, Frankie's mother was supervised in carrying out a comparable program at home. Five weeks were required in the school program and nine weeks at home to establish complete daytime control. At that point many layers of special underclothing were discarded, and Frankie no longer required close supervision of bathroom behavior.

Several weeks after the beginning of the daytime program, a nighttime home program was planned. A large "potty" chair was placed at the foot of his bed. He was coached and rewarded for using it just prior to bedtime and was awakened once nightly to use it. The chair was gradually moved farther away from the bed and closer to and into the bathroom. Soon he was getting up at night, walking to the bathroom and appropriately using the chair. Within a total of 11 weeks Frankie was completely trained during the day and bowel-trained at night. He still occasionally wet the bed at night, though by making sure that he urinated just before going to bed, this too was soon controlled. Regular follow-up checks for the next four years showed that all the control had been maintained, with no relapses.

There seemed to be several important results of this 11-week segment of the program. Most obvious was the achievement of toilet training, which seemed to have occurred surprisingly quickly in this older child. One inference is that he could have been taught much earlier in his life had anyone allowed him the opportunity and helped his mother to actively train him. Frankie seemed quite pleased with his belated achievement, one of the few of his restricted life, and it was unfortunate that previous professionals had not thought it important enough to work with.

Frankie's mother also was pleased at ending the cleaning tasks of many years. She noted an increased flexibility with Frankie, who could now be taken out more frequently and to more places, and even to stay overnight at relatives. Too, there were no longer family upsets centered around his incontinence. Not the least of the results was to convince Frankie's mother of the effectiveness of direct behavioral approaches and to establish her active, therapeutic role in our working relationships.

Most interesting, however, was the immediate improvement in Frankie's peculiar posture and gait which followed the removal of successive layers of tightly-bound clothing from around his middle. Why had Frankie walked in such a strange, bound-up fashion? Repressed hostility? No. He had walked that way because he had been so tightly bound up in clothing that it had simply been very difficult to straighten up!

Cathy

Cathy's parents were highly receptive to our direct advice on practical everyday management at home. As with other parents, this practical-management focus sharply contrasted with their experiences in earlier professional contacts and seemed to be immediately helpful in improving their morale and sustaining their commitment to help the children.

At first providing retrospective reports of the child's development, they gradually became more active in home training programs. They were sustained largely by their own successes—a powerful reinforcer. Their monthly interviews, which trained them to focus on behavior and to observe and report in detailed fashion, helped the parents to understand much of Cathy's behavior, particularly her tantrum and aggressive behavior, and also to see those home conditions requiring change. The discussions were aimed at helping the parents to become more consistently directive and goal-oriented, rather than continue to react to Cathy's extreme outbursts in an inconsistent manner or crisis-by-crisis basis. The parents were also advised on developing and maintaining firm limits and more consistent focus on specified goals. In short, we were teaching the parents how to apply our basic ideas at home. There were detailed discussions on how to best respond to Cathy's tantrums, how to help teach her more self-care in performing such activities as dressing, toilet training, washing, and eating, to control, reduce or avoid sources of great excitement like loud music, TV commercials, supermarkets, crowds of people, how to eliminate spanking as a means of control and how to reduce models of aggressive behavior as provided for example by TV, how to support language development by requiring and differentially reinforcing her use of language, and how to initiate brief, daily play sessions with Cathy to help develop interpersonal behavior.

The parents' work proceeded and, gradually, changes suggested in our regular meetings were made at home. The parents apparently gained greater control, the family setting became quieter and less chaotic, and life at home more pleasant. The parents reported a marked general improvement in Cathy's behavior. Tantrums, screaming and aggressive behavior had become rare, her aloofness was gone and she now readily interacted, even verbally, with the family. She no longer insisted on fixed routines or the sameness in her environment. Her behavior at the table was improved and she was somewhat more responsible for her personal care and cleanliness.

As will be discussed in Chapter 10, Cathy's fourth year was organized around a more intensive socialization program aimed at her part-time enrollment in public school the following fall. Her parents became even more involved in home programs, generating behavior goals for Cathy, such as personal self-care, helping around the house, meeting and playing with normal children, interacting with adults and gradually widening her conversations to more complete and appropriate levels. Steady improvement was observed as Cathy became a "part of the family." By April of the fourth year Cathy had gone far beyong the upper limits of the group and seemed ready to begin the public school program that had been arranged with the school officials.

Cathy's parents saw her functioning at a level far higher than ever before and were eager to help her in her next step, beginning public school. That summer, however, our program was abruptly dissolved, all of the supports for Cathy's new, high-level functioning were withdrawn, and the parents watched a summer of growing distress in the child, ending in a severe behavioral regression by the following December. Cathy's regression is discussed more fully in Chapter

11. For the next year and a half (mid-December 1967 through May 1969) we were again involved with the family, and our staff and the parents planned school and home programs to recoup Cathy's adaptive behavior.

Cathy's behavioral deterioration was severe, though not complete. During the nearly seven months in which our program did not operate, Cathy assumed a markedly negativistic and aggressive behavioral stance. She refused to cooperate or participate in any reasonable manner at home. She insisted on being left alone yet constantly forced the family to battle directly with her. In fact, every interaction became a major battle. She fought equally against getting out of bed or going to bed, dressing or undressing, going to school or returning home, eating, bathing, or any attempt to constrain her behavior, such as asking her to turn down the volume of the incessant TV. One day, for example, during a three-hour rampage, Cathy managed to lock her mother in the cellar, pour water on her father who was sitting on the couch, and run screaming through the house. She tyrannized her family with long, violent episodes of screaming and aggression, and they had lost all control over her behavior.

Our program resumed in mid-December, but because of Christmas holidays it was not until January that any programming began in school, and February, at home. Clearly, during the seven month suspension of our program, Cathy's aggressive surplus had been reshaped to a high level.

While the staff again worked with Cathy in the school program, her parents were supervised in re-establishing a home program. It was clear from the parent interviews that Cathy was now operating on a non-contingent basis, i.e., there were no consistent limits or applications of rewards associated with specific behaviors. Cathy maintained an aloof existence, spending much of her time with television cartoons, and interacted with her family only combatively to use them to get things for her, such as food. Her speech had become incoherent and inappropriate.

The parents were advised that their general task would be to reapply the earlier structures so as to bring about more social, cooperative behavior, to increase her participation in the family. The home program was to begin with two behaviors: (1) her refusal to eat meals with the family, and (2) her incessant hitting people with her dolls. Both behaviors were parts of complex behavior chains. At mealtime Cathy took her food away from the table and ate while watching TV cartoons. Attempts to change this resulted in major aggressive outbursts, so aversive to the family that they had soon stopped trying to change that behavior. As for the other behavior, Cathy was spending a great deal of time with her dolls, usually in conjunction with the TV cartoons. Any interruption precipitated an aggressive reaction that included screaming, throwing dolls, and attacking family members by beating them with the dolls.

To initiate the program, her parents informed Cathy that beginning in five days she would be required to eat at the table with the family. Cathy was reminded each day for five days and on the target day was not allowed to remove her plate or carry food to the TV set. Cathy, of course, had a tantrum that the family ignored, and she did not eat dinner that night. The tantrum was repeated the next day, but Cathy did eat some food at the table before quickly running back to her dolls and television cartoons.

Daily telephone conversations reinforced the parents for maintaining the limits they had set, and in only four days Cathy was eating a hasty, sometimes incomplete, meal at the table and in company with her family. Gradually, over the next five months, the parents used the mealtime setting to increase the time period Cathy remained with her family and to shape increased attention and verbal interaction. TV viewing immediately following dinner became contingent upon the duration and later the quality of her mealtime behavior. Eventually in this sequence verbal praise and tokens were also used as reinforcers. By June, five months after this mealtime sequence, the evening meal was a calm and pleasant situation in which Cathy participated, interacting verbally with the family. By maintaining the reinforcing contingencies, the parents next taught Cathy to help set and clear the table, thereby extending her cooperative interaction to both before and after the mealtime and enabling her to interact appropriately with them nearly an hour each day.

Two weeks after the mealtime sequence was begun, the parents began focusing on her hitting behavior. A similar procedure was used: Cathy was informed each day for a week that hitting would no longer be tolerated and that whichever dolls were used to hit people would be taken from her and thrown away. On the target day the first time she hit her mother with a doll she was again reminded of the clear contingency. In a short time she again attacked her mother; the doll was immediately taken away from her. Over the next few days this was repeated with another two dolls. The behavior then ceased and the parents began reinforcing alternatives for the hitting-when-upset. With the more violent hitting under better control, Cathy's mother and sister began entering into her doll play, reinforcing her talking to the family members and working to break up her intense preoccupation with the dolls.

Firm limits were gradually applied to the doll-playing. For example, when finished playing she had to clean up her toys. Previously, they had remained strewn around the living room or lined up against the front door. Touching or moving them, as when vacuuming the floor or answering the door, precipitated her usual violent reaction. Again the contingencies were made clear; a daily clean-up time was specified and any dolls remaining were to be thrown away.

Because she had already experienced having dolls thrown away Cathy did not test these limits. By bringing her doll-play under better control and limiting her use (and misuse) of rooms, many of the stimuli for conflicts were removed, and the number of tantrums decreased.

Similar limits were gradually applied to other examples of her surplus behavior, such as: (1) going into closets or drawers and throwing their contents around, which particularly distressed her teenage sister, (2) tantrums in stores, and (3) screaming.

Within four months (i.e., by May 1968) the more violent surplus behaviors were reduced, and the parents began to reinforce systematically adaptive alternatives, such as greater and better verbalizing, cooperative behavior, helping around the house, playing without violence or tantrums, demonstrating self-care, and socially interacting. By the fall, seven months after the home programs had begun, Cathy was again a more responsive, pleasant cooperative girl. There were still occasional tantrums, but not as severe or frequent, and her adaptive behavior still needed some polishing. To help in the more subtle behavior, the token reward system that had been operating successfully in school was extended to the home. The parents were coached in its application, and Cathy was happy at the chance to earn even more tokens at home. The tokens earned both at home and in school could be cashed in at either place, thus taking advantage of a wide choice of back-up reinforcers. In November, Cathy was told that the Christmas presents she had requested would be contingent upon tokens—50 tokens per present!

Cathy's behavior continued to improve and Christmas was very successful for the family that year. After Christmas, the tokens at home were faded out and gradually replaced by more social reinforcers, such as outings with the family to a McDonald's hamburger stand, a favorite of Cathy's. Thus by Christmas 1968, Cathy's severe regression had been reversed, and she was again operating on the high social level of a year earlier. In effect, she had lost a year. That she was able to regain her previous level was due in large part to continued efforts of her parents in their careful administration of the home program. Follow-up information over the next three years (to 1972) indicated continued social and academic development, and no further regressions.

Dori

At five-and-a-half years of age Dori was a non-talking, extremely hyperactive, aggressive child who exhibited grotesque posturing. During her frequent aggressive outbursts she jumped, kicked and punched anyone near, punched her own face until it was severely bruised, and pulled out handfuls of hair, creating a large bald spot. Her vocalizations during these episodes consisted of loud, nasal hooting and a horrendously loud roaring—one observer noted it "sounded like a lion in a subway tunnel."

While standing still, Dori would posture in grotesque positions (which could not be matched by staff when they tried them). All of her movements were awkward and rigid. Her behavior was so intensely disruptive that she was expelled from the cerebral palsy agency where she had been attending a daily group. Local pediatricians saw her as cerebral palsied and psychotic, and a psychologist found her to be completely untestable.

In an effort to obtain more definitive information and treatment, Dori's parents took her to a well-known children's hospital for two weeks of intensive diagnostic examinations. She was diagnosed as having diffuse brain damage and described as cerebral palsied, mentally retarded and psychotic. She was noted to be "an extraordinarily hyperactive child (who) certainly provided ample evidence of the desire to bite herself as well as people about her at every opportunity."

The two weeks of hospitalization and tests proved to be very disturbing to Dori, and surplus and deficit behavior seemed to have been intensified. Dori's parents described the four-hour drive back from the hospital as "a nightmare." Dori roared and hooted, threw herself around the back seat, slapped, punched, "dug into" and bit herself, pulled her hair, attacked both parents with feet, fists, nails and teeth, and tried several times to jump out of the car. By the time they reached home they were all scratched and bruised, and the parents were severely frightened by the child's new intensity.

Dori's violent behavior persisted over the next several weeks. A psychiatrist was consulted and prescribed tranquilizers and psychotherapy. Five months later, recognizing that there had been no improvement in her, he referred Dori to us with the recommendation that she be enrolled in a full-day program.

As there were no openings in any of our regular groups at that time it was decided to admit Dori to a pre-admission group for behavioral assessments and to train and supervise the parents in behavior modification programs at home. Although Dori was to be admitted to our program at the first opening, because of our program's disruption, an opening did not occur until more than a year later. Thus for the next thirteen months the major therapeutic work with this severely disturbed girl was carried out at home by the parents.

Parent training began in January 1967, six months after Dori's return from the hospital. For the first three weeks of training the parents met with their therapy supervisor once weekly for three-to-four-hour sessions. These meetings were used to teach the parents to focus on Dori's (and their own) behavior, to describe clearly the behavior and to sensitize them to the conditions immediately preceding and following the behavior observed. Every day, on an hourly basis, they recorded all Dori's behavior in a looseleaf notebook. From this, a clear picture of behavior patterns began to emerge. By the third week they were observing and recording increasingly specific behaviors, noting duration and making judgments about intensity. They were tracking specific conditions, such as signs of impending blow-ups, points at which targeted behavior increased in intensity and duration, their own conduct related to that behavior, and the prevailing atmosphere both immediately preceding and following the targeted behavior.

Dori's major surplus behaviors occurred frequently and often simultaneously. She grimaced, gestured, and rocked, assumed grotesque postures, all the while loudly hooting, roaring, screeching, attacking herself and others while (three or four times daily) defecating and urinating in her clothing. During the first several weeks the parents' daily narratives indicated severe levels of these surplus behaviors occurring during all Dori's waking hours.

The data gathered surprised the parents. For example, although they had reported some speech and some cooperative behavior, once they began to observe and record Dori's behavior they found over a three-week period *no* speech and far less cooperative behavior than they had estimated. A typical behavior that showed up clearly in their observation notes but not earlier in their retrospective reports related to Dori's eating. At suppertime, one of her presumably more cooperative periods, Dori did not sit at the table with the family, but walked around it grabbing fists full of food from the various plates. If not interfered with, she remained relatively quiet, and the family could complete their meal. Their overall perception of mealtime as peaceful led to their retrospective report of Dori's behavior as relatively good then and presenting no particular difficulty. Once they began making more specific observations, however, the social deficits associated with mealtime became very clear.

From their observations, a typical day was described as follows: Awakening on her own between 6:00 and 7:00 A.M. Dori immediately begins screaming and rushes into her parents' room where she attacks them, punching, kicking, scratching, biting, and screaming wildly. The parents' attempts to soothe and console her, or to restrict her by sending her to her own room, all fail. If she is sent out of their room, Dori screams louder, slams doors and rushes back in with even more intensity. A battle rages in the parents' room every morning and escalates to the point where the parents are shouting, Dori is screaming and finally is spanked hard several times. The spankings do not calm her. By 8:00 the father, angered and irritated after more than an hour of battle, leaves for work. By now exhausted, Dori often falls asleep for a few minutes, only to resume her screaming attacks on her mother when she awakens.

In the meantinme, Dori's mother has prepared breakfast, often while trying to fend off the still-attacking child. Breakfast time is a continuation of the battle. The child refuses to eat by herself, but nevertheless fights her mother's attempts to feed her. The scene, as her mother describes it, is noisy and chaotic: "I finally blow my stack and Dori screams even more. A good half-hour of this . . . . In between screaming and fighting and getting up and sitting down, and throwing food and spitting it out and gagging, (Dori) manages to eat something."

Shortly after breakfast, tired from the ordeal, Dori dozes on her bed until about 9:30, giving her mother a brief respite for cleaning up the kitchen.

About 9:30 Dori awakens screaming, seeks out her mother, and resumes the battle. For the remainder of the morning she follows her mother, screams, hits herself and her mother, throws herself on the floor against the walls and windows (she twice crashed through the windows, severely cutting her wrists and arms). The child does not play with toys, look at books or watch television. Her behavior consists of constant screaming and attacks on herself and mother, interspersed with brief periods of rest while she "catches her breath." Later, when medication was prescribed, (atarax and phenobarbital) the effect was to increase the duration of her drowsy and relatively quiet periods, giving her mother more respite. The medication did not alter her behavior otherwise.

About mid-morning Dori and her mother engage in another specific conflict, this time focused on dressing. Dori will neither dress herself nor cooperate with her mother's attempts. Her mother puts a blouse on the child who screams and rips it off, the "buttons flying in all directions." Some minor disarray, such as an untied shoelace or opened button, precipitates more screaming and ripping off of clothes. Within about a half hour the child is dressed, often at the cost of several torn pieces of clothing. Once dressed, Dori chews on her clothes, making holes in them and frequently tears them off. By mid-day she is in considerable disarray, and several articles of clothing are damaged.

Lunch is a repetition of breakfast. Following that, a 15 to 20 minute conflict occurs as Dori's mother tries to calm her enough to take a nap. Dori sleeps soundly for two to two-and-a-half hours, only to awaken screaming. She resumes her violent behavior which persists for the remainder of the afternoon. Her mother's attempts to calm her, to interest her in toys or books or to take a walk fail. Whether at home or walking outside, Dori's behavior is the same. They can neither visit others nor have visitors, nor can they do anything so normal as ride in the car or go shopping. Dori's mother is forced to contend with the bizarre, aggressive behavior all day, given respite only by Dori's naps and drowsy periods.

Her father returns from work at about 5:00 P.M. . . . to face the still-screaming, aggressive child and his harried, fatigued, literally beaten and bruised wife. Dori attacks him immediately on his return. He tries to contend with her for about half an hour, giving his wife some opportunity to prepare supper. This usually results in Dori's being spanked and sent to her room, where she stays briefly, but then returns to renew her attacks.

Suppertime, while quieter, is still tense and filled with conflict. Dori uses no utensils, but snatches food with her hands and requires spoon feeding by her parents. During supper there are usually no major tantrums; rather, as described by the parents, it is a period of prolonged misery with "a lot of hollering" as the parents try to teach her more acceptable mealtime behavior. Dori is corrected by being frequently yelled at, having her hands slapped and her bottom spanked.

Shortly after supper, by about 6:30, Dori's mother bathes and readies the child for bed. At this time, Dori is "withdrawn, seems tired and couldn't care less." However, dressing her in pajamas often precipitates a violent outburst, usually resulting in her father's entering, demanding her cooperation, sometimes spanking her and forcibly putting the child in bed. Once in bed her screaming continues. She gets up several times and is often spanked and forced back into bed.

Finally, Dori falls asleep. She sleeps poorly, awakening often and getting out of bed. The parents' sleep each night is frequently interrupted.

The next morning, between six and seven o'clock, Dori awakens, begins screaming, and another day begins.

The Home Program: Dori. None of Dori's severe behavior was new or different in kind, but had been present for much of her six years. The new aspect since her two-week hospitalization six months earlier was the enormously escalated nature of the behavior. Her bizarre and aggressive surpluses had increased in frequency, intensity and duration. Her deficits had deepened. For example, prior to the hospitalization Dori spoke a few words and could be at least tolerated in a group at the cerebral palsy agency. After the hospitalization, she did not speak at all and was so disruptive that she was expelled from the agency's program.

When I first saw Dori most of one forearm was bandaged because of severe cuts sustained when she crashed through a window. Her face was puffed and bruised, particularly the sides of her jaw, where she repeatedly punched herself, and the mouth, where she pulled the corners with considerable force. On her head where she had pulled out her hair was a bald spot nearly three inches in diameter and several smaller bald areas. Bruises and scratches dotted her body. Dori was a battered child, and only a few moments of observation were necessary to know that the battering was self-administered. Dori's mother too showed many bruises and scratches, particularly on her arms and face.

Violence had become a constant element in the family's life; there were virtually no interactions with Dori that did not include violence. Moreover, the complex chains of violence of the child and parents was reciprocally escalating.

The child's attacks raised the parents' excitement and anger, their alternative behavior, such as trying to calm, understand, or tolerate extinguished. Only two classes of parental responses were reinforced: (1) giving in and letting the child have her own way (for example, it was easier to let Dori eat with her hands than to try and correct her) and (2) spanking and shouting, which at least sometimes resulted in a cessation of her aggressive attacks and even a brief retreat to her room. In their own desperation, the parents alternated between tolerating and giving-in to her bizarre aggression, which probably led to its intermittent reinforcement, and lashing back with their own punishment, which was reinforced by its brief moderating effects on the child.

Although Dori had severe deficit and surplus behaviors, it was clear that the most urgent task was to reduce the violence in the family. Accordingly, the first behaviors to be modified were along the dimension of violence.

Reducing the parents' aggressive behavior toward the child was not difficult. We discussed the possible effects of their aggressive behavior toward Dori: (1) With all of their spanking, her behavior had not improved and in fact had worsened. (2) The spankings served frequently to anger Dori and escalate her own aggressive behavior. (3) Their shouting and spanking might serve as potent models for Dori to imitate. Thus, it was reasonable to eliminate the spankings.

The parents were advised to move from overt violence (spankings) of the child to a tactic of restraining her. They were coached to respond to Dori's violent attacks by holding her wrists and forcibly preventing her hitting, kicking or biting the parents. While preventing the blows, they were to repeat forcefully, "Dori, no! We don't kick (or bite, hit, etc.)." Frustrated, Dori fought hard against the restraint. As she tired and began slowing down, the parents verbally reinforced that behavior with such phrases as "Good job," "That's right," "Calm down." Dori's parents were being taught one of our group's methods for reducing aggressive behavior, as described in Chapter 7.

The parents' aggressive behavior was modified by simple verbal instruction. In addition, they became adept at substituting physical restraint for their former hitting. Within a week, Dori's behavior began to change. On the first day of the program her attacks and struggles increased in intensity, probably because of the frustration in being restrained and in not landing many blows successfully. Her production of bizarre sounds increased markedly. On the second day of this program Dori awoke and attacked her sleeping parents as usual. They held her wrists and repeated, "We don't hit." Their struggle continued from about 7:00 A.M. to nearly 8:30, during which time Dori screamed and struggled against the restraint which was apparently quite noxious to her. Whenever she began to slow down, the parents released her hands; as was predicted, Dori immediately tried to punch them again. After nearly one hour Dori echoed the phrase "Don't hit," but it did not affect her hitting behavior. About 20 minutes later Dori had calmed enough to be released and for the first time in six months she ate breakfast in a calm state. The remainder of the day was as difficult as any previous days, but the apparent success of this tactic after only one day was highly reinforcing for the parents. Dori's echoing of "Don't hit" and her later calm eating of breakfast were obvious changes. Regardless of how trivial they might appear here, at that time for the parents they were the first positive signs in more than half a year.

In the next two days Dori again repeated, "Calm down" and on the fourth day while battling her mother, her echo "Calm down" was immediately followed by an actual decrease in intensity.

The fifth day of the program was Dori's first "good day" since before her hospitalization more than six months previously. That day she had no tantrums, no attacks on parents, and was heard to echo many words and phrases. The next two days were mixed, with several tantrums and attacks, but at a lower frequency, intensity, and duration. When the parents returned for our discussion session after one week (daily telephone contact had been maintained all week) they were extremely pleased and obviously had been highly reinforced by their own successes.

In the next several weeks Dori continued to improve. Her tantrums and attacks had been reduced and mimicking words and phrases had increased. With the rapid reduction of tantrum and aggressive behavior, it was possible to begin teaching alternative behaviors. Accordingly, her mother was trained to initiate a positive social interaction dimension of training in which she maintained calm, pleasant, direct behavior with Dori. They sat together, looking at picture books, watching television, playing with the dog, and playing little infant games. These sessions were always brief, never more than ten minutes, and designed to include as much positive reinforcement as possible. The reinforcers were the nearness of the mother, food and the activities themselves.

As Dori's attacks on her parents continued to diminish, there was an accompanying increase in aggressive behavior toward the dog (i.e., she apparently imitated the parents' swatting the animal with newspapers as they tried to train it) and in imitation of the violent behavior she was watching on television. A judicious monitoring of TV programs was begun with no violent shows allowed, and the parents' own behavior of swatting the dog with newspaper was stopped. With these models removed, Dori's aggressive behavior decreased still further.

Within two months aggressive behavior had markedly diminished and there were many periods each day of pleasant interaction with her parents. Her tantrums and attacks on objects still occurred daily at a low level, but attacks on her parents had nearly ceased. With longer periods of good interaction each day Dori was gradually introduced to settings outside the home, such as walks up the street, visiting relatives, riding in the car and going into stores. Within ten weeks Dori's aggressive behavior had been markedly reduced, as had, though less dramatically, her screaming, gesturing and posturing. In addition, the facial bruises had cleared up and the bald spots were disappearing.

The parents reported an increasing number of good days in which Dori had no tantrums or battles and appeared relaxed all day. While the three-week baseline had revealed no good days, the subsequent weeks showed an increase to three such days in the ninth and tenth week. These breaks of calm behavior in the former pattern of unrelenting aggression were powerfully reinforcing for the parents.

After ten weeks in which aggressive behavior had been reduced and positive interaction and generalized control increased, two more dimensions were added to the program: Pre-Academic behavior and, two weeks later, Language Development.

The *Pre-Academic* dimension consisted simply of shaping attentive and cooperative behavior in brief 10 to 15 minute sessions. The parent and child "played school" every day much as we had done with our focal group (see Chapter 6). They sat at a specific table, with a large chalkboard and used clay, paints, and crayons.

For the language development dimension, the parents demanded more speech. They stopped reinforcing non-verbal communication and reinforced use of language promptly and lavishly. Dori began to use more single words and brief phrases, but interestingly only whispered them. Later in the program the parents focused on increasing the volume.

The work at home continued and the parents reported continuing success. Dori's tantrums and aggressive behavior had decreased, her speech was improving, she was interacting cooperatively with adults and children and, for the first time in her life, she was showing affectionate behavior. Dori was enjoying outings to stores, beaches, parks and the zoo, visiting relatives, looking at books, and becoming increasingly involved in small-muscle pre-academic activities. Overall, she was far less irritable, more alert, cooperative and interactive, and family life in general had vastly improved.

The parents worked at home with Dori for just over a year (January 1967 to February 1968) before we were able to add the child to our group.

There are innumerable descriptive details which could be presented about Dori's development, and perhaps at another time they will be given in a case study. At present, I would like to mention one incident. Dori had been speaking with increasing rate and complexity, but after six months still refused to talk above a whisper. One morning she and her mother were playing with their dog. Imitating her mother, Dori was giving a variety of commands to the animal (sit, shake hands), but because she was whispering softly, the dog was not responding appropriately. Alert for ways to shape louder speech, her mother remarked that the dog could not hear her and that Dori would have to speak louder. Caught up in the playing, Dori did speak louder, repeating "Sit, sit down" in a nearly normal voice. Fortunately, the dog obeyed immediately. Dori became ecstatic according to her mother, clapped her hands, laughed, and repeated more commands, many of which were obeyed by the dog. Obviously, the dog's response to her spoken command was powerfully reinforcing for Dori. After that fortunate incident Dori spoke more frequently in a normal volume. She still whispered much of the time, particularly out of the home or with non-family persons, but the characteristic whispering had been broken up by the dog's highly reinforcing behavior.

Summary: Dori. For 13 months Dori's total therapy or training program was carried out at home by her parents under our supervision. The parents worked along five major dimensions of behavior utilizing programming methods which included behavioral analyses, specific environmental structuring, application of reinforcers, and monitoring of behavior change. As the program continued, it became increasingly complex in two ways: (1) each dimension required increasingly complex behaviors, both of Dori and her parents; (2) the total program became more complex as each successive dimension was added.

The five major dimensions of training, in their order of introduction, were:

1. Aggression
2. Positive social interaction
3. Generalization of control
4. Pre-Academic behavior
5. Language

1. Aggression. This dimension was aimed at the *decrement* of aggressive behavior. The steps along the dimension were: (a) removal of all aggressive models; (b) physical restraint; (c) immediate reinforcement for calming down; (d) immediate reinforcement for verbalizing behavior rules like "We don't hit;" (e) reinforcement for increasingly lengthy periods of calm behavior while parents held Dori's hands (it should be noted that at this point the second dimension was initiated and operated in conjunction with the first as it continued); (f) differential reinforcement, i.e., restraint when behavior is aggressive toward self or others, no restraint when it is innocuous, such as slapping the table top, mild

reward when presumably tension-reducing, such as punching a pillow, bouncing on her bed; (g) specific relaxation training; (h) reciprocal inhibition, i.e., instructing Dori to relax when mild tension or impending upset is observed.

2. Positive-Social Interaction. This dimension was initiated after step (e) above when Dori had learned to remain calm for periods of about ten minutes while her hands were held by her mother. This dimension proceeded as follows: (a) sit quietly with Dori, hold her hands gently, talk softly to her; (b) gradually lessen and momentarily release hold on her hands while directing her attention to picture books, a quiet TV program, telling her a story, etc.; (c) the father begins (a) and (b); (d) reinforce longer quiet periods together without holding her hands, and by manipulating her hands, begin directing her use of objects; (e) begin similar sequences in other situations, i.e., reinforcing Dori for "helping" around the house. The emphasis here is on social cooperation and positive use of hands. At this point, the third behavior dimension was introduced; (f, etc.) continue adding more settings at home and lengthening them, in which child-parent interaction proceeds in a pleasant, calm manner.

3. Generalizing Control. As the first two dimensions proceeded it became clear that the parents and Dori were gaining greater control over a variety of cooperative social behaviors. They were, however, limited to the home and interactions with the immediate family. It was necessary to generalize this control to other settings and people. This dimension proceeded as follows: (a) take a walk together around the apartment; (b) walk downstairs and in front of the house; (c) walk around the neighborhood but not in other houses; (d) sit in the car together, then gradually take rides; (e) take a ride to the beach, a park or other area where there are few people; (f) ride to relative's house, stop only briefly, talk and return home; (g) have relative accompany them on ride; (h, etc.) the dimension proceeds to add increasingly social situations, such as spending a day at grandmother's house, going shopping, playing outside in the presence of other children, in which controlled behavior is reinforced. Later in this sequence in the program's fourth month, partly as a "test" of its success, a birthday party with 12 children was held for Dori. She behaved well, had no tantrums or fights, interacted nicely though on a very simple level, and maintained "a very happy, good mood" all afternoon. Her bahavior that day was on a considerably higher level than even before her hospitalization.

4. Pre-Academic Behavior. This dimension depended on the prior development of periods of calm interaction between child and parent, in which they could focus on some task. A school setting of a small table and two chairs was created, designated as "all Dori's," and used for the pre-academic training. The sequence here was not as specified as the other dimensions and it consisted of gradually lengthening periods of use of pre- and early-school materials. Gradually

the mother introduced a variety of Lotto, which required matching pictures and letters and word recognition. Dori's use of the chalkboard began with making large circles and lines, and then to forming letters and words. Many of these activities, particularly use of clay, picture puzzles, and a ball-point pen, were very reinforcing activities for Dori.

5. Language. There was already a fair amount of support for language development in the previous dimensions. However, until this dimension was specifically initiated, language development was secondary, incidental to the other training sequences. This language dimension, based primarily on the success of the first four, began with: (a) a generally increased and clearly-spoken modeling of speech for Dori; (b) much prompting and reinforcement for appropriate use of speech at all opportunities; (c) higher and consistent demands for speech, i.e., differential reinforcement, such as ignoring non-verbal requests of pointing, grunting or pulling, while responding to speech approximations; (d) prompting and support of normal volume in speech; (e) reinforcement of gradual increase in rate of speech and in a variety of settings. The language in this dimension was limited to spoken language (reading was to be developed later in school) and included much practice in practical, everyday use of language.

TIME RELATIONSHIPS AMONG THE BEHAVIOR DIMENSIONS

The five behavior dimensions in this home program were applied successively with each previous dimension continuing when the later ones were initiated. The program thus began with one dimension, Aggressive Behavior, and ultimately consisted of five simultaneously operating dimensions. As each successive dimension was initiated the program became increasingly complex, requiring more skill and time of the parents. Figure 4 shows the five dimensions and time relationships among them.

The home program, exclusive of initial interviews and retrospective reports by parents, operated for eight months, January to August, under our close weekly supervision. By August, Dori's behavior had improved markedly in all dimensions, and, according to the parents, she was functioning at a higher level than ever before.

Beginning in September, the parents' major task was to maintain the behavior gains, and our supervision was reduced to monthly meetings. In February 1968, 13 months after the parents' home program had begun, Dori was admitted to our school program where she remained for the next year and a half (to June 1969). At its termination, she was enrolled in a private school for children with learning disabilities.

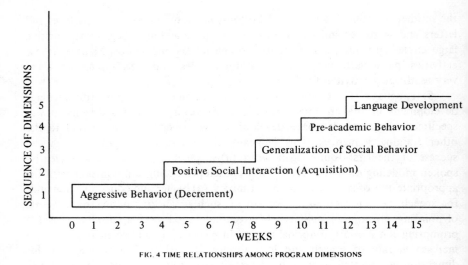

FIG. 4 TIME RELATIONSHIPS AMONG PROGRAM DIMENSIONS

CONCLUSIONS

All of the parents in our program were involved to some degree in carrying out home training programs for their children. The three cases presented in this chapter illustrate varying degrees of parent participation. The chapter also describes our own parent training attempts. For the work of other investigators, the reader is referred to the literature review by Berkowitz and Graziano (1972), which discusses some 30 papers on parent training and reports work with 179 children published from 1959 through 1971. The reviewers reported that a variety of parent training approaches has been applied to virtually all child problem behaviors. The children were primarily boys and in nearly all cases: (1) the mothers were the primary objects of training and bore the major responsibility for carrying out the home programs; (2) training consisted primarily of operant approaches, and (3) the home programs were aimed mostly at reduction of maladaptive surplus. Except for the direct treatment of enuresis, respondent paradigms were rare.

Parents were trained individually and in groups, through lectures, assigned readings, programmed materials, group discussions, modeling and direct coaching. Some of the training devices used were telephones, video and audio tapes, films, wireless communication, hand, sound and light signals.

Most of the reports, like our own in the present chapter, were descriptive case studies lacking sufficient controls. The body of the literature as a whole can be criticized for design limitations, such as inadequate controls and measurements, limited followups, poor evaluative techniques, as well as a general lack of details on training methods and parent and child behavioral changes. However, no one paper reviewed suffered from all of the methodological flaws, and many were sophisticated and controlled (Wahler, Winkel, Peterson & Morrison, 1965; Hawkins, Peterson, Schweid and Bijou, 1966; Wetzel, Baker, Roney & Martin, 1966; Hanf, 1968; Risley, 1968; Bernal, 1969; Johnson and Brown, 1969). The most complete and the largest scale parent training programs were reported in a series of papers by Gerald R. Patterson, 1971 and his associates; and by Leopold Walder *et al.*, 1972.

In light of the available evidence, there is little doubt that behavioral techniques can be applied to children's problem behaviors through the training of their parents. The direct and practical coping with the everyday realities of the disorganized family's situation may be an important therapeutic need not traditionally met by most child therapists.

The behavior therapist's emphasis on learning includes not only learning that occurs during therapy sessions, but also during the vastly more powerful and larger periods which make up the child's natural environment (Tharp and Wetzel, 1969). Thus, the behavior therapist finds himself concerned with details of the child's home or school and helping various important adults to become actively involved in the therapy attempts. For the therapist to move out into his client's real world is not a new idea—Witmer did this in his work with children starting in 1896 (see Brotemarkle, 1931). What is new is that the behavior therapist now has some systematic and objective ways of evaluating and modifying the child's behavior and environment. Additionally, like Witmer, many behavior therapists operate on the assumption that it is important to share professional knowledge and techniques in order to teach others to bring about and maintain improved behavior in the child. There are many moral and ethical aspects to this sharing of responsibility by the professional, but little written about those issues (Berkowitz and Graziano, 1972). In our own work we have maintained a position that the parents, by virtue of being parents, have assumed the major moral, ethical and legal responsibility for their children. The parents typically, but not always, have the greatest degree of contact with the children, the greatest concern over and personal investment in their welfare, and the greatest control over their immediate environment. We have found that parents are typically both willing and capable of assuming active roles and carrying out detailed and direct measures to help their children. Therefore, our task was not to accept the full burden of treatment and in the process allow parents to relinquish their responsibility. Rather, we maintained an emphasis on helping parents to be more effective in carrying out their own responsibility to help their children (Graziano, 1971).

In order to enter into a shared responsibility with parents the therapist must be willing to give up some of the mystical dazzle of an aloof expertise. The responsibility, we believe, must be shared and the parents must be actively involved as co-therapists in a very literal way.

CHAPTER 10

The Fourth Year

INTRODUCTION

In its fourth year, our program was moved to a newly-constructed center for retarded children where we had access to new group rooms, play areas, a swimming pool, and a wide variety of recreational and academic material. In addition to these comfortable facilities, we were well-financed through federal and state grants and contracts.

Four groups operated during the academic year (plus the additional six summer camp groups): (a) the focal group consisting of six children, (b) the young group of four children diagnosed as autistic, (c) the after school group of four public school children, and (d) a one-morning-per-week pre-admission group of four to six children who were being evaluated for eventual program placement.

The focal group and young group arrived at 8:30 A.M. and remained together until about 9:00 when the focal group moved into its classroom and the younger children stayed in the large playroom. These ten children also interacted again during the recess and snack time. Some of the younger children remained for lunch while others left just prior to lunch. By 2:00 all younger children had left, the focal group had completed its academic session, and the after-school group of four children began to arrive and interact with the focal group. By 3:00 the focal group had left, after more than six hours, and the public school children remained together until about 5:00.

The focal group now consisted of Freddie, Frankie, Cathy, Gerry, Billy, and a new boy, Allan. Mary would have brought the group to seven, but her parents had died in an automobile accident several months earlier and, with no one to care for her, she was admitted to a state institution with the expectation of permanent institutionalization.

Allan was an extremely difficult management problem, an intensified version of Billy of three years earlier. Would the expanded focal group be cohesive enough to both tolerate Allan's grotesque behavior and provide an organized social learning framework to help him develop higher levels of social behavior? We assumed that the other five children had already achieved significant social learning and were operating as a sufficiently coherent, organized, and cooperative group to tolerate bizarre behaviors which the children themselves had previously exhibited, and that they could serve as a therapeutic framework for a new child who appeared to be at least as disruptive and bizarre as Billy had been. These assumptions made heavy demands on the children, adding a large measure of therapeutic responsibility for one another, and severely testing the group's strength, cohesion, and power to shape adaptive behavior. In essence, we viewed this coming fourth year as a test of our previous assumptions and work; if the children developed during the year as we hoped, we could begin facing the next phase of our programming, moving them out to more normal or age-appropriate settings, such as special class placement in public schools. The suggestion that we might actually be coming close to achieving long range goals for some of these children whose prognoses had been so severely pessimistic was both exciting and highly reinforcing. Unfortunately, as will be seen, our excited anticipation was premature and with growing distress we saw the fourth year end in disorganization and dissolution of the program.

PROGRAM STRUCTURE

A. *Transition and Free-Play Period.* The six focal group children arrived at 8:30 A.M. and, in the same playroom as the young children, played quiet games, looked at books, drew pictures, played with the younger children, or talked quietly with staff or each other, making their own choices from a variety of activities. If anyone requested help from or interaction with a staff member, it was given; otherwise, they were left alone. As the year continued, this first period of the day became increasingly social and verbal.

B. *Relaxation Practice.* At approximately 9:00 A.M. the children moved to "the quiet spot," a separated area where relaxation exercises that had been developed over the previous year were carried out for several minutes. The children then lined up at the classroom door and, at a signal from the teacher, quietly moved into the classroom and to their seats. At first lining up was necessary as part of the structured, programmed, *small-step* sequencing that allowed much immediate rewarding and enabled the children to learn and anticipate the sequence easily. Later in the year, when the sequenced steps were much larger, lining up was dispensed with, and the children went directly into the classroom as each one finished relaxation.

The relaxation exercises ("relax time") served as a transition from physically active to quieter activities. Thus, the children practiced relaxation prior to entering each of the two academic sessions, prior to and after a walk or a trip, and at the end of the day prior to leaving. (It was important to return them to their parents in as calm a condition as possible.) We observed that frequent repetitions of relax time at carefully chosen points in the activity sequences apparently served to inhibit accumulation of tensions and helped maintain generally relaxed social interacting. Controlled research on the effects of periodically interpolated relaxation exercises for overactive children is needed. We can report our consistent observations that during the fourth year, excepting Allan, high excitability and frequent blowups were extremely rare, behavior was most calm during and immediately following relaxation exercises, and an apparent build-up of excitement and uncontrolled behavior in Allan would usually be interrupted and dissipated during relax time.

After repeated association with high reinforcement for relaxed behavior the quiet spot acquired stimulus control over that behavior and was effectively used as a contingency following disruptive outbursts. When Allan, for example, became disruptive, he would be removed from the class (time-out from social reinforcement) and sent to the quiet spot to calm down (stimulus control of relaxing behavior by the quiet spot cues). Reported observations suggested that this was an effective way of reducing disruptive behavior and teaching more appropriate, calmer alternatives.

C. *The Academic Session.* School sessions proceeded much as in the previous year, and with even greater progress. One teacher instructed the six children, who were now able to work increasingly independently of her. The two daily school sessions were expanded to approximately 70 minutes each and the academic work was generally on a higher and more consistent level. Cathy, Billy and Allan used a third-grade reader and Frankie, Freddie and Gerry used first and second-grade readers.

The classroom sequence, as in the previous year, usually included a pledge of allegiance, roll call, a check of the calendar, the time, temperature and weather conditions. Each child recorded this information in his own notebook. The children were then divided into two groups of three for seat work on individually-prepared programmed material and work with the teacher. After about half an hour, they all came together again for a whole class project. Each school session demanded appropriate behavior and moving on to the next sequenced activity, such as snack or recess, was contingent on completion of the assigned lessons.

At the end of the first school session, the children joined the younger group and the rest of the staff for a snack, followed by an outdoor recess. These periods lasted approximately 30 minutes. Another relaxation period followed and the children returned to the classroom for their second school session which continued another hour, until about 12:35.

By the end of this fourth year, school sessions totalled more than two and a half hours daily (see Fig. 2, Chapter 6). Each child received much attention, working for about 20 to 30 minutes with the teacher in the small groups of three, and another half hour with programmed material that had been specifically designed for him. The remaining hour or hour and a half was devoted to various class exercises and projects. In addition, each child received 20 to 30 minutes of individual tutoring during the day.

By the end of the fourth year, the duration of the academic sessions, academic level, cooperative behavior, as well as independent work had significantly increased, and the school group was far advanced over the brief and uncertain sessions begun in the second year.

D. *The Afternoon Programs.* After the second school session a brief recess and lunch were followed by various activities to widen the children's normal social experiences. We visited parks and playgrounds, museums, the zoo, a wildlife sanctuary, stores, restaurants, and even other schools. Weather permitting, there were three or four trips weekly. On the other days the children remained at school, using both the classroom and the large playroom to create a variety of social and group and individual academic settings. Toward the end of the afternoon program, the children interacted with the public school children who were arriving for their after-school program.

BEHAVIOR CHANGES DURING THE FOURTH YEAR

The fourth year opened with considerable staff excitement over our observations that we were approaching some of the long-term behavioral goals for the children. Much had happened during the past three complex years and, considering successes and failures, the children showed unmistakable progress. The initial goals, such as increasing general response rate and shaping simple approach behavior, decreasing aggressive and bizarre surplus behavior, teaching speech, encouraging simple social cooperation and beginning academics, had clearly been achieved. In addition, some of the later, more complex goals of sustained social cooperation, increased verbal interaction and flexibility of behavior—in general, greater social competence—were also seen as emerging.

The staff had labored to create a variety of behavior modification systems aimed at the behavioral goals already discussed. Those systems seemed to have been effective in modifying a variety of discrete and general behavior. Now, standing at the beginning of the fourth year, the staff saw as its major task the continued application of those modification systems, but with the added dimension of integrating their effects; the children had been taught to respond in a variety of ways—simple approach, control of aggressive and bizarre behavior, speech and reading, writing, drawing, social cooperation and so on, but, as remarked in one of our staff meetings at the beginning of the fourth year, *"Now, can we put it all together?"*

The fourth year, then, was of crucial importance. It was planned essentially to continue the same modification systems but with greater focus on complex social behavior in more normal social settings and on increasing flexibility and independence by the children.

1. Continued emergence of the group. As the focal group developed, particularly toward the end of the third year, there were many indications of developing perception of a group entity. The children, for example, referred to "our" school and "our" teacher. They indicated concern when a child was absent and often expressed a sense of group accomplishment. When visiting parks and playgrounds they answered pleasantries from strangers explaining, "He's in *our* class," or "We're from the SEDMIC school." In relation to children and staff in other programs in other parts of the building, the children clearly operated as a loose, but nonetheless real unit.

From repeated observation, we inferred the children's growing awareness of the size and organization of the social world. For example, they all showed interest in visitors, asking questions about each visitor's identity and purpose in being at the school. One day, Frankie was obviously puzzled, when the teacher announced, "We have a visitor today. This is Father Quinn." Frankie apparently thought about this for a moment and then, his face lighting up as he seemed to place the priest in some understandable social order, he exclaimed loudly, and much to the visitor's amusement, "Oh, a *daddy*!"

Cathy invariably asked about the marital and maternal status of female visitors ("Are you married?" "Do you have any children?"). During the third year, after a week or two in which Cathy had been obviously identifying and sorting out appropriate social roles and behavior gathered from observations at home and at school, she asked Jeff, who had been working closely with her for a year, "And Jeff, where do *you* work?"

In the emerging organization of her world Cathy had identified mothers and female school teachers as those responsible for child care. Fathers, however, went to work. My own role also corresponded to her model, for as she pointed out, I was "the boss." Frequently there early in the morning to meet with the

226 Child Without Tomorrow

staff and to greet the arriving children, I often left the group by 9:30 (to work with younger children, meet with parents, etc.) returning early in the afternoon. Apparently for Cathy, I, like other men, "went to work."

But how to explain this male group worker, obviously an important member of the group, and yet who stayed there all day? Hence, the reasonable question to ask one of our most important staff was, "And, Jeff, where do *you* work?"

2. Reactions to additional group members. Responding to one another as members of the same group had increased during the third year and, we assumed, had developed to a high enough level to allow us to return Billy and add Allan without disrupting the group's functioning. In Billy's case this was easily achieved. Although in a different group for the previous two years, Billy still had frequent contact with the focal group through often overlapping daily schedules. Happily accepted into the group, Billy was greeted on his first day by Freddie who hugged him and crooned, "mmmmmmmm;" Frankie smiled and said, "Billy is here. Billy is back again;" Gerry greeted him with, "Hello Billy;" and Cathy, after greeting him, happily announced that Billy, the tallest person in the program, would be "our big brother." Billy's welcome back into the group by the other children was spontaneous, affectionate, and highly reinforcing for Billy.

No longer highly disruptive, Billy, was easily integrated into the group. He was cooperative, controlled, and highly verbal, and quickly adjusted to the routines and to the children. The entrance of Allan, however, did not go so smoothly. Entering for the first time Allan behaved much as Billy had three years earlier. Allan was 13 years old, tall, behaved in a constantly agitated manner with sudden outbursts of wild handclapping, vigorous rocking, and loud giggling. At every opportunity he ran from the room and out of the building. His movements were stiff, rapid perseverations of jumping, pounding, and running wildly. When not giggling loudly, Allan made a long, ascending "whoooo!" sound or a repetitious "tshhh, tshhh." Allan also rapidly repeated words such as "generation, generation," "concentration, concentration," "cigarette, cigarette." Interspersed throughout this base of generally high excitable behavior were frequent peaks of explosive, intense and seemingly uncontrolled conduct, almost always aggressive and directed at other people. For example, Allan would suddenly erupt out of his seat, leap in front of or onto the back of another child and, with fists and teeth clenched, drooling profusely and making long, high-pitched sounds, leap rapidly up and down pounding vigorously and rapidly down on the child's shoulders and head. When staff pulled him off he kicked, bit, pounded and scratched them, until he gradually subsided, with lower and lower spurts of activity, finally sitting, rocking and perhaps crooning or giggling.

During his first three weeks in the program the staff concentrated on teaching Allan to remain in the room rather than run away as he had been doing.

They then focused on reducing Allan's wild surplus behavior, applying the various modification systems that had been developed earlier with the other children. Physical control and repetition of behavior rules, relaxation training, time-out from reinforcement including sending him home, and having his behavior ignored by the group were the most effective methods with Allan. In addition to these methods for reducing surplus behavior, a variety of contingencies both specifically designed for Allan and occurring naturally as integral parts of the group were applied to bring about social, cooperative, verbal, and academic behavior. As the year continued, Allan progressed more rapidly but otherwise much as the other children had done earlier. He became less intense, more cooperative and verbal. By Christmas (about fourteen weeks), Allan was far better controlled and he began showing academic improvement. With the marked reduction of disruptive surplus behavior, Allan's verbal repertoire became more apparent, and staff and other children could now interact with him on a verbal rather than almost exclusively a physical level. For example, he began expressing affection for the staff in a number of ways, including verbalizing, "I love you, Mrs. W . . . ." However, as he expressed this verbally, he became increasingly excited and soon was rapidly repeating, "I love you, Mrs. W . . . ." with great intensity, hopping, grimacing, and pounding upon the poor teachers. Allan was repeatedly disengaged physically, soothed, gently told to relax and to behave "calmly, Allan, calmly." With continued repetition and reinforcement, Allan made increasingly obvious efforts to comply by controlling his behavior. About mid-year, during a particularly successful day of self-control, Allan looked up and said, "I love you, Mrs. W . . . ." Then he paused, looked quite pensive for a moment, and added quietly, "I love you *calmly*, Mrs. W . . . ." He was, of course, well-reinforced for that.

Adding Allan to the group was, among other things, a test of the strength of the group—would the children be able to tolerate wild, bizarre, disruptive behavior such as they had so recently emitted? It had been less than two years earlier when an upset by one child effectively stimulated the others into wild and disruptive behavior. Now adding Allan effectively re-introduced those powerful stimuli and at an even more intense level—because of his age and size.

Despite the high intensity and frequency of Allan's outbursts, the children's behavior was not disrupted and the overall group functioning, while often interrupted, was not disorganized. After being caught off guard a few times by Allan's attacks, the children became alert to signs of an impending blowup, and they tended to stay away from him and to warn each other. The children began to observe his behavior and to discuss it, pointing out that they had previously acted in a similar manner. Most interestingly, the children clearly tried to help him, talking to him, repeating behavioral rules, directly demonstrating appropriate behavior and verbally rewarding him whenever he succeeded. They perceived Allan as being ill-behaved, "a baby" and in need of learning proper behavior, just as they themselves had been. They frequently expressed optimism that in "our school," because we would "be nice" to him and "know how to teach," Allan would, undoubtedly "learn how to behave."

Thus, instead of wild loss of control in response to Allan, the children tolerated him, accepted him in a remarkably calm manner, recognized his behavioral difficulties and responded with help and even sympathy.

3. Development of mutual helping behavior. A significant development planned and actively shaped by the staff was the growth of helping behavior, a refinement of earlier-developed general cooperative behavior. The older children gradually began assisting staff with the younger children, and aiding each other in a variety of ways. To do this, their awareness of each other's behavior had to be sharpened and their recognition that the other child needed assistance developed. It was a complex social act, and it clearly was shaped during this fourth year. Examples include situations in which Cathy helped Frankie and Freddie in school work by correcting their spelling and printing; Allan later became very gently solicitous of Randy, a five-year old, calming him when he cried and all of the older children except Freddie helped to watch the younger children in the playground and on walks in the park or at the zoo. Increasingly frequent spontaneous acts of helping were noted as the year progressed and by the end of the year had become a normal occurrence, with general sensitivity to the various problems of each other and a variety of appropriate and effective helping behavior. Freddie, however, did not develop in this way, and the rest of the group far surpassed him in most respects by June.

4. Development of special social learning settings. In the preceding three years we and their families had observed significant changes in the children. Bizarre and aggressive surplus behavior had decreased significantly and in the cases of Billy and Cathy had ceased completely. Deficits, such as lack of speech, academic and general social behavior, had been corrected so that all of the original children could maintain long periods of socially appropriate behavior and all except Freddie could now read, write and converse. It was surprising to see these children operate quietly, cooperatively, appropriately for several hours each day, to observe their mature behavior and control during our field trips to public places, to watch them spontaneously help each other or the younger children in a variety of situations, and to witness their academic progress.

Nevertheless, however helpful our program may have been for the children, it was far from a normal social setting. The program was "special," the children segregated from age-mates. While apparently dealing effectively with much of the children's grossly bizarre surplus and debilitating deficit behavior, the learning settings within our program were many steps away from age-appropriate or normal settings. The children progressed at different rates and some children, particularly Cathy and Billy, more closely approximated the behavioral goals defined for them than did others. The "modal direction" of our program was to bring psychotic behavior under control and that emphasis would continue as we brought in new, younger children with severely maladaptive behavior. But Cathy and Billy had progressed beyond these goals and were now ready for more subtle social and academic learning which our program could only approximate. In this fourth year, then, we particularly attended to those more subtle socializing processes and planned for each child's eventual move from our program to other more normal social settings.

Much of the children's deficit behavior had been corrected and nearly all of their maladaptive surplus behavior was under good control, leaving more subtle deficits to be removed. Frankie, for example, could now probably function acceptably in a public school special class. He was now alert, cooperative and verbal, he interacted with others, and could read and write. Of his remaining deficits, the most serious was his markedly slurred speech which was at least partly due to a noticeable dental problem. Frankie's program for the fourth year included: (1) continuation of his academic and social learning programs, (2) consultation with a speech pathologist and (3) a pediatric dentist, and (4) gearing his daily program to emphasize development of clear speech. The major goals for his fourth year were (1) continued improvement through the socialization program of his generalized deficits so as to more closely approximate age-appropriate functioning, and (2) specific improvement in speech. If these goals were successfully achieved by the end of the fourth year, then Frankie would be moved out of our program during the next year, his fifth in the program, to a special class public school setting.

Similar plans were made for each of the children, including an approximate date for leaving the program. For Billy, the major goals of his fourth year were improved academics and elimination of several specific fears. We expected that Billy would be able to leave the program early in the next year though placement for a 16-year old would be difficult.

Having made considerable progress in verbal development, academics and in reduction of the massive, intense and prolonged outbursts, Gerry still required help in further reducing his general level of excitement responses. This behavior was far less in intensity, frequency and duration than it had been and no longer appeared to interfere with his academic development. However, because of its persistence, even at a low level, it imparted a consistently bizarre quality to his general functioning, making him easily identifiable in all situations except our classroom as a disturbed child. Reduction of this behavior had clearly come under the control of the classroom setting, but had not generalized to other settings. Accordingly, the program for Gerry was focused on the decrease of his generalized excitable behavior. It appeared to us that control would have to be developed specifically in a setting-by-setting manner that would require considerable time. Thus, we did not expect that Gerry would be ready to leave the program the following year, and no new placement plans were begun.

Of all the children, Freddie had made the least progress. Compared with his earlier behavior he was more responsive, interactive, verbal, and cooperative. He was less excitable, had lost his various sharp fears (of water, dogs, cats, thunder), and no longer exhibited bizarre or grotesque behavior (arm-flapping, sudden shrieking, head-banging and other self-injurious behavior). Despite his gains, his development was at a generally lower level than that achieved by the other children and was still characterized by severe generalized deficits. Because we could not predict a probable termination point for Freddie, his program was planned around continued attempts to overcome his various and general deficits, the most important of which was his verbal behavior. Speech development, therefore, was the major focus of his program.

Allan was new in the program and it was too early to assess his progress. However, if he progressed more rapidly than the others had, we could anticipate about a two-year stay in our program to be followed perhaps by a public school special class placement.

As described earlier, Cathy had improved the most during the preceding three years, from a wild, screaming, autistic child to a pleasant, lively, cooperative and bright but socially naïve little girl. Although she had developed a large repertoire of basic social behavior, she was nevertheless a ten-year old girl who for most of her life had lived apart from normal social experiences. She knew how to converse and how to play, but had virtually no experience with the things that ten-year olds normally play and talk about. Her behavior was no longer bizarre and uncontrolled, but was markedly innocent, naive, gauche, childish. What Cathy needed at this point was a wider range of normal, age-appropriate social experiences.

Whatever we might program for Cathy would necessarily be incomplete. Now that her bizarre surplus behavior had been removed and, many basic deficits corrected, the best setting for her acquiring age-appropriate sophistication would be in a normal peer group, specifically a regular public school third grade class. Accordingly, in this fourth year, Cathy's program was aimed at continuing the academic learning as before, but with the major emphasis on preparing her to move eventually from her current disturbed peer group to a normal one. This move would have to be programmed and monitored carefully.

School officials were cooperative and eager to help Cathy succeed. Several conferences were held with public school personnel to assess Cathy's academic work in terms of that required in public school; it seemed clear that she was doing adequate third grade work and would have no difficulty academically in public school. To further insure her eventual success, we borrowed appropriate material from the public school for Cathy's use in our program.

Our expectations were that Cathy's major problem area would not be academic behavior, but social behavior. If Cathy could successfully meet the demands for appropriate social behavior, then her academic behavior presumably would also be successful. Thus, while we continued to improve Cathy's academic development, the primary focus of her program was on providing a wide range of normal, age-appropriate social experiences that would teach her a more ordinary "little girl" role.

It is difficult to describe adequately Cathy's mixture of age-appropriate, mature behavior, and her pervasive social naivete. In our group she was by far the most sophisticated, but compared with a regular third grader, she was strikingly naive—like someone who had been away for several years and was subsequently out of touch with the subleties and nuances of social behavior. For example, Cathy had seldom worn dresses or skirts, as shorts, slacks and jeans were more appropriate for her activities. If she were to attend public school, she would have to be taught to wear dresses. As part of the planned program, Cathy's parents began sending her to our school wearing dresses. One day she wore an exceptionally pretty pink and white dress, and was obviously pleased with it and the many compliments it evoked. This was a "going out" dress. At noon she and a group worker were going for a ride, to a restaurant for lunch and perhaps to a store or two, and Cathy was dressed for this occasion. Waiting for the group worker, Cathy sat down for a moment. Every inch a lady with her pretty dress, white gloves, purse delicately held on her arm, a gentle look of sophistication on her face, Cathy slowly reached down, delicately grasped the hem of her skirt between thumb and forefinger of both hands and, with both pinkies gently extended, lifted the skirt and petticoat high above her head. She stood poised for a fashionable few moments and then after sitting down slowly and carefully so as not to wrinkle it, she fluffed and arranged her dress around her.

In her fourth year, then, Cathy was taught to wear a wider variety of clothes, to keep herself reasonably neat, to assume more responsibility for the younger children in the program, to assist the staff, to help out at home, to buy in stores, and behave in restaurants. Later in the year she was introduced to the public school class she would join the following year. She visited the class several times, where she sat in on lessons, joined in recess, interacted with the teacher and some of the children. By the end of the year she was to have attended one or two afternoon sessions each week. This sequence of visits was designed to prepare Cathy for a partial involvement in public school the following fall, that would develop into full-time involvement by the winter or spring. Cathy's transition to the public school was to be systematic and gradual, a gentle easing accompanied by our gradually fading support.

These plans were discussed with Cathy's parents and their active roles defined. Up to that point they had served primarily as sources of information and as supporters for behavior changes brought about in our program. Now, for the first time they were to be very actively involved. They were asked to keep records at home, a running diary of Cathy's behavior. The parents were instructed in generating behavior goals for Cathy, such as adequately dressing herself and other self-care activities, helping around the house, meeting and playing with normal children, interacting with adults and gradually widening her conversations to more complete and appropriate levels. The parents carried out simple reinforcement schedules, using as rewards verbal praise, playing with dolls, and visiting other families, etc. They learned to maintain limits so as to be consistent in making the variety of rewards contingent on Cathy's good behavior. For the first time in years, they took Cathy to a wide variety of settings, including stores, church, homes of friends and relatives, playgrounds, museums, and diners. Throughout all of these experiences Cathy was reinforced for age-appropriate behavior. The parents developed a new consistency with Cathy and new skills in helping her to continue learning. The parents reported steady improvement at home. Cathy was much more "a part of the family," the daily crises and screaming rages were over, and family life was markedly more pleasant than it had been two years earlier. Cathy had become a pleasant, contributing member of the family. Thus, there were several major, simultaneous and converging directions to Cathy's program for the fourth year, all geared to increasing her social competence.

The proposed program, including its goals and methods, was discussed with Cathy. Her obvious hesitation disappeared after only a few weeks. In school also Cathy continued to improve, and, in the final ten months of that year she had no rages, no outbursts, no screaming tantrums. She appeared to be extremely relaxed, was making good academic gains, and took in stride easily the new complexities of her program. Just two years earlier even minor changes in schedules or activities would precipitate major outbursts. Now Cathy moved easily through school in the morning, an outing to a store one day, the park the next day and a visit to public school the next. Last-minute cancellations and changes were infrequent, but when they did occur they occasioned no outbursts in Cathy. Cathy conversed with adults, played with the children, and looked forward to her new regular outings with staff. She anticipated continuing her visits to public school the following year, speaking often of the children she would meet. With individual attention and specific programming, Cathy was becoming an increasingly poised girl and she rapidly progressed beyond the other children. By April of her fourth year she had obviously gone beyond the upper limits of our group, and often seemed to be patiently marking time until the next fall and her more complete involvement with public school. She more frequently verbalized differences between herself and the other children: "Allan, you behave the way I used to. In this school we learn how to behave better. I learned and you can too;" "We have to help Allan learn how to behave;" "Mrs. W . . . , they're acting like babies."

Our program to prepare Cathy for public school seemed to have succeeded very well, and we expected that at her current rate of progress, Cathy would be in public school full time nearly six months sooner than we had planned. In our highly supportive and structured settings she was exhibiting behaviors necessary for public school success and for nearly a year had not shown any of the bizarre or strange behavior that would occasion failure in the public school. She seemed both ready and eager to begin.

Cathy's program was planned to continue without interruption throughout the summer, thus strengthening her emerging adaptive behavior. However, as will be discussed in the next chapter, our entire program, including all the plans for Cathy and the other children, collapsed in June, and Cathy did not enter public school in the fall.

PLANS FOR EVALUATION

Through the fourth year our program had been exploratory and our reports descriptive. We had observed changes and noted apparent relationships between those changes and the program structure. In short, we had observed that the operations were apparently successful in bringing about positive behavior changes in these severely psychotic children. The data on which we based this judgment were comprised essentially of our own experiences, our countless daily observations, the cumulative effects of repeated observations by many persons over a four year period. We now had little doubt that we could analyze behavior, specify goals, program the learning environments, and successfully guide the children to significant and observable behavioral improvement.

By the middle of the fourth year we were fully convinced of the effectiveness of our program. However, questions remained: could the results be repeated or even approximated, and could more precise measurements and data be offered to lend increased support to our conviction? Accordingly, we began to focus on developing adequate tests of the effectiveness of the various approaches we had developed. Simply, we were convinced, but aside from describing our program we could offer little additional evidence to support our approaches. Other professionals had not shared directly our experiences and the entire endeavor had been far too complex and personalized to be replicated and tested elsewhere. By virtue of our explorations we could now offer a systematic clinical program for severely disturbed children—but that program still required further testing, evaluation and refinement.

PLANS FOR THE FIFTH YEAR

Therefore, plans for the fifth year were organized around two major goals: (1) a continuation of the plans already in effect for the currently enrolled children, and (2) the formation of two new groups of children, test groups, for whom careful baseline, treatment and post-treatment measures would be taken. Care would be taken to assess both validity and reliability of the measures, to clearly and specifically define relevant variables and test their relationships as thoroughly as possible. In other words, we now planned to refine and test the procedures we had developed during the previous four years.

It was our belief that we could bring together a new group of severely disturbed children and, by avoiding the previous mistakes and by carefully programming from the beginning of their program, we could more effectively and in less time bring about significant behavioral improvement while offering convincing quantitative data. Early in the fourth year was a very optimistic time, and we were estimating that two or three years would be necessary to bring about significant changes that would be clearly specified at the beginning of the new group's program, and validated by the end.

Children were being referred to us at a fairly high rate and, by the middle of the fourth year, we had already established our new groups for the next year. Developmental histories, medical information and baseline observations were taken; parents were apprised of their active roles in the children's programs and education of the parents in behavior modification was begun. By May we expected to have all the evaluations, the program planning, and preparation of the parents completed and two new groups each consisting of four children would be ready for programming. We anticipated gathering enough reliable data within two years to adequately evaluate our methods.

From the vantage point of about the middle of the fourth year, our assessment of the previous work and plans for the next two years were decidedly positive. We were convinced by our own observations that significant improvement had occurred in less than four years under exploratory conditions including many errors, blind alleys and much time-wasting backtracking to undo mistakes. It was reasonable to assume that without the major delays, the processes of behavioral change would occur considerably more quickly, and it might be possible to bring severely psychotic children to a level of complex social behavior within only two or three years of intensive group behavior modification. The progress of our new groups over the next two years, along with the success of the parent-training programs, would test these assumptions.

Our expectations for the next two years, then, were that Cathy would be in a regular public school class and Frankie in a special class, with Gerry and Allan probably moving to a special class the following year. Billy had improved to a point where he could function in a special class, but at 16 he was too old to be considered by his local school system for inclusion in their programs. No predictions were made for Freddie, who had fallen far behind the others. We expected the younger children to develop in much the same way as had our focal group, but hopefully at a faster pace. Our project, to develop effective approaches to the modification of severely psychotic behavior in children, was nearing its end, moving into the last two or three years, which were to be the testing phase of the program.

CHAPTER 11

The Program's Dissolution

OPERATIONAL DIMENSIONS AND PUBLIC IMAGES

We return to a theme presented in Chapter 1. Mental health programs operate on at least three major dimensions: (1) a practical, applied dimension of everyday operations, encompassing applied methods, facilities, staff and clients, that draws its major rationale from (2) a conceptual dimension of abstractions, i.e., theory of human behavior, humanitarian-philosophical assumptions, that is supported by (3) a social-political, business dimension of finances and access to appropriate decision-making groups. Agencies operate simultaneously along these three dimensions (see Figure 5) which vary in strength between agencies and across time within agencies.

The most positive aspect of these dimensions are selected and assembled by the agency, incorporated into its public image, and projected through various media, primarily the local newspapers. This is a selective, manipulatable projection with a potentially high degree of distortion. Thus, a primarily political agency with only a thin conceptual patina and superficial applied program can project a deceptive public image of an effective, humanitarian and scientific program, guided by a devoted board of directors and hard-working professionals (see Figure 5). It is unfortunately true that uncertain programs with weak conceptualization can project and maintain high positive visibility as long as they rest on powerful social-political systems. Such agencies are primarily shaped by politics and their major decisions, such as concerning the types of clients treated, fees, and even definitions of mental illness, must be responsive and acceptable to the local power structure.

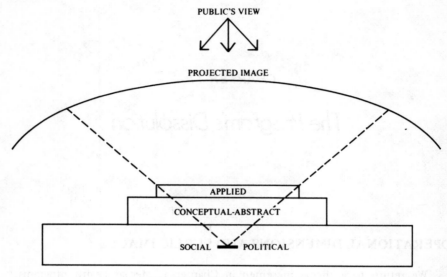

FIG. 5 DIMENSIONS OF AGENCY FUNCTIONS

A program without powerful social-political support, however, regardless of how well-conceived or effectively operated it may be, cannot survive long in our essentially political climate. The critical survival factor is the social-political dimension.

Likewise, in the present case, the program's demise was rooted in the weakness of its social politics—specifically its internal politics.

SEDMIC'S DISORGANIZATION

The antagonists, for such we had become, were the board president and the program director; the central issue was control of the agency and its programs; the result was disorganization; the major victims were the children and their parents. Ironically, the applied program had become firmly developed, well-supported and recognized, when destroyed by the political discord of the last two years.

In the next few pages we will attempt to identify the critical issues that led to the destruction of the program just as it had achieved its highest level to date.

LAYMAN-PROFESSIONAL ISSUES

A general, initially muted atmosphere of layman-professional distrust was ever-present, stemming, perhaps, from a combination of SEDMIC's earlier unfortunate experiences with the mental health power structure and the board president's proprietary and fiercely protective attitudes about the agency. The first two years of our association were extremely—and misleadingly—harmonious. However, as already discussed in Chapter 1, the director failed to recognize and to deal with the different expectations held by laymen and professionals, i.e., application versus inquiry. Within two years the program had been firmly established, expanded, and was operating smoothly and apparently successfully. As the laymen saw it, the major goal—direct services for children had been realized and, except for some future expansion and improvement of facilities, they were generally pleased with the program's achievements. The program director, on the other hand, believed that only the most basic goals had been achieved and that the program should continue its systematic inquiry toward refinements of effective applied methods. Therefore, the laymen were puzzled when the director continued to modify what appeared to them to be an already adequate program.

Another important element enters here; in order to maintain systematic inquiry and develop the high-structure program described, the director had to maintain control over all program decisions and events. As the program grew in size and complexity so too, of necessity, did the scope of the director's program-related decision-making. The director's actions, consistent with his assumptions and expectations, in continuing to modify the program and rapidly assuming greater decision-making scope, awakened some of the board members' old distrust of professionals and led to the eventual confrontations over who would control the program—the president and her faction of the board or the director and his staff.

SEDMIC'S UNEVEN DEVELOPMENT

Four years earlier when the new director had joined SEDMIC there had been agreement that he would be responsible for all programming and professional developments while the board would continue to raise money and recognition. Their roles were thus somewhat defined. In terms of the discussion above, the director and his staff were to develop the conceptual and applied dimensions while the board of directors would attend to the social-political dimension.

The roles did not remain separated and the director quickly found himself pulled into the political aspects—meeting with government officials and local agency representatives, giving testimony to legislative committees, interviews in the public media, and presentations to state and local business, professional and lay groups.

The director functioned in all three dimensions—political, conceptual and applied—and also contributed to the agency's public image, but had been accorded legitimized responsibility in only two areas (conceptual and applied). He could not make political decisions, and his political activities were always at the initiation of the board who called him in when needed for his "expertise." For example, the director would be called upon to produce reports and present them to the United Agencies to request funding, but only the board could accept or agree to the terms of any such support.

The conceptual-applied tasks facing the director were complex but reasonably circumscribed—developing effective services for severely disturbed children —and the director had the educational-professional training to enable him to develop the necessary rational, systematic inquiry.

In many ways, however, the laymen had a more difficult task. They had clearly assumed responsibility for the political development, and the tasks facing them were diffuse rather than cirucmscribed, and were mainly controlled by other people who were not sympathetic to SEDMIC. Furthermore, the laymen had no professional training to help them develop and evaluate rational, systematic approaches. Consequently, they functioned largely on an emotional, trial-and-error basis. Determined, energetic and well-intentioned, they were, however, ill-prepared for a heavily demanding task.

It should not have been surprising when after two years the conceptual and applied dimensions had progressed far beyond the development of the political dimension. This clearly disparate development added to the laymen's unease.

For the first two years there had been harmonious cooperation among the board, the staff and the parents, and an apparently good balance of the program dimensions existed. The staff developed the conceptual and applied dimensions; the board helped provide financial support, while the parents paid tuition and cooperated enthusiastically. By the start of the third year, however, the conceptual and applied dimensions had become far more sophisticated and complex than the agency had previously experienced, gaining good local visibility, and increasing success in drawing state and federal funding many times the amount raised by the board. The number of children increased from four to more than 60 while the staff grew from the original one person to more than 30. (The large summer programs accounted for half of these increases.) Decisions, such as selection of staff and children, involvement of parents, and use of facilities and equipment, were now being made by the program director and staff rather than the board. Further, in accordance with the conceptual model being developed, children were being admitted who would previously have been excluded. Specifically, a large percentage of Black and poverty level children were admitted as well as many who defied traditional diagnositc labels. The applied program, directly under staff's control, had grown rapidly in the first two years, surpassing any of SEDMIC's previous programming.

During the same time, however, the board of directors did not fare well in the local social-political arena. Raising local money was difficult for any agency and SEDMIC's membership and fund-raising drives were likewise disappointing. The local United Agencies refused to give support. The board's political power status within the local mental health field remained at a low level.

The size and character of the board did not appreciably change; the same small group of charter members largely controlled it; the same person was repeatedly elected president and the powerful assumption operated that this was her organization. The president, members of her family, and several old friends who had founded the agency formed a perpetual nucleus, seemingly identifying the agency as theirs with ancillary people volunteered or hired to help.

The rapid development of the conceptual and applied dimensions compared with the board's slow progress in the political area created an intolerable gap. The president's faction saw program control slipping from them. Marginal in the local agency arena, failing to spur high public support for their efforts and now sensing that they were being outdistanced by the program they had themselves created, they moved to regain their previous control by reducing the magnitude of the program, bringing it back to a narrow scope and slow pace that they could readily manage. The director continued to develop the program in ways he considered necessary and resisted all attempts to diminish it. The two factions clashed and, in the conflict that lasted two years, the program was destroyed.

THE LAYMEN'S UNDERESTIMATION OF THE TASK

In the process of alienation each adversary viewed the other as being of decreasing value. In the director's opinion the board was long past due a new president; the president believed the director had outlived his usefulness. This latter point is important for it developed, by the fourth year, into the president's assumption that *any* professional director was superfluous.

Ironically, the very success of the program had contributed to the president's underestimation of the difficulty of working with the children. By the fourth year, the groups were operating smoothly and the obvious, dramatic encounters between children and staff no longer occurred. A layman's casual glance into the focal group's room would reveal an orderly interaction of adults and children, giving the impression that even an untrained layman could now effectively handle the group. After all, how difficult could it really be to take those children for walks, play games or continue teaching them to read and write? Now that the children were better socialized, the remaining tasks could harldy be beyond the ability of well-intentioned laymen. More specifically, the president's faction believed that a reduced program could be maintained by one or two key staff (who had by then been well-trained by the director) under the board's general supervision. They now underestimated the task, overestimated their own ability, and assumed they had the requisite skill to supervise a complex program. Originally so impressed by professional expertise, these laymen now believed that the director and most of the staff were superfluous and their departure would pose no threat to the board's program.

There was an element of retributive justice in this development, for the director himself had contributed to that point of view by his earlier—and apparently successful—attempts to disabuse the laymen of their awe of applied professional expertise. Further, he simply failed to communicate to the president's group his assumptions that conceptualization and rational, systematic inquiry are essential to the development of effective applied programs, and the professional's most important contribution lies in that conceptual dimension.

THE ISSUE OF "COMMITMENT"

While the majority of the board accepted the director's position on the importance of systematic inquiry and evaluation, the president's minority perceived it as further evidence for the director's lack of "real" (i.e., emotional) commitment. A brief examination of the laymen's commitment will clarify this issue.

SEDMIC's board had made a significant contribution to the community. Despite heavy odds against success, this small group alerted the public and the professional community to the lack of services for severely disturbed children and they stimulated local and state-wide interest and activity. Subsequently, a number of special programs for severely disturbed children were created as direct or indirect results of the activity of those laymen. Although often abrasive, contentiously demanding and ultimately given little credit, they brought about significant change in the community.

Their vehicle for change was the agency, SEDMIC. They created, nurtured, "raised" the agency and gave it a character and identity long before the program director joined. In this process they developed a proprietary, perhaps even parental, regard for the agency's well-being and they often said they would "never give up" the agency "to the professionals." They accepted their almost entirely emotional commitment as proper and they described it as a "genuine," "from the heart," and "permanent" concern for the children.

Anyone not so emotionally committed was characterized as less "genuine," not "really" concerned, and of only temporary "loyalty." Thus characterized were professionals who insisted on any large measure of objectivity, and the director's position on systematic inquiry was clear evidence of his lack of "real" commitment.

The president's minority believed that because of the nature of their commitment compared with that of the director, it was in the children's best interest for control to remain clearly with the founders.

As the program grew, the director increased the scope of his program-related decision-making power. This occasioned a parallel increase in alarm among the president's faction and a hardening of their position into an implacable determination to "protect" their agency from further encroachment by the director or any future professional.

NEAR-RESOLUTION OF THE CRISES

Although powerful, the president's faction was a voting minority and was unable to convince the whole board to support the president's determination to take program control from the director. However, they were powerful enough to maintain, during the third and fourth years, an unrelenting, essentially emotional, critical assault on the program, the director and some staff.

Many of their numerous criticisms were petty and insubstantial; some were valid and important. Few, however, were presented in a constructive spirit of solution but all had high disruptive value. The board meetings for those two years assumed a character of perpetual crisis. The director was repeatedly called in to answer criticisms and the moderate board members increasingly found themselves mediating between the growing antagonists. An angry, two-year stalemate ensued; the usual business of the board evaporated and the moderate board members grew weary of the sustained conflict.

After more than a year of such conflict these moderate board members nearly brought about a resolution of the crises. Correctly perceiving the central issue of program control, they saw the difficulties as complex but solvable problems generated by the rapid growth of the program during the first two years. Concluding that the agency's informal structure was no longer adequate to support the more complex levels of the current program, they developed an extensive clarification of SEDMIC's organization and tasks, including the roles of the officers, board, staff and program director. As a result, virtually all of the substantive issues of conflict were resolved and the president had little choice but to cooperate in allowing the fourth year to proceed, despite her unabated personal concerns over program control.

INCURSION OF A RIVAL AGENCY

The fourth year began in an atmosphere of uneasy truce, and the past year's conflicts within the board had not yet affected the conduct of the program. The board was relatively quiescent for the first two months of the fourth year and it appeared as if the moderate board members' work in clarifying the agency structure and resolving substantive issues, might have been effective. Had it continued, this truce might have helped the agency to develop into a mature and stable organization. However, just at this point of near-resolution a new and sharply-disruptive event occurred that became a focal point for all of the residual anger that battered the agency into disorganization at the end of the program's fourth year. Many of the president's criticisms had focused on the summer programs and those issues provided a rival agency with the opportunity to propose a merger of the two programs. The incursion of the rival agency at the start of the fourth year was the event that led finally to the program's dissolution.

The president's earlier criticisms of the summer programs were clearly related to her more general concerns about program control, but were focused on the immediately available and emotional issues of the director's inclusion of a high proportion of poverty level children in the program. The president's faction asked, "Why should *they* come in free, (i.e., under federal grants) while our own kind have to pay?" "Our program is no longer *ours*, it is being turned over to *them!*" "Why is the staff nicer to *them* than to our own?" "I have nothing against the Coloreds, but. . . ." The complex issues were highly emotional and not easily resolved.

Although wrapped in racial emotionalism and although some of the president's supporters were clearly behaving from a racist's position, the essential issue was not a White-versus-Black struggle. The point being contested through the racial vehicle was whether the president or the director was going to decide what children were to be accepted into the program. The president's faction did not appear to have particular animosity toward Black children; rather, it was a convenient and effective issue to be used in the power struggle, providing points around which the board minority could criticize the program and force power struggles over program decision-making.

Anger and harsh accusations prevailed and positions hardened. In time, the substantive issues of camp were resolved, and emotionality subdued by the efforts of the moderate board members and the brief truce referred to earlier followed. However, it was at that point, early in the fourth year, that the truce was broken—the director of the rival agency stepped in with support for the president and reignited the entire dispute over program control. Whether he was called into the dispute by the president or he initiated the move himself is unclear. What is clear, however, is that any sharp dispute within SEDMIC was to his agency's advantage.

The rival agency, a city-owned program, derived its strength from the local political machine. Only three years old, it was among the most heavily-supported local programs, receiving good financial support, ample city-owned space and equipment and heavy and favorable press coverage. Its projected image grew rapidly, rivaling those of much older agencies.

Its director had been unsuccessful in several attempts to bring SEDMIC under his expanding jurisdiction and several times had clashed with SEDMIC's program director. More recently, he had begun to compete directly with SEDMIC for clients, arguing that all emotionally disturbed public school children were rightly under his jurisdiction. For example, SEDMIC, and not the city agency, received the public school's annual contract for special summer programs for emotionally disturbed poverty level children—the very program around which so much dispute had raged within SEDMIC. Furthermore, those programs were held in an ideal setting—a large, city-owned building, custom-renovated by us, located on a sandy-beached ocean peninsula and surrounded by trees and grass. For its expansion the city agency wanted the public school contract and could certainly use the summer facility. The director had failed before to gain control of both, but now our internal bickering provided a new and ultimately successful opportunity.

He proposed that SEDMIC and the city agency operate joint programs, sharing SEDMIC's beach-front summer quarters and in the fall his agency's quarters. Pooling staff while maintaining administrative independence would presumably also be achieved. The president's group supported this "generous offer" while many of the other board members viewed it suspiciously as a maneuver to control SEDMIC.

The resulting debates over whether to join the city agency the next summer became a series of forums that revived and intensified the earlier debate over the summer program. The messy, racial issues were heated to boiling. The discussions became increasingly hostile and personalized on both sides and all appearance of rational debate dissolved. The intense antagonism continued throughout the entire fourth year and spilled out of the board meetings to affect the staff and the parents.

THE PRESIDENT GAINS FULL CONTROL

Despite the increasing political turmoil within the agency the program, now into its fourth year, was operating smoothly. Although still able to keep politics separated from their daily work with the children, the staff soon found that greater efforts were needed to maintain the program stability in the face of the president's continuing and constant criticisms. The board meetings also required greater effort and about this time the final process began that led to the president's faction gaining full control. As hostilities grew, the moderate board members became increasingly uneasy and pessimistic. One by one, quietly and, usually without notice, they dropped out, shedding a major irritant from their lives, and leaving the president's faction in clear uncontested control. Now effectively the whole board, the president's group had control and proceeded to undercut the program by freezing funds already obtained, refusing to accept new children it had not screened, refusing to enter into contracts based on proposals prepared by the staff or to support staff proposals and plans, particularly for the next year's research programs.

The parents were upset by the intra-agency conflicts and greatly concerned with the possible loss of the program. However, they had never been an organized group and had no effective decision-making role in agency policy. In the political crisis, the parents were no better equipped to resolve issues than anyone else. Neither board nor staff members, they found themselves uncomfortably squeezed and powerless to divert the destructive currents.

In growing distress, the staff watched the children's program consumed in a power struggle among the adults—ironically occurring at a point when these children were achieving major behavioral gains that needed continued support if they were to be maintained and when resources (staff, money and facilities) were ample. As the fourth year drew to its close, it became clear that the program, as we had developed and planned it for the next year, would not be allowed to continue. Thus momentum would be lost and continuity destroyed.

When the fourth year ended, the demoralized and intensely disappointed staff resigned from the agency. This group of colleagues, now close personal friends, separated, some leaving for jobs or school in other states. Their carefully developed programs for the children were cancelled and the children, at a point when they appeared to be doing so well, also were to be separated.

The Program's Dissolution   247

SEDMIC'S FINAL PROGRAM

By June of the fourth year, SEDMIC had lost its director and staff, its applied program, its summer contract and its moderate board members. Now unopposed, the president and her faction had complete control and were free to accomodate the city agency, which moved into and shared SEDMIC's summer camp facilities. The few children who remained with SEDMIC for the summer were incorporated into the city program operated by city staff. The president had succeeded in tying SEDMIC to the agency that had the highest political status in the city, and for those few summer weeks the president seemed vindicated.

SEDMIC's new status, however, was brief, for it discovered in the fall that the city agency would not in fact provide help with staffing, programming or physical facilities. Further, the beach house somehow became the city agency's beach house for its own future summer programs which would not include SEDMIC.

The summer moves had been fruitful for the city agency. It had courted SEDMIC's president and helped to disorganize its board and alienate it from its own staff. Consequently, SEDMIC became dependent upon the city agency's program. However, having helped put SEDMIC in that dependent position, the city agency then neatly withdrew its support, letting SEDMIC collapse. Then the city agency stepped in and claimed the beach house as its own, arguing that SEDMIC no longer had any programs to be housed there. With SEDMIC removed as a competing agency, the city agency's status and power were greatly enhanced within the local mental health power structure.

The local bureaucratic field had shifted. SEDMIC had owed its status primarily to its applied programs, but once it lost those programs it was reduced to a marginal agency. Further, the remaining members of the board had lost much of their credibility with the community.

In contrast, the city agency flourished. Its power was derived almost completely from its political support by the local government rather than from its applied programs. Its strong political support enabled the agency to maneuver boldly and quickly in the competetive mental health field.

However, only two years later the city political alignments changed, and significant decision-making power was redistributed—a common occurrence in the world of politics. As a result, the city agency and its director found themselves no longer supported. The director left the agency which was reduced in scope, and his own status and power collapsed.

THE STAFF'S FINAL PHASING OUT

In the final year of SEDMIC's program there had been 13 private school children enrolled full-time and 45 public school children part-time. With the end of SEDMIC's sponsorship, the staff, with no formal supporting agency or legal status, lost contact with nearly all the private school children who were ineligible for public school programs. However, after its separation from SEDMIC, the staff carried out its summer program under the direct sponsorship of the public school therefore maintaining contact with the public school children. That summer program was intended to serve as a model for the public school's continuation of special behavior modification programs the following fall.

While the former SEDMIC staff carried out its summer programs for the public schools, SEDMIC's board moved into its summer program partnership with the city agency. With SEDMIC's breakup, the children had been separated into several groups: 36 of the public school children entered the former staff's summer program; four of the private school children (Cathy, Gerry, Frankie, Freddie) joined the SEDMIC-city summer program; the four pre-admission group children were maintained in home programs; one child was accepted into a local summer program for retarded children; the remaining 13 public and private school children had no summer programs or were lost track of by circumstances, such as moving out of town.

That summer while working with the public school children, the staff heard rumors about and caught brief glimpses of the children in the SEDMIC-city program. A disturbing picture emerged as our staff reported seeing Billy slapped, yelled at, and shaken by an irate teenage camp counselor, or seeing an untrained adult holding Cathy, screaming, down on the ground, calling loudly and with great irritation, "Somebody come and subdue this child!"; or seeing Freddie swoop into camp, giggling and arm-flapping as he had not done in a year; or Gerry grimacing, posturing, spitting and swearing as of a year ago.

The available indications were distressing, for they suggested that the behavior of the children in the SEDMIC-city program was deteriorating. There was no way of learning, however, if these observations were valid, for we no longer had any professional jurisdiction in those cases.

In the fall the public school children went to their various special classes, but no programs were available for the private school children. It was not until mid-December that we were able to arrange administrative support by a small local private school, and thereby reassemble the remaining children and continue their programs for nearly another two years. By giving us its support, the private school achieved an important goal. With the sizeable funding and staff we brought, the school qualified for state recognition and support as competent to work with severely emotionally disturbed children, a recognition it had not previously been able to achieve.

The plan was for us to at first operate autonomously, then in time provide services for the rest of the school, until we were gradually integrated with it. Eventually, therefore, our program was to lose its autonomy. For the next two years we were to continue working with the focal group children still available and to find suitable future placement for them, while simultaneously planning for our own dissolution as an autonomous group. We hoped after ending our program to leave enough trained staff, ideas and structure in the community so as to help maintain a behavior modification direction.

By December, only two of the original staff members and the former SEDMIC director were available, and only on a part-time basis. Together with two untrained, part-time staff hired through the private school, we comprised the staff for our new program. The following year, responding to pressure from the schools, additional groups were added, two members of our previous staff returned for full-time employment and additional staff were hired.

Of the previous year's 13 private school children, eight were still available. Billy had moved to another city, Frankie and Allan had been accepted in public school special classes; one child from the previous young group and one from the pre-admission group had been enrolled in a program for mentally retarded children. Of the eight remaining, only three, Cathy, Gerry and Freddie, were supported by state financial aid. For the other children several more months of discussions were required to convince the state and various local school systems to support them, and those children were eventually admitted too. By early 1968 we had the beginning of two groups—Cathy, Gerry and Freddy in one, and the five younger children in the other. Over the next academic year (1968-1969) four children were added to the older group, and several brought into the younger group. For 18 months (December 1967 through June 1969) we again operated our behavior modification group programs for severely disturbed children. In that time the program became increasingly integrated with the rest of the private school, sharing rooms, teachers, and activities. With the end of the school year in June 1969, it ceased to function as an autonomous program. Nearly all of the staff remained with the private school, becoming integrated with other groups and programs. This history of our development of group behavior modification programs for severely disturbed children, having begun early in 1963, ends with the closing of school in June 1969.

Before ending this chapter, I would like to briefly describe the program's final year and a half, pointing out particularly the problem of behavioral deterioration.

BEHAVIORAL DETERIORATION

The staff had grown concerned throughout the summer over suggestions of behavioral deterioration in the children, but had no direct contact with them. In December, as the children began returning to our program, it was immediately apparent that gross deterioration had occurred, and that only those children who had remained in the home-training programs throughout the summer had not deteriorated. The five others had, and to a remarkable degree.

Cathy was back to her isolation, tantrums, destructiveness, self-injury, toe-walking, screeching and humming, bizarre fingering and "peering," and screaming refusals to cooperate in any program activities. Gerry was again involved in his high rate of intensely grotesque posturing, spitting, guttural vocalizing, loud and frequent belching and regurgitation sounds, swearing, self-injury and destruction of objects. Freddie was again intensely afraid of animals and loud noises, and resumed his screeching, arm-flapping and sporadic intense, teeth-clenching excitement. Randy, one of the young children, had resumed his high rate of severe head-banging, constant crying and aimless running. Karl, another young child had resumed his intense isolation and aggressive striking out whenever approached.

After a seven-month interruption in the program there had been a marked reinstatement of the severe surplus behaviors that had been previously eliminated or reduced greatly in some instances for as long as two years. Our first impression of the children was that all their maladaptive behavior had been reshaped, suggesting that our four years of behavioral treatment had been of no lasting value. The behavior modification program had been designed to shape and maintain particular classes of new and adaptive behavior. Could it be that the new behavior was so transient that when removed from the specific structure of the program, the children quickly reverted to their previous behaviors? We had become convinced in the previous four years of work that even the most bizarre behavior could be modified. Now, however, our initial observations of the children returning to the program after their nearly seven-month absence forced us to look carefully at the problem of *maintenance* of the behavioral changes. It was clear that we had demonstrated behavioral change in severely disturbed children. It was equally clear that a major weakness of our previous program, revealed by its forced interruption, was its apparent failure to produce adaptive behavior that could remain at a high level independently of the structured program. This suggestion was supported by the further observation that those children for whom behavior modification programs had continued at home did not show behavioral deterioration. In fact, they had continued to improve.

Over the succeeding weeks of the revised program our initial judgment of the apparent failure of the program to have brought about permanent change was modified. Continuing our detailed observations, we noted that the deterioration was virtually all in terms of the reshaping of the childrens' previous maladaptive *surplus* behaviors such as screaming, hitting, spitting, and posturing. However, the complex social and academic behavior that they had acquired was still present. For example, despite Gerry's renewed high rate of bizarre behavior, he still spoke appropriately, could read, write, and respond to verbal instructions and to subtle social cues. For all of the children, their previous maladaptive *surplus* behavior had been largely reshaped, but their former behavior *deficits* had not been renewed.

Our program had moved in both directions, toward the acquisition of adaptive behavior and the decrememt of maladaptive behavior. Observations on the children returning to our program suggested that our efforts toward acquisition had resulted in stable, seemingly permanent, changes, while those toward decrement had resulted in only temporary modification. Apparently, the greatest value of our program to the children, and the area in which it produced its most enduring results, was in teaching them a large array of complex motor, social, and academic behaviors and skills that they could retain despite the ending of the program.

In contrast, despite the reduction in maladaptive surplus, its low levels were not maintained at home but quickly spiraled again during the program interruption. Our overall conclusion was that the acquisition of adaptive behavior results in more stable improvement than the decrement of maladaptive behavior, or, to generalize, behavior once learned is highly resistant to extinction. Thus, behavior reduced in rate under special conditions can be quickly reshaped to its previous high levels. In terms of clinical approaches to severely disturbed children, our conclusions suggest clearly the value of extensive work toward the direct acquisition of adaptive behavior and the necessity of developing systems not only to *modify* behavior, but to also maintain adaptive behavior, particularly outside the treatment program. They suggest further that in developing maintenance programs, special attention be given to preventing the reshaping of maladaptive behaviors. Maintenance programs must be sensitive to the re-emergence of maladaptive surplus behavior and must move quickly to prevent any strengthening of it. These implications are particularly important for the development of maintenance programs in the home.

In summary, our initial observations of behavioral deterioration were only partly correct. Deterioration did occur in terms of the reshaping of previous surplus behavior, but it did not occur in terms of loss of adaptive behaviors previously acquired in our program—suggesting that the direct acquisition of adaptive behavior may be of greater clinical value than the decrement of maladaptive surplus and it should be emphasized more. Both directions of modification must of course be employed; we are suggesting however that one be given greater weight. Our suggestions apply also to maintenance programs developed in the home.

The forced termination of the program and the subsequent six months without behavioral programming might be seen as an unanticipated "return to baseline" condition. Moreover, the children's high level of surplus behavior had the effect of masking their previously acquired adaptive skills. Careful attention was directed through detailed retrospective reports by the parents to try to determine why the surplus behavior had been so markedly reshaped. A comparison of that information with the data we had gathered during the summer on the children who had remained in supervised home programs suggested that the major general difference between the two groups was in the gradual loss of control over the child's home environment by the unsupervised parents. Without supervision the parents gradually began to react to their children as they had years before, thereby unintentionally reshaping the old maladaptive surplus behavior. This was particularly clear with very discrete behaviors, such as Randy's severe head-banging, Gerry's swearing and bizarre posturing, Cathy's tantrums and Freddie's arm-flapping and screeching. By the end of the summer the families were again reacting massively to and strengthening those behaviors back to their original high levels.

It was in the families without supervision during the summer that the greatest deterioration occurred. Further, they were also those families in which the *least* parent training had taken place. Parent training (see Chapter 9) was most developed in the two years *following* SEDMIC's breakup while the earlier focal group parents had received little training for independent work with their children. In fact, parent training was one of the program dimensions that had suffered earliest from the board's conflicts.

Cathy appeared to have been most severely affected by the program interruption. She had been the most advanced of the group, rapidly moving toward public school placement. The factors underlying her reversal, however, seemed clear. She had been receiving tremendous stimulation and attention; her world had been expanded to include new directions to which she had responded with highly enthusiastic cooperation. Each step of the program had been carefully discussed with Cathy. Involved in the planning of her own program, Cathy began anticipating some of its future aspects, particularly the goal of entering public school the following fall, and this clear, future orientation was a significant advance in her development.

When our program ended in June, Cathy reacted not only with concern, but with anger—exhibiting her first upset behavior in a year. Although her anger was fully justified, she knew no way to express it except by exhibiting a pale copy of her own former tantrums. Her concern also became apparent in her many questions: "What's going to happen to our school?" "Will we have summer camp?" "Are you (staff) going to stay with us?" "Will we (the children) stay together?" "Will I still go to public school next year?" Cathy's clearly defined program and expectations suddenly turned vague. The abrupt ending of her current program, along with the new uncertainties about her future public school placement, constituted an abrupt withdrawal of the major supports for the highly adaptive behavior that she had been maintaining over a long period.

That final June, Cathy said "so long" to our staff and shortly after was enrolled in the SEDMIC-City summer program—a very different situation, with unfamiliar people and procedures. Probably the greatest change was from the carefully planned sequencing and intense individual focus of our program to the largely unorganized setting in which staff reactions were inconsistent, unpredictable, and sometimes angry and punitive. Despite marked changes in her environment and the way people treated her, Cathy's behavior did not deteriorate immediately. Neither did her apparent expectations for the fall. Each day, her parents later reported, Cathy talked about *her* school opening again in the fall, when she would resume her contacts with her friends among the children and staff and continue her program toward public school placement. In many ways Cathy expressed her view that summmer camp was only temporary, a "vacation" from her own school, and she frequently talked about school, clearly indicating her eagerness to join her friends again. Her parents later reported that as the summer progressed Cathy seemed to become increasingly focused on the resumption of school in the fall.

In camp, faced with the array of new people, demands and inconsistent rewards and punishments, Cathy's tantrum and isolate behavior began to increase. By mid-summer, her parents noted more "restlessness," "aimless activity" and "touchiness," although the severe tantrums now occurring at camp had not yet erupted at home. When camp ended in late August, Cathy appeared to her parents to be "excited" and "happy." She had successfully completed the summer without major disruption at home, and was intent on resuming school in

mid-September. Cathy's parents had known all summer that there would probably be no school program for her in the fall, but had refrained from telling Cathy
on the chance that some program might still be arranged. In response to her
questions about when *her* school would resume, they could only answer, "We
don't know." All ambiguity was removed for Cathy in early September when she
saw her sister and neighborhood children going back to school while she
remained at home. Her reaction was immediate and violent. Cathy's parents
reported. "It seemed the only thing that kept her going all summer was (her
expectation of) going back to school. When she found out she wasn't going back,
she seemed to go all to pieces, all at once." Experiencing strong sympathy for
Cathy's intense disappointment, helpless in being unable to provide school for
her, and alarmed at the intensity of her reaction, Cathy's parents were unsure
how best to respond. Cathy's reaction was intense, tearful, and accusative and
her maladaptive behavior which had been reshaped at camp, began to occur at
home. The parents' distress and inconsistencies resulted in a gradual and unwit-
ting intermittent reinforcement of the maladaptive behavior, and it began to
escalate sharply. The general home situation deteriorated, with the parents
becoming increasingly distressed and decreasingly successful in coping with her
behavior. This pattern of the transfer of maladaptive behavior from camp to
home, its subsequent escalation and the parents' growing distress and difficulty
coping with the children, was found with each child. The pattern appeared
similar but less intense for those who did not attend camp, and it did not occur
with those children who remained in supervised home programs of behavior
modification.

BRIEF REORGANIZATION

In mid-December, when our program was resumed, Cathy was again behaving in massively maladaptive fashion. She was highly negativistic, flatly and
usually screamingly refusing to cooperate in even minor ways. She had many
severe tantrums, throwing and breaking objects as she had years before, and even
physically attacking staff. There was no doubt that she was profoundly angry
with us and was showing it. The staff's reaction was much like that of her
parents! We felt distressed and partly responsible for her deterioration. We
sympathized with her anger, recognizing that she had much about which to be
angry.

Despite our sympathy, which perhaps made us tend to be too tolerant of
her bizarre behavior, our task was clear. The major goal with Cathy and the
other children was to return them as quickly as possible to the level at which

they had been functioning the previous spring. By the end of May, five months later, that goal had been achieved with Freddie, Gerry, and those young children who had not been in home programs over the summer, and nearly achieved with Cathy. Thus, one major effect of the seven month interruption in programming was the halting of progress for a full year (June 1967—June 1968) for most children and some loss for one (Cathy). The former pre-admission-group children who had remained in supervised home programs had no deterioration to over-come when they returned to our re-established program. A year after the program interruption, those children were functioning at a higher level than during their previous year. Having brought the children back up to their level of a year before, we were to have one more year (to June 1969) to try to bring about further progress. In the remainder of this chapter the last year and a half (i.e., our resumed program) will be described briefly.

The resumed program continued for an 18-month period, less eight weeks of vacation. The first to return were the three former focal group children (Cathy, Gerry, Freddie). Over the next year four additional boys, each about 12 years old, were added, and these seven children formed the "academic" group. A non-academic or social learning group for young children ranging in age from five to eight was also formed, consisting of four children formerly in the young or pre-admission group, and two newly-referred youngsters. These six young children were much like the focal group had been, having no usable speech and being characterized by severe deficit and surplus behavior.

For the final year and a half our approaches were essentially the same as those we had developed earlier with some refinements, such as the expanded use of a token reward system for the academic group, specific training of mothers in the groups for independent work with their children, and some attempts at highly systematic discrimination training for the young children.

The setting too was different than before and held several advantages. As part of a private school we were surrounded by other children and teachers and had available to us a variety of programs, materials and skills. For example, our groups had weekly periods with both an art teacher and, in the gym, with a physical therapist. Freddie received individual and group language training from a language teacher, while Cathy and some of the new academic group children were able to join higher-level classes in reading, mathemetics and science. Having our program in the midst of this variety of resources gave us added flexibility in programming for individual children, particularly in the academic areas.

The academic group of seven children was structured as the focal group had been, with continued social learning programs and a heavy empahsis on academics. All but Freddie had good speaking skills and were to read at least at a third grade level by the end of the year. All of them, however, had gross maladaptive surplus and deficit behavior, and they rarely functioned well, either socially or academically.

For example, Bob, a tall, slow-moving and slow-talking 13-year old, was an accomplished shoplifter who explained in his slow, matter-of-fact drawl, "I do my best work at Kresge's." He openly urinated and masturbated in class, destroyed books, papers, pencils or any other breakable equipment with a slow, careful, deliberateness. Bob persisted in taunting and goading other children into rages, particularly Cathy and Gerry, and he spent a great deal of time mumbling, laughing, crooning, making bizarre motions and remaining withdrawn from the group.

Jack was an intense, highly-explosive 13-year old with an exceedingly high-pitched voice that climbed to rapid and screech-like speech when provoked. He often physically attacked children and teachers, tore up his work in raging frustrations and devoted a good deal of time drawing amazingly good and complex pictures of dinosaurs, insects, machines, bridges, and roads. Many were detailed and imaginative works consisting, for example, of a crew of ants operating heavy equipment to build a complex system of roads and bridges, or an anesthetized stegosaurus on an operating table, about to undergo surgery.

For the first two months, Cathy, Gerry and Freddie, with all of their renewed disruptive surplus behavior, comprised the group. When Bob and Jack were added, the compounded surplus behavior arising out of their interactions was truly immense, leaving not a day unscarred by some new form of grotesquerie.

The program for this new academic group, structured much the same as the earlier program, had less of a trial-and-error quality and focused quickly on specific goals and approaches. After a new start-up time of about three weeks, which included detailed interviews with parents, daily observations of the children and planning of group and individual programs, the new programs were started (January 1968).

The immediate goal for the academic group was to reduce as quickly as possible the nearly constant surplus behavior of the three returning children. This was necessary because persistence of the surplus behavior would interfere with the further acquisition of social and academic skills.

By restricting and tightly structuring the physical space, specifying and clearly sequencing activities, reducing extraneous stimulation, keeping demands low and rewards high, removing as much as possible the more apparent reinforcers for the maintenance of disruptive behavior, we achieved about a 50 percent reduction of surplus behavior within the first four weeks. That is, instead of some major upsets occurring virtually all of the time, they were occurring about half of the time, giving us about three hours of relatively calm periods each day. As we had noted very early in the previous program, the reduction was primarily a reduction in duration of upsets and some lessening of intensity, while the number of upsets remained high. Further reductions were achieved by the use of relaxation periods throughout the day and the more refined removal or modification of stimuli that were clearly controlling many of the violent reactions. A good example of the latter is the modification of Cathy's reading material. After the first few weeks Cathy was calmed down enough to sit at a desk and focus on academic work. Her reading was accurate, but after only a few minutes she would erupt into a violent rampage. The same behavior occurred at times with arithmetic assignments. Since there seemed to be no clear reason for this consistent behavior, the teacher believed it to be a "willful" disobedience aimed at avoiding work and disrupting the class. Close observation revealed that as Cathy read (1) she soon became increasingly tense, her hands clenching, arms and shoulders tightening and facial grimaces beginning to appear. Within only a few minutes of the start of the growing muscular tension, Cathy erupted, frequently screaming "I can't, I can't," knocking over her desk, tearing and throwing the material and often running out of the room; (2) this behavior was under the control of the reading material itself, since all else in the situation was common to other settings in which she did not react tensely; (3) her reaction was less when the reading material was brief or there were few arithmetic items on each page. Based on these observations, we hypothesized that Cathy's reaction was to the stimulus complexity of the material and that she had not yet regained enough of her former attentive skills to deal with the resulting perceptual complexity. The solution seemed apparent: make reading a more clear, less complex perceptual task. Accordingly, we retyped her reading material, at first with only one short line per page, and found that Cathy was able to read many consecutive one-line pages without upset. Her successful attentive reading behavior was highly reinforced with verbal praise and tokens given immediately on her successfully completing each line. Gradually more lines were added to each page, reinforcement continued and soon she was reading a full page of text without any upset at all.

One of the more important developments of this year was the refinement and full use of a token reinforcement system[1] that had been partly used during the previous two years. The large array of back-up rewards included toys, games,

---

[1] I was introduced to token reinforcement systems in 1952 by Dr. Ralph Hefferline who described to his undergraduate abnormal psychology class at Columbia College a token system used in a summer camp. It included an inventive psychology-student camp counsellor, cardboard tokens and an array of back-up reinforcers (small toys) stored in an old trunk—the lid judiciously opened periodically and briefly just enough to establish it as a tantalizing treasure chest!

books, art supplies, as well as free time and a variety of activities. The immediacy of the token rewards were highly effective in reinforcing academic behavior particularly. Special contingencies were also set up for individual children. For example, in our only punitive use of tokens, Bob was "fined" for his destruction of property and he soon stopped. For the rest of the children the token rewards were used to shape a variety of social and academic behavior. Tokens were distributed immediately upon completion of some specified task and on a variable interval schedule for general classes of adaptive behavior. At first, the tokens were exchanged for back-up items at the end of each day. After three weeks, the "token store" was open only three days and, eventually, only one day per week. Initially, children immediately exchanged their tokens for low-cost items, usually toys. It was interesting to note how quickly all but Freddie began saving tokens and delaying their purchases so as to accumulate enough to buy special items, such as toy binoculars for Gerry, some science kits (plant-growing, making crystals in solutions, wiring bells and small electric motors) for Jack, and phonograph records of The Supremes for Cathy.

Some of the children, particularly Cathy, later reduced their purchases of concrete objects, preferring to spend their tokens to buy a variety of activities and "free time." Further in the program, free time was also contingent upon completion of specified tasks. Thus, a child would be shown the academic work to be completed and then left alone to work. Upon completion, he could then choose from a variety of highly reinforcing activities. Cathy, for example, frequently chose to go off by herself into another room and play with a large doll house. Jack often used the opportunity to draw complicated pictures. For each child the activities chosen were obviously highly reinforcing, and he worked well to attain those free time periods. The principle is Premack's (1959) in which one behavior is reinforced by the child's own behavior of a more highly reinforcing order.

As the program continued, the academic group became more orderly, verbal and cooperative. The children's academic and social behavior continued to improve and the setting took on a normal appearance. The loud outbursts had ended and bizarre behavior had been eliminated for all but Gerry and Bob, who maintained a low rate of bizarre behavior. For those two children our program succeeded in reducing, but not eliminating bizarre behavior.

During the final year, the programs for individual children in our group had become complex. The children spent part of their time together, for example, in the academic group, gym and art. In addition, at various points in the day individual children left our group and joined other classes. For example, Freddie went to a language class, Jack attended science and math and Cathy went to Math and English. In those classes the academic demands were greater than in our group, as were the demands for appropriate, cooperative, social behavior. Generally those classes much more closely approximated normal public school. It was our aim to prepare the children in our group for their full-time inclusion in those more normal classes. Toward that goal the final year saw the addition of two more boys to our group, the continued refinements of the program, and plans for its complete absorption by the private school.

THE LAST DAY

On our program's final day in June 1969 I saw all the children for the last time. I remember in particular a quiet conversation with Cathy, who was then 12 years old. We had worked together—and so many times in opposition—for more than five years, and I felt a special fondness for her. In a sunny little room, seated on two comfortable chairs, we talked. This was no interview carried out by a professional, but just a quiet, desultory conversation between a child and an adult who had known each other for several years and who had both traveled a goodly distance in that time. Our mood was reminiscent, and our conversation nibbled selectively around "remember when. . . ?" We stayed clear of the numerous painful conflicts of the past, and instead focused on the friends we had known and the happy, nice or humorous things we remembered.

At one point Cathy began to cry softly. "It's about Gerry," she explained. There had been some discussion of Gerry's possibly going to another school after our program ended. "What will happen to Gerry?" she asked. "Will the other school treat him right?" "They won't know how to treat him like we do."

As our conversation continued, Cathy, among other things, asked about my daughter, Amy.

"Um, what does Amy do in nursery school now?"
"Amy? Oh! You know, Cathy, Amy's in kindergarten now."
"Oh! Well, what does she do in kindergarten, play all day?"
"Mm, no. They play some of the time, but they also do some work. Some writing, some arithmetic . . . ."
"Oh, yeah, I know. Easy stuff. You mean like one and one and stuff like that? We used to do that. But now they give harder stuff, Mrs. Wendell does."
"Yeah, that's right, you're doing a lot harder work than that."
"What time does Amy go to kindergarten?"
"She starts about 9:30. But you know, Amy's not in school this week."
"No? Why not?"

"Because she has the mumps."

"Oh! How long will she be out? Two weeks, isn't it?"

"No, only a week, and then back to school. Tell me, Cathy, did you
   ever have the mumps?"

"Oh, yes. About, umm, two years ago. That would make it, let's see,
   1967." Cathy pauses, swings one leg a little, and watches dust
   motes sparkle in a shaft of sun, and then asks:

"Did Amy have the, um, the German mumps?"

"German mumps? (I smile.) No, Cath, she had plain, old-fashioned,
   American mumps."

(Cathy laughs at this.) "Plain old-fashioned, huh? I guess that's what I
   had. Amy can't play with any kids until the mumps are all out."

"That's right, not until she's all over the mumps."

We were silent for a while. Cathy picked up a stop watch from the table
next to her. We clicked it into movement, watching the minute hand on the
small dial and the large sweep second hand. Cathy looked up, smiling:

"Can we put wings on it and see how it flies?"

"How it flies? The watch?"

"Yeah" (Cathy beams.) "How time flies!"

"Oh" (We both laugh.)

"I fooled you. That's a moron joke. Morons do silly things."

"Yeah," and to myself, repeated slowly, "and time flies."

Soon, as if on cue, we heard the going home sounds of children gathering
their things, and cars and busses pulling up to the door.

And as quickly as that, our program was over.

CHAPTER 12

Summary and Conclusions

We have tried to describe in detail our six-year effort to develop special services for children labeled "severely disturbed." The project, which operated from May 1963 to May 1969, began in response to a clinical service need and maintained a primary service focus throughout. We began with the facts of the behavior of four children and the failure of local professionals to provide adequate services. Our initial general assumptions were (1) previous psychodynamic approaches had been ineffective with severely disturbed children and alternative approaches were needed; (2) the alternative we chose to explore was the systematic application of behavioral principles. Our overall task was to develop effective children's services through exploring the clinical applications of behavioral concepts.

The exploratory program developed well for nearly four years, at which point it dissolved in political turmoil. Seven months later, with only a small portion of the previous year's staff, the program was reactivated, operating under many constraints for nearly 18 months before it was terminated. It was during the first four years that we had the most opportunity to develop our ideas, and we have drawn primarily on that period in preparing this book.

Our major intent in this book has been to share our experiences and conclusions with parents, teachers, mental health workers, and students. We hope these readers have found some helpful and some thought provoking ideas.

Our presentation has been primarily descriptive, utilizing an essentially case study approach that will not satisfy those readers who demand more experimental validation. The criticism is well taken; we have developed, described, demonstrated, and discussed our approaches, but have not tested or confirmed them. The program's complete disorganization at the end of the fourth year

261

prevented the evaluation research planned for the following year. In fact, those plans for evaluative research provided one of the issues in those conflicts which destroyed the program.

We are left then with our exploratory observations and tentative conclusions and these are offered in the hope that they can be useful despite their inconclusiveness.

In this final chapter we will briefly summarize the program, touching on the major developments of each of the six years. Following that will be a brief summary of our main conclusions, suggestions for future children's programs, and a note to the parents of exceptional children.

A SUMMARY OF PROGRAM DEVELOPMENT

First Year

The first year focused on organizational problems and community status of the agency (i.e., the political-professional level) and the conceptual and applied level of programming. Our basic position was that children's maladaptive behavior can be largely accounted for by their learning history and understood in terms of learning concepts. All children, regardless of their degree of behavioral disturbance, are capable of learning complex, socially adaptive behavior; it is the professional's task to provide those conditions under which even the most severely disturbed child will learn complex, adaptive social behavior. The main problem is *learning* and the main task becomes *teaching*. Accordingly, the agency must become a highly specialized teaching situation in which the staff develops specific techniques for teaching adaptive behavior to children. In this endeavor, it was assumed that a group setting would facilitate adaptive social learning and its transfer to other situations, that behavioral approaches can be readily taught to non-professionals including parents, that parents require training in reality-oriented, concrete, everyday methods of childrearing and *active* involvement in the child's therapy or educational program, that active, consistent *modeling* of adaptive behavior by staff is crucial, and that modifying complex behavior requires an analysis of its more specific constituents and their reinforcement in carefully-planned sequences of successive approximations of the behavioral goals.

Most of the first year was devoted to developing working systems that translated those assumptions into concrete procedures. A children's group was formed, staff hired, (Chapter 2), and the parents' cooperation obtained. Observations of deficit and surplus behavior were made from which we identified the major behavioral goals and programming directions (behavior acquisition or decrement). Behavior goals and program dimensions common to the focal group of four children as well as those specific to individual children were defined (Chapter 2). The teaching programs entailed behavioral assessments, a structured setting to manage stimulus control and reinforcement contingencies necessary to bring about adaptive behavior, and the assumption that maladaptive behavior would decrease as a direct consequence of increased adaptive behavior. Thus, initially, we focused directly on the acquisition of adaptive behavior and indirectly on the decrement of maladaptive behavior.

The program structure consisted of specific strategies and organization of the daily program (Chapter 4) in order to facilitate stimulus control and contingency management and maximize stimulus values so as to increase discrimination by the children. The major dimensions of program structure were (a) time scheduling and sequencing of activities, (b) determining and controlling content of activities, (c) zoning physical space, (d) setting and maintaining clearly-defined behavioral limits, and (e) systematically controlling important discriminating, eliciting and reinforcing stimuli. These dimensions were all aimed at providing stable, clearly-discriminable limits.

Based on our assumptions, trials and errors and intensive work, there began to emerge a reasonably consistent approach to the children. Behavioral goals were specified that defined programming dimensions and directions of change. These dimensions consisted of a range of goal-constituent behaviors, to which were applied techniques to stimulate and reinforce those responses in small-step sequences progressively approximating complex behavior goals. Planned in detail for each child, the programs were applied in a group setting to maximize overlap of common goals and take advantage of the presumably powerful social-learning value of a group. The major programming dimensions specified as common to all children were:

A. Acquisition Sequences (i.e., increases in)
    1. Social interaction, including general positive response to others, social cooperation, verbal and non-verbal communication
    2. Physical involvement with the environment, including appropriate use of common objects
    3. Appropriate verbal behavior
    4. School, social and academic skills
    5. Independent or self-care behavior
    6. Behavior flexibility, i.e., using alternative behaviors
B. Response-decrement sequences
    1. Repetitive and stereotyped behavior
    2. Inappropriate vocal/verbal behavior
    3. Aggressive and destructive behavior
    4. Inappropriate eating behavior

5. Hyperactivity
6. Fears

The initial six months were devoted to organizational problems and preliminary analyses after which several more children were added to our project, new groups organized, and the behavioral programming was begun. The first general programming goal was to reinforce all approximations of social behavior, and then gradually shape higher levels. The situation was structured presumably so that minimal social responses could readily occur; i.e., at least the initial, low-level social responses expected of the children were assumed already to be part of their behavior repertoire. Accordingly, the staff waited for children to emit desired behavior that could then be reinforced. However, it soon became clear that this strategy would not work. The children simply did not emit sufficient social behavior that could be reinforced; their initial operant level was far lower than we had thought. Secondly, even if they occasionally did emit desired responses, reinforcement could not be applied because the stimuli intended by us to be reinforcers were either too difficult to readily administer or, when applied, were ineffective (Chapter 4). In essence, ineffectual reinforcers were being used in an attempt to strengthen behaviors which were not even being emitted!

Thus, early in the program we had run into our first blind alley and had to develop alternative goals and procedures. The direct shaping of adaptive social behavior was postponed while we moved to a more basic level of achieving a program whereby we would (a) stimulate a higher rate of general behavior and (b) identify and later develop effective reinforcers. To accomplish these goals, the staff assumed a highly active role in stimulating the children until they finally made their first—and unexpected—consistent response to staff: they retreated whenever a worker came near.

The constant stimulation was apparently noxious and by moving away the children effected a presumably reinforcing cessation of noxious stimulation. The same reinforcement was used to teach them to reach a hand toward and touch people and approximate words. In a few weeks they had acquired a variety of new, simple responses. However, they became increasingly aggressive and difficult to control because, in developing their new, high response rate, all behavior, including aggressive behavior, had been reinforced.

A high rate of behavior had been established and a variety of reinforcers identified (Chapter 6). With those basic tasks completed, the staff began to focus on differential reinforcement, actively selecting only adaptive behaviors to be reinforced, shaping increasingly social behavior. It soon became apparent that selective or differential reinforcement aimed at shaping social behavior of severely disturbed children is a highly complex task requiring an intense focus on programming details.

More generalized reinforcers, such as verbal stimuli, were needed in this complex social-learning task, and one of the important learning settings established was snack time, a reward-dispensing social situation. Snack time soon acquired its own high positive reinforcement value and was used to directly shape cooperative social and verbal behavior and to develop secondary reinforcers (i.e., generalized verbal reinforcers, see Chapter 6).

The acquisition of secondary, generalized reinforcing value by verbal stimuli was a major achievement. Dependence on primary rewards decreased as use of verbal reinforcement increased, and interaction with the children became largely verbal. That first year was one in which basic organizational and programming goals were sought, simple social behaviors begun and reinforcers developed, all of which would be used as the program continued.

The Second Year

Utilizing the previous year's developments, the second year focused more heavily on the development of complex social behavior in the focal group. Several new dimensions were added, the most important of which were: (1) continued strengthening and generalizing the learned social behavior within and beyond the immediate group structure, (2) adding school time, an academic dimension (Chapter 6), and (3) dealing specifically with the extremely high rate, intensity and duration of aggressive behavior that reached its peak just after the middle of the second year. A variety of methods were developed to bring aggressive behavior under control (Chapter 7).

By the beginning of the third year, the children were far more socially interactive and at a more sophisticated level. Their aggressive behavior had begun to decrease in intensity and duration, though not in incidence. School time had increased to nearly a half hour daily.

Thus, the second year saw an intensification of direct shaping of social and verbal behavior through both primary and secondary reinforcement and a utilization of the basic reinforcers and behaviors previously developed. In this second year snack time was used as the basis for developing school time; the secondary reinforcers developed during snack time were used to strengthen behaviors during school. The range of learning social behaviors increased and attempts were made to generalize the newly-learned social behaviors to wider aspects of the world, such as the home, and walks in town where the children visited stores, parks and playgrounds. Also in the second year, the staff and children began to come to grips with the children's highly aggressive behavior. By the end of the second year, the children had developed to a far higher and more stable level of social behavior; their aggressive behavior was under somewhat better control, and school time had been initiated.

In addition to those programming developments, the agency was beginning to receive more significant support and recognition, particularly from the field of education. Many referrals were coming in and the program and agency were growing.

The Third Year

The third year continued to build on the first two both in terms of the agency's growth and the clinical programming. Both the summer camp and the regular program were expanded and included many poverty level children. The duration of daily school sessions increased and a second daily school session was initiated, giving the children about 45 minutes of school each day. The children's behavior during school sessions had improved markedly, and they were beginning simple pre-academic skills (Chapter 6). By the middle of the third year, the children had developed beyond the curriculum knowledge of the group worker and a certified teacher was hired to conduct the two daily school sessions. Employing the previously developed structure, the teacher introduced a variety of learning settings to teach reading, number concepts, printing, and an expanding use of verbal phrases. Teaching was also carried out through trips, including the familiar daily walks in the city which gradually developed into informal and highly enjoyable expeditions to stores, playgrounds, the zoo and a bird sanctuary.

By the end of the thrid year, school time was lasting nearly an hour and half in a program that had developed to nearly six hours daily. The children were using standard pre-primer books and lower first-grade reading material and were able to work in school with few severe upsets.

On the latter point, the use of relaxation training had been introduced to reduce the still high incidence of aggressive outbursts and our data at the end of the year indicated that it was a successful method (Chapter 7).

By the end of the third year, all of the major program dimensions had been developed and the overall program was functioning well, with the children obviously operating at higher levels than previously. The program had expanded and was receiving good support and recognition. Paradoxically, at the start of the third year, when all seemed to be progressing well, conflicts became apparent between the board president and the program director. The general conflict was over control of the program. Specific issues related to the proposed research plans, the controversial inclusion of poverty-level children, and a proposed merger with another agency (Chapters 1 and 11).

The Fourth Year

The fourth year began against a background of political conflicts that became increasingly severe as the year progressed. The program nevertheless continued to develop and operate well. The daily academic sessions, now totalling more than two and a half hours, included six children with one teacher and employed second—and third-grade reading material. Clearly the time, cooperative behavior and independent academic work in these sessions had all increased appreciably and the school group had progressed far since its brief and uncertain sessions in the second year (Chapter 6).

Despite the political infighting, the fourth year had opened with considerable staff excitement and optimism in that we were actually approaching some of the long-term behavioral goals for the children. The initial goals, such as increasing general response rate and shaping simple approach behavior, decreasing aggressive and bizarre surplus, developing language, social cooperation, and beginning academics, had clearly been achieved. In addition, some of the later, more subtle behavior goals, especially sustained social cooperation, increased verbal interaction and flexibility of behavior—or general social competency— were emerging. The "modal direction" of our program had been to bring psychotic behavior under control and that emphasis continued with new children enrolled. Some of the focal group children, particularly Cathy and Billy, had progressed beyond our goals and were ready for more subtle social and academic learning that our program could only approximate. Accordingly, in the fourth year we began planning for each child's eventual move from our program to more normal social settings, such as special or regular classes in public school.

A complex, stepped up social learning program involving her parents as well as herself was developed for Cathy. Its aim was to prepare her for public school placement the following year. Plans for similar programs were begun for Billy and Frankie, with the goal of moving them out of our program a year after Cathy.

Another important programming development of the fourth year was the active involvement of parents as therapists.

Early in the fourth year, it was clear that the major programming dimensions had been developed and a coherent program with systematic approaches had been created. By virtue of our exploratory work we could now describe a systematic clinical program for severely disturbed children. The program required further refinements and careful evaluation. Accordingly, plans were made to carry out a two-year evaluation of our methods with two new groups of children for whom careful baseline, treatment and post-treatment measures would be taken. These children would be given the best possible clinical program we could devise and would provide reliable, controlled, evaluative data.

The fourth year began with a highly optimistic staff, excited by the obvious improvements of the children. Plans were made for moving some children into public school; parents became more active and responsible in home programs, and clear research plans were made and data-gathering begun. However, by May of that year the political conflicts had become so intense that the program ended in bitter disorganization (Chapter 11).

The Fifth and Sixth Years

After its disorganization, our program for the focal group did not operate for seven months, May to December, although the summer program for poverty-level children was carried out. By the time the regular program was reorganized in December 1967, key staff and many children had left and we began to work primarily with new children. The program continued, but under many constraints and, in a year and a half, was finally phased out.

In the attempted reorganization, two related factors were clear: (1) the crucial program continuity and group organization that had developed over four years had been destroyed and could not be easily retrieved; (2) the seven-month program suspension acted in some ways as an unfortunate "return-to-baseline" condition, and the children suffered severe behavioral deterioration. Adding some validity to this is the observation that four children whose parents continued to maintain supervised home programs did not deteriorate.

It required at least six months for our renewed program to bring the children who rejoined us back to their behavioral level of a year earlier. Thus, because of the adults' bickering, the children had lost at least a full year of development. More crucial was the timing of the disorganization that prevented completion of the plans to move some children to public school.

The final year had new children added to the program, active involvement of parents, and, mostly, a final phasing out, as the program was gradually integrated with a private school.

Our efforts to develop services spanned six years and two months, within which children's groups operated for five years and six months. Subtracting vacations, the time in session totalled four years and seven months.

THE FOCAL GROUP

Our program included 161 children, 66 staff, many parents and other lay people. In the present work we have used a particular group of children—the focal group—as a vehicle for describing the development of our ideas and approaches. That group consisted of ten children, three of whom entered during the final 15 months. Two years after the program ended the focal group children were enrolled in a variety of programs.

Mary, whose parents were killed in an automobile accident, is in a state residential school for retarded children. Billy's family has moved to another city, where he is enrolled in a private day school. Cathy, Freddie and Gerry are enrolled in a private school. According to her parents, Cathy has reached the sixth grade academically and appears to be doing well socially. Gerry has achieved a third to fourth grade level but his bizarre surplus behavior has not diminished. The private school does not appear to be working on control of that behavior. Freddie apparently has reached a plateau, making few gains beyond his level of two years ago.

Frankie and Allen are both in public school special classes, but we have no other information about them. Roy, Paul and Jack entered our program for the final year and a half. Roy's family has moved and we have no information about him. Paul and Jack are both in public school regular classes.

MAJOR CONCLUSIONS

The six-year project yields a mixture of success and failure; our equivocal results are largely unsatisfying in light of our originally stated goals: (1) develop practical clinical-educational service programs for severely disturbed children that would be achieved by (2) developing and (3) evaluating behaviorally-based methods. The first two goals were clearly achieved; the third was not. Behaviorally-based clinical programs for children were developed and, even after the program ended, other agencies, stimulated by our work, incorporated behavioral methods.

The third goal, evaluation, was clearly not achieved, and although the program can be evaluated, the evaluation falls short of our original expectations. When evaluated several times by mental health and educational professionals, the program compared very favorably with other clinical and educational programs. It was judged to meet all professional standards and to operate at least as well as other acceptable agencies. These evaluations assessed at least some minimal professional competence for programs, supposedly providing some safeguards for the public. The evaluations were made by teams of professionals who visited the program for one or two working days. They observed children's group sessions, interviewed staff and some parents, inspected our record-keeping systems, lines of inter-agency cooperation, and considered the nature of our evaluative procedures. They tried to assess:

1. *Physical variables and general policy* — (a) meeting state and local fire, health and safety codes, (b) meeting minimum staff-child ratios, (c) having access to adequate outdoor play area, (d) having adequate educational and play equipment and furniture, (e) observing non-discriminatory child enrollment and staff-selection practices;

2. *Professional support* — (a) access to professional consultation in related fields (e.g., neurology, opthalmology and optometry, audiology, dentistry, etc), (b) form and quality of staff selection, training and supervision, (c) adequacy of record-keeping, (d) direct help to parents, (e) inclusion of state licensed or certified professionals (e.g., teachers and psychologists);
3. *Quality of program operation* — (a) number and ratio of children and staff per group, (b) number of per-child and group hours in weekly sessions, (c) program goals, (d) consistency of staff functioning, (e) methods of case evaluations, (f) processes of child-program planning,
4. *Theoretical base* — (a) assessing presence and degree of consistent theoretical base underlying the work, (b) determining whether eventual evaluation of methods is feasible, (c) determining whether the program's theory and/or methods have been presented to colleagues through journals and paper presentations.

From several evaluations the program was judged to be of acceptable quality, functioning at least as well as other older acceptable programs. In addition to meeting the state's evaluative criteria, the program also had several dimensions that made it unique and of greater interest to the evaluators. Compared with other agencies, the program offered alternative theory and methods; it included evaluation based on more discrete variables; parents were far more actively involved; there was a major focus on training and employing sub-professionals; the program sought to work specifically with the most-disturbed children in the area; it integrated treatment and educational goals; the per hour cost of services, while only slightly under that for public school special education, was considerably less than that in other mental health agencies. In the estimation of the evaluating professionals, the program offered several different interesting dimensions. When judged by evaluative standards typically used in the mental health field, the program compared very favorably with others and clearly met or surpassed even the most demanding criteria applied by the state.

When we apply still more demanding levels of criteria for effectiveness—levels that are not typically applied in clinical and educational operations—the program failed to meet our evaluation goals. Our failure to carry out the planned evaluation during the fifth and sixth years or to have obtained more quantitative data during the first four years leaves us with descriptive, observational data gathered under largely uncontrolled conditions, and thus restricts our conclusions. The data do, however, reflect a mass of direct and indirect observation of children and their families. The focal group, for example, entailed more than 4000 hours of programs in which the children were directly observed for highly discrete behaviors by at least 18 different staff over a period of six calendar years. It is primarily from these observations that our conclusions are drawn.

A major limitation of the largely uncontrolled nature of our observations is that we cannot specify precise antecedents to our major conclusions. Most of them are the results of accumulated observations and impressions over the several programming years. They are, therefore, tentative and not intended to suggest the specificity and power of confirmed hypotheses. The major conclusions presented here are largely summaries of what has already been discussed earlier.

1. Observed Behavior Change. Our first conclusion is presented with a great deal of confidence: the focal group children, who began with severe deficit and surplus behavior, obviously and significantly improved. Sophisticated measures are not needed for this assertion. Rather, observations that previously aloof, aggressive, non-talking children are now interacting with affectionate and co-operative behavior, that children with no academic skills now read and write, or that the swollen, discolored faces, lacerated skin and bald spots of self-abusive children have cleared up provide sufficient evidence that their behaviors, most of many years' duration, have changed.

It can be concluded too, but with less confidence, that the observed improvements were brought about specifically by our program. This appears particularly true of the decrease in bizarre and hyperactive behavior, the initial development of positive social interaction and the development of the wide range of academic behavior, all of which were highly program-specific. Also, the unfortunate reversal-to-baseline-conditions that occurred after the fourth year suggests the earlier improvements had been controlled by our programming.

We cannot conclude that our methods were more effective than traditional psychodynamic approaches, since that comparison was not made directly.

While obvious in all of the focal group children, these observed improvements cannot be considered to constitute over all cures. All of the children, even those who improved most, retained some of their previous surplus and deficit behavior. We suggest that had the program continued, the observed improvements would have been greater. That, however, is speculative. The fact is that none of the focal group children overcame all of their maladaptive behavior.

2. The Personal Significance of the Behavioral Changes. Because none of the children were "cured" the question remains whether those observed changes for which we so long labored were significant. Again with confidence, we conclude that the behavioral changes were significant for the children and their families. The development, for example, of speech and language, social and academic skills, and control of aggressive behavior were major developments that altered the children's interactions with their families, generally improving them. For example, a large reduction in a child's aggressive behavior, the development of toilet training, the reduction of his fear of water (and thus of bathing) might alter those child-parent interactions around which conflicts had previously developed. These changes in the child's behavior frequently occasioned greater positive approaches and rewards by parents, which then led to a mutual shaping of positive interaction.

Our repeated observation is that changes in discrete behaviors which at first glance seem to have little "real" value result in *generalized* rather than isolated effects when introduced into the family system. The inference is that the child's personal and family systems amplify the discrete behavior changes through complex behavioral chaining. Our conclusion is that carefully selected, discrete behavior changes can have significant *generalized* effects. They are therefore of therapeutic importance and should be sought in children's programs.

3. The Need for Skill Training. Many of the behaviors can be viewed in terms of the active development of skills. As the program continued, we became more impressed with the importance of teaching specific skills that make up larger, more generalized behavior categories. Each new skill (e.g., how to speak clearly, use crayons, or the bathroom) provided the child with greater potential success in and control over his environment. Presumably, the accretion of skills will increase the child's ability to solve problems. The point may seem obvious but is emphasized here because in our experience it appears *not* to be taken at all seriously by clinical agencies which typically focus on "insight" and "self-understanding," while doing little to help the child actively develop skills to cope with his immediate and future world.

The importance of programming for discrete behavior change, including a major focus on direct teaching of skills, must therefore be emphasized. This teaching can be best accomplished by providing the child with daily, detailed practice in the specific behaviors being taught. It requires a great deal of *detailed* and hard labor on the part of the helping professional; suits and ties, careful coiffures, high heels, white shirts, and professional dignity are not part of the labor picture. "Love is not enough," according to Dr. Bettelheim, to which we must add, "neither is insight."

4. Importance of Behavior Maintenance Systems. Initially in our work, as in most behavior modification, our attention was focused primarily on developing and applying systems to *change* behavior, with relatively little attention given to *maintaining* the new behavior. Behavior maintenance systems became increasingly important as the children developed to higher levels of behavior. Our seven-month disruption taught us the necessity of developing systems to maintain both newly-learned and previously-existing adaptive behavior. Maintenance systems become important after behavioral gains have been made and are particularly needed outside of the treatment program where special attention must be paid to preventing the reshaping of maladaptive behaviors.

5. Parent Training and Home Programs. The above point emphasizes the necessity of developing behavior modification *and* maintenance programs in the home. Parental involvement is necessary in nearly all cases. In our work we found the parents to be both willing and fully capable of assuming active roles and carrying out detailed and direct measures to help their children. We conclude that active parental involvement, even to the extent of their being trained to assume a co-therapist's responsibility, is not only feasible, but is necessary and highly valuable when carried out, for both behavior modification and maintenance.

6. Selecting and Training Paraprofessionals. We found that when selection is carried out with care, potentially good child workers (i.e., teachers, therapists) can be identified in the general population and, their lack of professional background notwithstanding, trained in a short time. The importance of careful *selection* is underscored as being at least equal to and perhaps of greater importance than training. We conclude that cities can yield an abundance of potentially effective, non-professional child workers to provide services for *all* of its exceptional children. We suggest that all child health professions devote a large portion of their efforts to selecting and training such paraprofessionals.

7. The Modeling Task. We are convinced that direct, consistent and unambiguous *modeling* of adaptive behavior by staff is of crucial importance. Staff should be selected for, trained, and supported in successful modeling skills. Sharp alertness and monitoring by staff of their own modeling behavior is necessary. A major message of staff to the children is "Do as I *do*."

8. The Political Nature of Helping. We conclude that helping is tightly entwined with the non-scientific social context of the helpers, the helped and all of the surrounding culture. Mental health programs may conceptually begin as humanitarian and scientific endeavors. However, when these ideals are confronted by the realities of working with people, the effort becomes redefined as the art and application of politics. The development of the mental health profession has been essentially the politicizing of the original scientific and humanitarian ideals.

To a degree, such politicizing is necessary if the humanitarian and scientific notions are ever to be applied to populations generally. However, the process has gone far beyond a level of politicizing in the service of humanitarian and scientific ideals. In fact, there seems to have developed a reversal of priorities so that those ideals are now used to develop social and political power. We maintain that the practical result is that the helping agencies' major commitment of resources and effort is to the preservation and enhancement of their own social power, which conflicts with and largely blocks the task of delivering effective helping services.

One of the major aims of this book is to help both laymen and professionals to recognize the importance of this issue.

9. Psychodynamic versus Behavioral Concepts. One of our most important initial assumptions was that professional attempts to help severely disturbed children had failed because of the limiting constraints imposed by the psychodynamic framework. However, we soon became convinced that the major limitations were political and not conceptual. That is, the application of psychodynamic theory was itself constrained by the professions' own politics, just as were our own behavioral programs. It is a gross failure of those persons who have been operating clinical agencies not to have recognized and dealt with the political constraints which have been, after all, of our own making.

At this point we must maintain our position that psychodynamic approaches to severely disturbed children still have not been clearly validated and, based on admittedly incomplete evidence, we would still choose to apply behaviorally-based programming. Controlled comparisons between approaches are needed.

SUGGESTIONS FOR FUTURE PROGRAMMING

Our major conclusion is that severely disturbed children with gross, long-term maladaptive deficit and surplus behavior can improve significantly. They can be taught complex, cooperative social behavior, academic achievement, self-control and appropriate use of language. There is no doubt that our focal group children made significant gains and that they no longer displayed the earlier levels of autistic characteristics such as aloneness, preservation of sameness (Rimland, 1964), or severely aggressive, destructive, stereotyped or bizarre behavior.

We also conclude that behavioral concepts and techniques can be (1) effectively developed and applied to *groups* of severely disturbed children and (2) taught to highly selected non-professionals who have high school education but are without previous mental health training. Potentially effective therapists exist in great numbers in the general adult population, and with careful selection and approximately one year's training, there need be no scarcity of personnel for children's services.

Further, it is important to note that the observed improvement over the first four years was brought about in just over three years of actual programming (three years and four months). This was achieved under exploratory conditions that included many errors, blind alleys, and time-consuming back-tracking to undo mistakes. It seems reasonable to suggest that under more stable, less exploratory conditions, a similar level of improvement could be achieved in considerably less time.

We therefore suggest that it is possible through detailed, behavioral programming operating five or six days weekly to bring these severely disturbed children to levels of complex, adaptive social behavior well within only three years. Such improvement, while clearly significant for each child, nevertheless does not constitute "cure" or total change in functioning.

Further, but even more speculatively, it seems reasonable to suggest that (1) uninterrupted programming continuing for more than three years might produce higher levels of change and (2) a residential program of even more intensive and total programming might produce still more rapid and complete changes. An effective combination might begin with a brief intensive residential program, followed by an integrated day care and home program, gradually moving toward the child's disengagement from the day care program into more normal settings, such as public school. To us, in light of our experience, these predictions appear reasonable. But whether such improvements can actually occur through behavioral programming, in so short a time and to higher levels must be answered empirically through future programs designed to test the predictions.

If given the opportunity to test the suggestions of this book, we would organize a group behavior modification program for a small number of children, select and train non-professionals and maximally involve parents in helping roles. Our programming structure would be much as has been described in our previous work, with primary focus on the active, direct teaching of adaptive behavior in structured, high-reinforcement behavior-contingent programming.

To overcome the major weaknesses of our previous program we would emphasize the research and evaluation functions from the beginning, specifying and clarifying them in the original contractual arrangements as an *essential* basic component of any service program. Objective observational data recording would begin immediately to determine quantitative as well as qualitative-descriptive baselines, treatment and post-treatment data which would be evaluated in terms of the single, within-subject designs used in behavioral research (see

Sidman, 1960; Gelfand and Hartman, 1968; Tharp and Wetzel, 1969; and Browning and Stover, 1971).

Each group would have four to six children, with a 1:2 staff-child ratio. The entire program itself would be small to enable a detailed, individual focus on each child to be maintained. Further, to maximize and support high parental involvement, the program would be *local*, i.e., near the children's homes. A large, centralized hospital or school far from a child's home is not conducive to close relationships with the parents and home or easy transfer of shared programs across settings. Within cities the population density is great enough so that neighborhood programs could be located within walking distance of the children's homes.

The underlying goal of this program would be to modify children's behavior so that they develop a sufficiently wide range of behavioral choices to eventually exercise control over thier own lives. The essence of behavior modification as we have used it is the development of varieties of skills so as to increase not only the child's functional effectiveness, but primarily his *freedom to act as an independent person in control of his own life.*

This program would operate in a highly concentrated fashion, a major prediction being that concentrated, consistently-applied programming, with maximal parental involvement will produce significant and specified improvements in three years. The controlled data collection would yield a sufficient basis to accept or reject that prediction.

Initial baselines would include physical dimensions (general health, height and weight, growth rate), sensory-perceptual dimensions (neurological, visual, auditory evaluations) as well as the behavioral dimensions. Where necessary, physical problems, including nutrition, would be treated so as to control as much as possible variables that might result in physical illness.

Programming would be intensive, carried out for six-to-eight hours daily at least five days weekly, plus the parents' work at home. Because of the program's intensity, demands on parents would be high. To provide them some respite, special staff would be trained to take care of the children 24 hours daily and maintain programs for weekends or up to two-week periods. These "home-maker" programs could be carried out in residential centers or summer camps as well as in the children's homes.

What has been outlined here is essentially the program we had planned but could not carry out for the last two years. It is hoped that some readers of this book will be sufficiently stimulated to do what we could not—to carry out what might be a definitive test of the effectiveness of behavioral programming for severely disturbed children.

ACTIVE MENTAL HEALTH CONSUMERISM—
A NOTE TO PARENTS

Our final comments are for the parents of all of those children who have been variously labeled as autistic, schizophrenic, psychotic, or severely emotionally disturbed. Whatever differences are suggested by the various labels—for example, it appears to be fairly clear that autism is a condition which differs from schizophrenia—(see Rimland)—we know that there is a commonality of behavior. All of these children share elements of grossly severe deficit and surplus behavior, and in fact the behaviors are indistinguishable a large proportion of the time. In the present book we have focused on the similarities of behavior rather than differences, and thus have paid little attention to differential diagnoses. Allowing that children labeled differently might in fact be different we nevertheless believe they can all (including many children labeled "retarded") be grouped together, based on each child's observed functioning, in the same program. Our intense *individual* focus in program planning should take care of many differences that might be related to diagnostic categories.

In this book too we have focused on the *behavior* of the children, ignoring for the most part any physical factors. All of the children had regular pediatric examinations and at least one neurological examination. Other medical treatment, including dental treatment, was obtained by the parents whenever recommended by their pediatrician. By our lack of detailed discussion we do not wish to minimize the importance of medical treatment. We urge parents to see to it that their children have regular, complete medical examinations and treatment for any medical conditions. Medical evaluations are particularly important in ruling out or treating a physical problem that may be contributing to the behavior disorder. In our experience we have often found that parents overlook some physical problems that could be treated, because the problems were masked by the children's behavior. For example, dental and visual symptoms were assumed to be part of the children's behavioral problems and thus not investigated. Because of these children's poor ability to communicate discomfort or pain, parents must be particularly alert to physical problems and strive to keep their children in good physical health.

In the future, researchers may discover some clear physical variables that account for the disturbed conditions of these children and specific medical treatment for the overall condition might become available as another aid in providing help. Such specific treatment, however, does not at present exist and there is little indication that it will exist in the near future. Meanwhile, behavioral programming can be started and might even constitute all of the child's treatment. Therefore, parents are also urged to seek the best educational-training programs.

That last point, however, poses some problems. It is generally easier to obtain competent evaluations than it is to find competent, long-term treatment or training. Unfortunately, programs do not exist in sufficient numbers, scope or quality. When we began our work early in 1963, we attributed such lack to the mental health professionals' continued use of psychodynamic theory and approaches, a model which we believed had clearly failed in the past and was simply not working with severely disturbed children. We established our program, therefore, as an alternative approach; our six years' experience has convinced us that highly structured behavior modification programming is an effective approach with severely disturbed children; though it did not "cure" them, it improved them in significant ways.

Behavior modification is one of several approaches and, while it appears to be effective, it remains to be seen through careful research which approaches are best for which children, and under what conditions. In the meantime without definitive research we can offer our professional opinion of the current state of knowledge, based on our own direct experience: *for severely disturbed children we recommend that the current treatment of choice is long-term, intensive, daily behavioral programming, organized around the task of teaching adaptive behavioral and cognitive skills.* Before any behavioral programming is undertaken, the children must have thorough physical evaluations and, when necessary, treatment. *A psychiatric examination is not sufficient to evaluate the child's physical condition!*

We have mentioned our original assessment that the generally poor service picture was primarily due to the generally unquestioned use of psychoanalytic or psychodynamic theory. Our subsequent experiences convinced us that this is only a small part of the problem, and the major reasons for the professions' failure are *political* not conceptual. We argue that the mental health field has become an essentially political field in which agencies struggle to survive. If they do succeed in surviving, they necessarily do so by enhancing their own social power; providing sufficient and effective services becomes of secondary importance. Moreover, within the meager service area, children's programs seem to be given the lowest priority.

Thus the professions' earlier failure to provide effective services was more the result of the professions' own entrapment—being caught up in political struggles to enhance their own social power and, in the process, focus on their own welfare first, and clients' welfare secondarily—than it was their "bad" or "weak" theory.

I am confident that the following blanket statement is correct (and would be most pleased to learn that it is not): in no city or town in the United States are there any clearly effective, long-term services readily available for these children. Parents who have been through the agency maze know this from experience. Unfortunately, there is no reason to expect the mental health profession to improve itself in the near future. It is not that individual professionals are unwilling to help, but they have become so tightly locked into bureaucracies, rigid procedures and roles which focus on maintaining professionalism and provide powerful reinforcement, that they are generally unable to see their own failures; moreover, those who do perceive the professions' weaknesses are generally unable to develop alternatives because of the control imposed by the bureaucratic and professional power structures. Countless professionals who have tried know that it is extremely difficult to change the long-established procedures of an old, politically successful clinic or hospital, regardless of how ineffective or wasteful its procedures may be.

Despite the many professionals who desire change, the mental health profession will not on its own initiative develop better programs for your children. Ways must be found to jar loose the profession's commitment to itself and shift its concern to its clients.

Parents may hold an important key to solving this large problem, but first must recognize the hard reality that the mental health professions operate primarily politically and are most responsive to political pressures. Parents can exert a major influence primarily by exerting this pressure. A million-and-a-half children in the United States require special psychiatric or psychological programs.[1] There are thus nearly three million parents actively or potentially seeking mental health programs—and this group of parents comprises a potentially powerful political force particularly at local levels where parents can immediately increase their impact by calling in relatives and friends to support their activities. We urge parents to become politically active in demanding better services for their children. If parents do not assume that responsibility, *no one else will,* and our current inadequate situation will continue.

We need highly aggressive demanding groups of parents committed to the welfare of their children working together to mount heavy and sustained political pressure on the local mental health agencies, funding organizations and political office holders. Specifically, we urge parents

1. to contact other parents of children in their community who have special program needs and form an aggressive group fully willing to press the issues.

[1] This is the ". . . most conservative estimate" for the year 1966, made by the National Institute of Mental Health, and reported in the Final Report of the Joint Commission On Mental Health of Children, Inc., 1969, page 4.

2. to pay particular attention to maintaining the new group's task orientation, i.e., developing effective services for children, being careful to avoid "sidetracking" on irrelevant and potentially disastrous conflicts such as racial issues. Any parent group must be fully committed to representing *all* children and must consist of parents from *all* the diverse groups which make up a community.

3. to utilize their strength in numbers and their most aggressive members as spokesmen to bring pressure on the local mental health agencies and political office holders. They must demand to know what those agencies have been doing, to see and question their evaluation reports in order to understand procedures for staff selection and training, to learn their future plans, and to review their budgets to see, for example, how and on what basis tax money is being used.

4. to assume and argue that research is a *major and basic part* of the profession's responsibility to their clients because the agencies have abdicated responsibility for evaluation. Without research, we cannot know which approaches are effective, and can hardly develop more effective programs.

5. to contact local and state elected officials, particularly those who control budget allocations to the mental health agencies, for control of the money is probably the most powerful single variable involved.

6. to aggressively investigate the local United Fund or other cooperative money-raising agencies for any evidence of conflicts of interest in their staffing and boards and favoritism in their allocations to agencies.

7. to investigate the entire system of mental health services in the locality, including the involvement of private practitioners who are answerable to no one, and are never under any circumstances evaluated. Yet if they receive public monies or support from public agencies (such as the free use of offices, telephones, secretaries, etc.) in their private practice, they should be evaluated.

8. to not lose sight of their essentially constructive and cooperative goals (although we suggest an approach of aggressive demands, criticism and evaluation) and to seek professionals who are willing to join in their efforts to develop better services. It is at this time that care is needed to define the layman-professional working relationships so as to leave no hidden assumptions and expectations (see Chapters 1 and 11). Cooperative development of a written contract is recommended to help identify potential conflicts and specify the details of the layman-professional agreement.

9. to maintain their "critic-evaluator" role and to begin to focus on the constructive details of good programming if the political drive does succeed in

obtaining professional commitment to helping their children. This requires close cooperation with professionals who should assume the major responsibility in defining the program. The programs developed will vary depending upon the details of the individual children and families and the particular biases and skills of the professionals. Hopefully, there would be variation between programs, allowing many alternatives to develop. Whatever those variations, we urge that long-term behavioral programming along the lines summarized in the preceding section of this chapter be included.

10. to maintain their critical alertness, once a program is developed, to insure the continuation of the program at a high level of quality. Particular attention must be paid to the political dimension where, we submit, the major factors in program failures develop.

Underlying these proposals is a basic assumption that has also been expressed in earlier work (Graziano, 1971): *parents, by virtue of being parents, have assumed the major moral, legal and practical responsibility for helping their children develop as best as possible.* I emphasize this because there appears to be a general acceptance of the idea, fostered in part by the mental health profession, that only professionals are qualified to help emotionally disturbed children. Children are too often taken away from their families and placed in professional settings such as hospitals or outpatient clinics where, clearly, responsibility is yielded by the family and turned over to the agency.

There are at least two major problems with this approach. First, the work of the professional is rarely monitored or evaluated. Parents must rely on their faith and feelings about the professionals rather than any hard assessment of results. Parents typcially do not really know what is happening to their children in those settings and are allowed little input. Although professionals are concerned with the welfare of the children under their care, an element of impersonality invariably must creep in; simply, the professionals' commitment to the child cannot be as strong as that of the parents!

The bureaucratization and politicizing of mental health programs have fostered that impersonality by rewarding the professional's commitment to his agency far more than his commitment to his clients. We see this most distressingly in some large institutions where professionals—and all other staff—have become inured to horrendous conditions such as those depicted in Blatt and Kaplan's *Christmas in Purgatory* (1967). In these settings the professional is not outraged—and he should be! We do not argue that the professional must have the same intensity of emotional commitment as the parents, but clearly a realignment of values is badly needed in the field so that we will value the child's welfare above that of the institution. The parents' emotional commitment to their children, given weight in the development of programs, provides another element in the decision-making mix that might be of sufficient influence to pull the professional system toward that realignment of values.

A second problem with turning over responsibility to professional agencies is that it might interfere with the general goals of teaching these children to control their own lives successfully and to maintain themselves *in their natural environments*—i.e., their normal and gradually-widening environment with family, home, relatives, friends, etc.

Accepting the idea of the importance of the family, programs should be developed to interact with the family across many dimensions. The professionals' programs should be immediately accessible to the parents who, in turn, must remain involved in the planning, operation and evaluation of the programs developed. Maintaining strong parental responsibility and involvement, the program must help teach parents to be consistent and effective models of adaptive behavior.

What I am advocating is a model of professional services in which the parents, professionals, and paraprofessionals become co-workers in small, neighborhood centers, sharing a common concern for the children, sharing the responsibility and the very hard work involved in helping the children. This would require that the professionals teach their skills to both parents and paraprofessionals. In this model, parents cannot abdicate their responsiblity to the professional agency; likewise, professionals are required to clearly communicate concepts and procedures to parents and not hide behind jargon, mysterious "expertise," or constant complaints about lack of money, staff, or office space. In this model, parents and professionals are required to produce results in an honest, open, mutually-monitored, cooperative setting. In essence they are required to "put up or shut up!" And if we can, in fact, hold ourselves to that so-simply-stated demand, then, we submit, the mental health field will have been significantly improved.

REFERENCES

1. Ayllon, T. and Azrin, N. *The token economy: A motivational system for therapy and rehabilitation.* New York: Appleton-Century-Crofts, 1968.
2. Berkowitz, B.P. and Graziano, A.M. Training parents as behavior therapists: A review. *Behavior Research and Therapy*, 1972, **10**, 297-317.
3. Bernal, M.E. Behavioral feedback in the modification of brat behaviors. *Journal of Nervous and Mental Disease*, 1969, **148**, 375-385.
4. Bettelheim, B. *Love is not enough.* New York; Free Press, 1950.
5. Blatt, B. and Kaplan, F. *Christmas in Purgatory: A photographic essay on mental retardation.* Boston: Allyn & Bacon, 1967.
6. Branch, C.H. Preparedness for progress. *American Psychologist*, 1963, **18**, 581-588.
7. Brotemarkle, R.A. (Ed.) *Clinical psychology: Studies in honor of Lightner Witmer.* Philadelphia: University of Pennsylvania Press, 1931.
8. Browning, R.M. and Stover, D.O. *Behavior modification in child treatment.* Chicago: Aldine–Atherton, 1971.
9. Cowden, R.C. and Ford, L.I. Systematic desensitization with phobic schizophrenics. *American Journal of Psychiartry*, 1962, **119**, 241-245.
10. Cruickshank, W.M., Bentzen, F.A., Ratzeburg, F.H., and Tannhauser, M.T. *Teaching methodology for brain injured and hyperactive children.* Syracuse, N.Y.: Syracuse University Press, 1961.
11. Dollard, J. and Miller, N.E. *Personality and psychotherapy.* New York: McGraw-Hill, 1950.
12. English, H.B. and English, A.C. *A comprehensive dictionary of psychological and psychoanalytical terms.* New York: Longmans, Green, 1958.
13. Eysenck, H.J. The effects of Psychotherapy. In H.J. Eysenck, (Ed.), *Handbook of abnoraml psychology.* New York: Basic Books, 1961.
14. Eysenck, H.J., and Rachman, J.S. *The causes and cures of neuroses.* San Diego, California: Robert R. Knapp, 1965.
15. Gelfand, D.M. and Hartman, D.P. Behavior modification with children: A review. *Psychological Bulletin*, 1968, **69**, 204-215.
16. Ginott, H.G. *Group psychotherapy with children: The theory and practice of play therapy.* New York: McGraw-Hill, 1961.
17. Graziano, A.M. A behavioral day-care and treatment program for psychotic children. Preliminary Report, mimeograph, 1963.
18. Graziano, A.M. Clinical innovation and the mental health power structure: A social case history. *American Psychologist,*, 1969, **24**, 10-18. (a) Copyright 1969 the American Psychological Association.
19. Graziano, A.M. The reluctant client: Counterpoint to a "pop" theme. Paper presented at U.S. Public Health Association, Philadelphia, 1969. (b)
20. Graziano, A.M. Mental health, psychotherapy and the new psychotherapist. *Journal of Psychiatric Nursing and Mental Health Services*, Mar.-Apr., 1969, 69-72.
21. Graziano, A.M. *Behavior therapy with children: A book of readings.* Chicago: Aldine-Atherton, 1971.
22. Graziano, A.M. On mental health. *Psychology Today*, 1972, **5**, 8, 12-18.

284 Child Without Tomorrow

23. Graziano, A.M. The consultant, the client and hidden assumptions. In J. Zusman and D.L. Davidson (Eds.), *Practical aspects of mental health consultation.* Springfield, Ill.: Chas. C. Thomas, 1972, 52-70.

24. Graziano, A.M. (Chairman), Ayllon, T., Franks, C., Ullmann, L., and Wolpe, J. Training Behavior Therapist. Symposium presented at American Psychological Association, Washington, D.C., 1967.

25. Graziano, A.M. and Kean, J.E. Programmed relaxation and reciprocal inhibition with psychotic children. *Behaviour Research and Therapy,* 1968, 6, 433-437. (Also as a paper, presented at 75th. Annual Convention, American Psychological Association, Washington, D.C., 1967.)

26. Guerney, B.G., *Psychotherapeutic agents: New roles for non-professionals, parents and teachers.* New York: Holt, Rinehart and Winston, 1969.

27. Hanf, C. Modifying problem behaviors in mother-child interactions: Standardized laboratory situations. Paper presented at Association of Behavior Therapies, Olympia, Washington, 1968.

28. Haring, N.G. and Phillips, E.L. *Educating emotionally disturbed children.* New York: McGraw-Hill, 1962.

29. Hawkins, R.P., Peterson, R.F., Schweid, E., and Bijou, S.W. Behavior therapy in the home: Amelioration of problem parent-child relations with the parent in a therapeutic role. *Journal of Experimental Child Psychology,* 1966, 4, 99-107.

30. Holzberg, J. The companion program: Implementing the manpower reommmendations of the Joint Commission on Mental Illness and Health. *American Psychologist,* 1963, 18, 224-226.

31. Homme, L., C'deBaca, P., Cottingham, L., and Homme, A. What behavioral engineering is. *The Psychological Record,* 1968, 18, 425-434.

32. Jacobson, E. *Progressive relaxation: A physiological and clinical investigation of muscular states and their significance in psychology and medical practice.* Chicago, University of Chicago Press, 1938.

33. Johnson, R.M. and Brown, R.A. Producing behavior change in parents of disturbed children. *Journal of Child Psychology and Psychiatry,* 1969, 10, 107-121.

34. Joint Commission on Mental Health of Children, Inc., *Crisis in child mental health: Challenge for the 1970's.* Washington, D.C.: Joint Commission on Mental Health of Children, Inc. 1969.

35. Kanner, L. Autistic disturbances of affective contact. *Nervous Child,* 1943, 2, 217-250.

36. Keller, F.S. and Schoenfeld, W.N. *The Principles of Psychology.* New York: Appleton-Century-Crofts, 1950.

37. Kozol, J. *Death at an early age.* New York: Houghton Mifflin, 1967.

38. Lang, J.P. Experimental studies of desensitization psychotherapy. In J. Wolpe, A. Salter, and L.J. Reyna (Eds.), *The conditioning therapies.* New York: Holt, Rinehart and Winston, 1964.

39. Levine, M. and Graziano, A.M. Intervention programs in elementary schools. In S. Golan and C. Eisdorfer (Eds.), *Handbook of community mental health.* New York: Appleton-Century-Crofts, 1972.

40. Levine, M. and Levine, A. *The time for action: a history of social change and helping forms.* New York: Appleton-Century-Crofts, 1970.

41. Mowrer, O.H. and Mowrer, W.M. Enuresis—a method for its study and treatment. *American Journal of Orthopsychiatry,* 1938, 8, 436-459.

42. Patterson, G.R. Behavioral intervention procedures in the classroom and in the home. In A.E. Bergin and S.E. Garfield (Eds.), *Handbook of Psychotherapy and behavior change.* New York, Wiley, 1971, 751-777.
43. Polsby, N.W. *Community power and political theory.* New Haven, Connecticut: Yale University Press, 1963.
44. Poser, E.G. Training behavior therapists. *Behaviour Research and Therapy,* 1967, 5, 37-41.
45. Premack, D. Toward empirical behavior laws: I. Positive reinforcement. *Psychological Review,* 1959, 66, 219-233.
46. Rimland, B. *Infantile autism: The syndrome and its implications for a neural theory of behavior.* New York: Appleton-Century-Crofts, 1964.
47. Rioch, M.J., Elkes, C., Flint, A., Usdansky, B., Newman, R., and Silber, E. National Institute of Mental Health pilot study in training mental health counselors. *American Journal of Orthopsychiatry,* 1963, 33, 678-689.
48. Risley, T. The effects and side effects of punishing the autistic behaviors of a deviant child. *Journal of Applied Behavioral Analysis,* 1968, 1, 21-34.
49. Sarason, S.B. *The creation of settings and the future societies.* San Francisco: Jossey-Bass, 1972.
50. Schermerhorn, R.A. *Society and power.* New York: Random House, 1964.
51. Selznick, P. An approach to a theory of bureaucracy. *American Sociological Review,* 1943, 8, 47-54.
52. Sidman, M. *Tactics of scientific research.* New York: Basic Books, 1960.
53. Skinner, B.F. *The behavior of organisms.* New York: Appleton-Century-Crofts, 1938.
54. Skinner, B.F. *Science and human behavior.* New York: Macmillan, 1953.
55. Strauss, A.A. and Lehtinen, L.E. *Psychopathology and education of the brain-injured child.* New York: Grune and Stratton, 1947.
56. Terrace, H.S., Stimulus control. In W.K. Honig, (Ed.), *Operant behavior: Areas of research and application.* New York: Appleton-Century-Crofts, 1966, 271-344.
57. Tharp, R.G. and Wetzel, R.J. *Behavior modification in the natural environment.* New York: Academic Press, 1969.
58. Wahler, R.G., Winkle, G.H., Peterson, R.F., and Morrison, D.C., Mothers as behavior therapists for their own children. *Behavior Research and Therapy.* 1965, 3, 113-124.
59. Walder, L.O., Cohen, S.I., Breiter, D.E., Warman, F.C., Orne-Johnson, D., and Pavey, S. Parents as agents of behavior change. In S. Golan and C. Eisdorfer, (Eds.), *Handbook of Community Mental Health.* New York: Appleton-Century-Crofts, 1972.
60. Walton, D., Experimental psychology and the treatment of a tiquer. *Journal of Child Psychology and Psychiatry,* 1961, 2, 148-155.
61. Wetzel, R.J., Baker, J., Roney, M. and Martin, M. Outpatient treatment of autistic behavior. *Behaviour Research and Therapy,* 1966, 4, 169-177.
62. White, J.G. The use of learning theory in the psychological treatment of children. *Journal of Clinical Psychology,* 1959, 15, 227-229.
63. Wolpe, J. *Psychotherapy by reciprocal inhibition.* Stanford, California: Stanford University Press, 1958.
64. Wolpe, J. *The practice of behavior therapy.* Elmsford, New York: Pergamon Press, 1969.

Index